Thinking about the Lifecours

Thinking about the Lifecourse

A Psychosocial Introduction

Liz Frost and Stuart McClean

First published 2014 by
PALGRAVE MACMILLAN

Palgrave Macmillan in the UK is an imprint of Macmillan Publishers Limited, registered in England, company number 785998, of Houndmills, Basingstoke, Hampshire RG21 6XS.

Palgrave Macmillan in the US is a division of St Martin's Press LLC, 175 Fifth Avenue, New York, NY 10010.

Palgrave Macmillan is the global academic imprint of the above companies and has companies and representatives throughout the world.

Palgrave® and Macmillan® are registered trademarks in the United States, the United Kingdom, Europe and other countries

ISBN: 978-0-230-24965-3

This book is printed on paper suitable for recycling and made from fully managed and sustained forest sources. Logging, pulping and manufacturing processes are expected to conform to the environmental regulations of the country of origin.

A catalogue record for this book is available from the British Library.

A catalog record for this book is available from the Library of Congress.

Printed in the UK by Charlesworth Press, Wakefield

Contents

List of boxes and figures

Boxes

Figures

Acknowledgements

The author and publisher would like to thank the following publishers and organizations for permission to reproduce copyright material:

David Gadd for Box 1.1 on page 6 from D. Gadd: Murderer, mad man, misfit? Making sense of the murder of Zahid Mubarek, *Journal of Psychosocial Studies* (2011, 5(1): 139–62)

International Catholic Child Bureau for Figure 6.1 on page 114 from S. Vanistendael: *Growth in the Muddle of Life: Resilience Building on People's Strengths* (1998)

Introduction

This book concerns itself with *thinking* about the lifecourse. Thinking often requires that we take what we know about a subject, sometimes from different perspectives and traditions, and put this together in new and surprising ways. *Psychosocial thinking* is an emerging art and is not 'finished' and so we have been careful to include some existing ideas and approaches, but we have also had to create ideas for the purpose of the book: to put together theories and approaches to lifecourse issues that in combination say more than the sum of their parts.

Achieving this bringing together of different ideas and traditions is no easy task. In the book we consider big questions about individual and social lives, about who people are, how people change, how their lives have been shaped and grow, and what has shaped those lives. We ask the question of how we can better understand this process through *psychosocial inquiry*. The questions posed here are indeed vital questions within what we might call 'traditional' psychology and sociology texts that address the issue of growth, development and identity, but these questions are not always satisfactorily answered in a way that 'connects up' both the socio-cultural contexts (e.g. sociology) and the psyche, or inner life of the individual (e.g. psychology). Some texts achieve the combining of approaches but not necessarily integration and connecting up. To try and achieve this bringing together we highlight the very inter-connectedness between the internal, intimate concerns of individual lives and the external social, economic and political order that largely governs and shapes those lives.

In this book we argue for an integrated and interdisciplinary introduction and discussion of the individual or person located within the social setting, one that tries to find a balance between the individual capacities to act and the structural constraints that limits those acts: between agency and structure. Central to our text is the exploration and interrogation of the nature of the human lifecourse, and at its heart is a psychosocial approach. For those of you keen to find out more about this approach we suggest moving along to Chapter 1.

This book is an introduction to an integrated approach to theorizing the lifecourse. It is aimed at anyone interested in or studying issues to do with the lifecourse from an integrated perspective: one that aims to bring together social/cultural contexts with the inner life and individual experience. Primarily aimed at an introductory level the book contains sufficient depth of discussion and analysis to be useful beyond this level.

The scope and outline of the book

This book is divided into chapters that explore in more depth themes and theories connected to the lifecourse. Psychosocial theory is used to understand and set in context the kinds of changes, concerns and issues associated most with that particular stage of development. Each chapter highlights some of the key psychosocial theory that can be useful and explores some of the themes that are central to that period of the lifecourse.

In Chapter 1 we begin by outlining what we mean by a psychosocial approach. We start by providing an example of what a psychosocial approach looks like by way of illustration – a psychosocial criminologist writing about a murder case. The chapter then goes on to discuss the elements that make up this perspective and how psychosocial might be defined. It will explore the underpinning and history of these ideas and key thinkers in the twentieth century. It then considers some contemporary developments of psychosocial theory emerging from within, for example, critical psychology and criminology, and some deployments of these ideas, for instance as research methods. It offers a full discussion of how a psychosocial approach can help us to understand the inner life of people located within their social worlds.

Chapter 2 highlights key areas of psychosocial thinking about babies and early childhood. In this chapter we consider the work of key twentieth-century psychosocial theorists such as Winnicott, Erikson and Bowlby. In addition, the psychoanalytic work of Freud and Klein is explored. It considers the social and familial context of early childhood in thinking about babies. Familiar themes such as attachment are reviewed and psychosocial implications discussed. The social context of baby and young childhood are reviewed: ideas such as socialization and the making social, as well as identity formation and the social construction of childhood. The chapter also considers how our own conscious and unconscious sense of ourselves as babies impacts on how we respond as

adults and workers to small children and their parents, and more generally.

In Chapter 3 we continue the process of looking at some of the themes
from the previous chapter – psychosocial understandings of babies – with
the emphasis on how they move towards greater independence from their
primary care giver, through to childhood generally, developing identities.
We draw partly on the 'new sociology of childhood' (James and Prout,
1997) and psychoanalytical approaches, such as Freud and Lacan. We
explore themes of the child in the body and the child in the context of
friendship. Furthermore, how the child is located in the family in the contemporary West is given some thought.

We move on to the broad psychosocial theme of love, marriage and the
family in Chapter 4. How is love, marriage and the family pursued in
contemporary Western society, and how can we understand this better
through an approach that integrates psychic, emotional themes with the
social and interpersonal? We also explore the broader aspects of those
connections in terms of being in families and becoming a parent. The
family is an important area of discussion here, for example: what kinds
of families exist now, and how do they work? What does it mean to be a
parent? Here we borrow a range of theories and approaches from social
constructionism and psychoanalysis to make sense of these lifecourse
issues.

How are people occupied and engaged with the world? How is this
influenced by the lifecourse? These key questions form the backdrop to
Chapter 5. We explore the different ways in which people are engaged in
activity through the lifecourse, and how we can approach this psychosocially. What does it mean for children to be occupied by their education?
The issue of work and the main ideas about being occupied in the middle
period of life are considered, and these continue into late life decisions.
Work and its role in identity formation and sustaining are considered.
The psychosocial theme of work – being occupied – is central here, and
we try to make sense of what it is to do well in the world of adult identity.

How is it that some people 'do well' in the world and some struggle?
Chapter 6 considers how a 'base-line' of well-being can be conceptualized, and what kinds of theory can be usefully consulted. Positive psychological and psychoanalytical approaches to well-being are examined
and work on the capabilities approach to welfare are also discussed. An
outline as well as a critique of self-help and self-oriented 'methods' for
fulfilment is offered. In addition to thinking about well-being, resilience
and its opposite, vulnerability are explored as important and influential
in seeing who is 'doing well'. We highlight theories of psychosocial
resilience and vulnerability as well as discussing why social connections
and friendship are necessary for this. The psychoanalytical perspective

of 'normal everyday misery' versus the contemporary perfectionism of self-help psychology is considered here.

Chapter 7 should be read alongside the previous chapter as it concerns the disruptive and negative life events that individuals experience, that overwhelm and threaten individual health and identity, and that ensure that for some struggling and suffering is more likely to occur. The relationship between physical illness and long-term depression on the one hand, and social deprivation, poverty, and all kinds of illnesses on the other is given considerable consideration in Chapter 6. That being a member of any undervalued group – working class, black, female etc. – is likely to correlate with poor health across most dimensions is crucial to the debate. That 'social suffering' and exclusion, regardless of the life stage, is damaging is discussed. Examples such as research into depression in women are drawn upon. How the mechanisms of stigma and other forms of exclusion, stress, anxiety and powerlessness create physical and mental distress and 'ill-being' is examined.

The book moves on to a discussion of how people hurt and hate in Chapter 8. For many people in contemporary society, anger, violence and/or abuse are the emotional and physical context in which their lives, or some part of their lives, are led. From babies being shaken to political 'dissidents' being tortured, from being jeered at by a teacher for poor work, to being dismissed as 'too old', the various kinds of damage which are inflicted on individuals and communities are discussed. This chapter looks at what there is to be known contemporarily about the impact of abuses across the lifecourse, and how these are variously responded to. Domestic violence and child abuse are two central areas of focus. Youth violence, 'gangs' and 'knife crime' are considered. Anger, damage, suffering, protection, hope and hopelessness and moving on are discussed from psychosocial perspectives.

How can we best understand the later stages of our lives and those of others? This is the key question in Chapter 9. Here we psychosocially explore the meaning of later life, ageing, and death and dying. A range of theories are discussed, such as psychoanalytic and identity theory, as well as Erikson's life-stage approach, to help us shape an integrated and interdisciplinary psychosocial perspective. The various losses of status, power, income, looks and physical capacity are considered here. Losses of contact through leaving work, grown up family, bereavement of friends, and the psychosocial impact of these are looked at, as are the fluctuations in relationships within communities and the possibility of loneliness and aloneness. We examine death and dying in the context of grief and loss; psychosocial themes emerge as part of the discussion about loss.

1

Psychosocial theory: being and becoming

The issues with which this book concerns itself – of the formation and revision of identity as people experience being in the world; of development, transition and change – are also central to many traditional psychology and sociology texts on the lifecourse and on human development. However, it is not usually the concern of those texts to link the disciplines and 'connect up' both psychological and sociological perspectives, for example both the socio-cultural contexts and the psyche, or inner life, of the individual.

In this book, and particularly in this chapter, we explore the central premise that we can better understand who people are, what they can do and be, by integrating knowledge about the social context of how people live their lives, with knowledge about how their personal ways of thinking and being, develop. Or, to put it more strongly, we argue that it is not possible to really understand how people negotiate their lives without understanding that both the unconscious and conscious elements of their personalities, their relationships with other people and the social and cultural environments in which these transactions and understandings take place entwine. Interdisciplinary thinking is invariably at the heart of this approach. Put simply, a psychosocial approach involves integrating what are traditionally seen as psychological and sociological paradigms.

This chapter starts with an illustrative example of what a psychosocial approach looks like; it goes on to discuss the elements that make up this perspective and how we might define psychosocial. It will then present some of the history of these ideas in the twentieth century, and proceed to look at the contemporary process of building a body of psychosocial theory in the UK. Following this there is some consideration of the contribution of some primary disciplinary areas to the psychosocial approach:

psychoanalysis and child psychiatry, psychology and sociology. Finally, applied psychodynamic thinking for welfare practice is given some consideration, as is the role of the theorists themselves.

A psychosocial scenario

The short scenario provided in Box 1.1 shows a psychosocial approach 'in action' as it were, to demonstrate to the reader what, if we think about a person and/or a situation psychosocially, it might look like. Even this approach – offering a holistic scenario first to mull over, and then considering its elements – fits with 'psychosocial'. The extract below, then, forms part of a discussion of this tragic murder, taken from a paper by the psychosocial criminologist Professor David Gadd

---

Box 1.1

A psychosocial scenario

Deep down Stewart must have wanted to change, however much this prospect must have frightened him. No longer a juvenile, the criminal justice system had given up any pretence of being able to settle him back into a law-abiding life. Far from where he had grown up in Manchester, Stewart was friendless in Feltham. In prison his menacing appearance invited ridicule. He had nightmares. He wrote incessantly. He begged his 'girlfriend' to forgive him for implicating her in his vile fantasies of miscegenation. Her loss of interest in him can only have underscored what an unlovable person he had become. Even as he became aware of how outrageous his miscegenation fantasies were, Stewart could not let them go. He felt consumed from within and overwhelmed from without. He tried to talk to his cellmate about his girlfriend and – remarkably given how unnerving he found Stewart – Zahid Mubarek tried to listen. We know Stewart saw Mubarek as both a 'paki' and someone who was alright and safe with him. Given they were both 19 year olds who had been excluded from school with histories of problematic drug use and involvement in car crime, the two of them did have things in common. In considering this commonality, Mubarek may also have reminded Stewart of everything he would have liked to have been: good-looking, easy going, untroubled by a chaotic love life, and about to be returned to a family who missed him and still loved him dearly in spite of his bad behaviour. But Mubarek could not identify with Stewart's murderousness, or contain his pain. He was, in Gilroy's (2004: 137) words 'half-different' and 'partially familiar', perceived by Stewart as smuggling uncomfortable thoughts into his head, being better than him, judging him, making him feel 'shitty', no longer the safe cell-mate but yet another ethnic 'gangsta' reminding him how insignificant he was. For Stewart, as for many incarcerated killers, murder was '...the ultimate act of self-defense, a last resort against ... losing one's mind' (Gilligan, cited in Gadd, 2011: 154–5).

Stewart murdered Mubarek in their shared prison cell in March 2000.

In the above scenario Gadd offers us a disturbing but useful example of thinking about the theme of violence psychosocially, something we return to in Chapter 8. His powerful evocation of a young man whose 'hatred' is a product of a socially reinforced sense of worthlessness and his particularly loveless upbringing, the persecuted psychic world through which and within which his racism and pain percolates and the confusion and ambivalence in his thinking and actions, give a strong sense of the highly complex and multilayered subject that psychosocial theory proposes. It demonstrates how a psychosocial approach is useful as a framework for understanding the inner life of people located within their social worlds.

The scenario also to some extent explains the importance of understanding psychosocial approaches to people in their contexts. It is very hard to see how someone like Stewart could be understood without recourse to psychosocial thinking. Sociology, for instance, would allow us to consider the implications of factors such as: he was gendered 'male'; came from a poor background, a 'broken home'; was let down by the school system and had been in and out of custodial institutions where aggression can be reinforced. This offers a social context in which violence and hatred might well flourish, but most young people in this context do not murder. Psychology might offer the lack of familial love reinforced by the various rejections and failures producing an unconfident self-critical person with low self-esteem, and that too is helpful. And yet neither of these approaches in isolation provides enough of an understanding of the complexity and is not somehow 'strong' enough to make sense of this life situation. Gadd's evocation drawing on social context, psychoanalytic understanding and positioning the human at the centre of the discussion seems to offer the best possible chance we have of understanding, for example, such extreme violence.

Background to the psychosocial approach

The psychosocial approach this book is offering, including Gadd's work, is both new and historical, building on a tradition laid down in the mid-twentieth century by a range of European thinkers and social theorists. Thinking first about the historical dimension, it is important that such work came out of the era of the destruction and cruelty of the World Wars and the Holocaust in Europe. In the light of broad concerns with social justice, liberation, truth, understanding of the nature of violence and persecution, and the nature of human 'depth and surface' and repression, a group of theorists commonly referred to as 'critical theorists', or what has also been known as 'the Frankfurt school' established themselves (see Box 1.4 below).

Key thinkers central to this approach and still of importance in contemporary psychosocial studies are Theodor Adorno and Jurgen Habermas, whose attempts to understand human nature and social injustice exactly draw on this unique blend of sociology and psychoanalysis. That such concerns as racism and other forms of social conflict can only be understood as the product of individual affect and social structure (see Adorno *et al.*'s *The Authoritarian Personality*, 1950) have continued to be a major driver in psychosocial thinking and research (Clarke, 2005; Gadd and Dixon, 2010).

Following on from this tradition, what psychosocial theory does, then, is to strive to understand the human subject and their lived experience, and to make this the starting place, that is to say, the key concern within social theory inquiry.

Whereas psychology traditionally has mostly concerned itself with individuals, taken in isolation, and sociology mostly with the social contexts and institutions surrounding individuals, psychosocial studies argues that you cannot think about individuals without their contexts, or 'contexts' without engaging with the person for whom these exist. The individual and their social 'contexts' are therefore connected up though thinking through a range of important themes in development. We are thinking, then, about:

> Subjects whose inner worlds cannot be understood without knowledge of their experiences in the world, and whose experiences of the world cannot be understood without knowledge of the way in which their inner worlds allow them to experience the outer world (Hollway and Jefferson, 2000: 4).

Psychosocial theory in process

Building psychosocial theory is an ongoing project: unfinished and in the process of identity formation. Psychosocial theory is currently being written and developed, so the edges of what it looks at and what its scope is, are still flexible (although this is true of some other subject areas up to a point – exactly what is in, say, media studies or even geography is not always clear). This tells us something about the transitional nature of boundaries and identities within disciplinary subject areas; psychosocial studies are no different.

Over the last two decades, particularly in England and the USA, an interest in psychosocial theory has emerged. In the UK, for example, there is now a UK Psychosocial network, a psychosocial sub-group of the British Sociological Association, and a 'learned [academic] society' called The Association for Psychosocial Studies. Core academic journals have been founded such as *Psychoanalysis, Culture and Society* (Palgrave Macmillan) and the online *Journal of Psycho-social Studies*. Moreover, significant groups of psychosocial theorists, researchers and practitioners can be located at, for example, the Centre for Understanding Social Practices (CUSP) at the University of the West of England; the Department of Psychosocial Studies at Birkbeck College, London; the Tavistock Institute for Human Relations; the Institute for Education, the Open University, Cardiff University, Brighton University; and the University of East London. Recent years has seen a burgeoning of higher education institutions across the UK engaging in psychosocial studies.

Perhaps even more important is the written contribution of psychosocial theory to understanding contemporary social life. In the UK a substantial body of psychosocial literature and research has been generated from within the disciplines of sociology, criminology, psychology, social policy, psychotherapy, psychoanalysis and social work over the last decade or so.

Paul Hoggett and Lynn Froggett, for example, radically introduced the notion of emotion as constitutive of the emerging neo-liberal 'turn' in social policy in the twenty-first century (in other words, increased privatization, reduced public services, emphasis on organizational profit not human need). They produced work such as *Emotional Life and the Politics of Welfare* (Hoggett, 2000) and, *Love, Hate and Welfare: Psychosocial Approaches to Policy and Practice* (Froggett, 2002), and their themes are also developed in Cooper and Lousada's (2005) *Borderline Welfare: Feeling and Fear of Feeling in Modern Welfare*. The emotions generated by neo-liberalism, for example divisive resentments and populist anti-welfarism, are also being subject to psychosocial analysis (see, for example, Hoggett *et al.*, 2013).

Research methods and research practice have become core topics in the psychosocial approach, for example in terms of theory, such as Hollway and Jefferson's (2012) revised *Doing Qualitative Research Differently: A Psychosocial Approach* and *Researching Beneath the Surface* edited by Clarke and Hoggett (2009). Research-based studies drawing on such approaches have also contributed to how we are able to think psychosocially about the lived experiences of, for example, class and gender, unemployment and 'shame', and these original studies have helped to develop the field: for example, Walkerdine *et al.*'s (2001) study of 'Growing up girl: psychosocial explorations of gender and class', and recently, *Gender Work and Community after De-industrialisation: A Psychosocial Approach to Affect* (Walkerdine and Jimenez, 2012). Social problems and social practices have also become of core concern to psychosocial theorists, with racism providing a particularly rich focus, in for example, Clarke's (2003) *Social Theory, Psychoanalysis and Racism*, and

Gadd and Dixon's (2010) *Losing the Race: Thinking Psychosocially about Racially Motivated Crime*.

Box 1.2

Psychosocial research methods: Wendy Hollway

Wendy Hollway and Tony Jefferson first published *Doing Qualitative Research Differently*, essentially proposing a form of research that focused on the relational, psychoanalytic and social aspects of the research process.

The interview method developed to facilitate this was the free association narrative interview method, which involved giving the subject a great deal of self-direction in the interview, not offering interpretations but essentially helping the subject to tell their story in their own way.

Analysis of the interview material is conducted in a group, and the focus is on the latent and surface content in the interaction of the interviewer and the interviewee. Social political and 'under the surface' material is all considered relevant to the 'findings'.

Currently Hollway's exploration of 'scenic analysis' as research method is pushing back more frontiers in psychosocial investigation by drawing on the psychoanalyst Lorenzer's notion of 'the scenic', which is the concept he uses to describe how we as babies absorb the undifferentiated totality of our life worlds.

Hollway's recent research, for example, on young mothers in East London used this technique for data analysis, primarily by offering the researcher a responsive space to make sense of their material affectively and rationally (Hollway, 2011). This means in practice that initially, instead of switching on the tape recorder and asking questions in a research interview, the researcher writes a free-hand descriptive and impressionistic account of the research scenario – the setting, the subject: clothes, demeanour, anything – then returns to it later to see what perhaps less than obvious thinking and understanding it prompts.

A common feature of psychosocial theorizing is its cross-disciplinary approach, which has become one of the ordinary leitmotifs of psychosocial thinking. So, if we bring our knowledge of 'x' together with our understanding of 'y', what kind of picture of 'z' emerges? For example, why is unemployment often correlated with depression? Social-structural issues around, perhaps, poverty (the broader socio-economic and political context) may be important, but the lived experience notions of shame, isolation, lack of recognition might give us more clues as to what happens for individual people when they are made redundant or cannot find work (Walkerdine and Jimenez, 2012).

Psychosocial is a theory in process; it is currently being developed and borrowing what it can to flourish. There is something here of what we might term the '*bricolage*' approach to social theory and social thinking, which is new and experimental, and brings together traditionally different subject domains. For example, in education: if we start with sociological theories about education, and bring them together with psychodynamic thinking to look at how children might actually experience their education, we can think about issues such as group membership, or being left out at school, psychosocially. In other words what is it to do with the institution – reflecting things about the society in which it is placed – that gets into the children, and what in how the child perceives this and can be in this, is also part of them in this institution (Lucey and Reay, 2002).

This volume constitutes another such example. Oftentimes in our writing we use psychosocial theory that has already been forged by the writers mentioned above, amongst others, but sometimes we find ourselves constructing the theory, or at the very least piecing together the theory from the different approaches we know. We use ideas and theories that we find helpful to underpin ways to think psychosocially. This chapter now looks at some of the disciplines that have generated psychosocial theory and/or have become its building blocks.

Psychosocial theory from psychoanalysis and child psychiatry

Later in this chapter we briefly discuss psychosocial theory and welfare practice; presently we are going to look briefly at the traditional and to some extent historic practices which both built the theory and also incorporated this theory: those existing in an intersection between psychoanalysis, psychiatry and child psychiatry/psychotherapy.

The notion of 'psychosocial' approaches in, for example, human growth and development (developmental psychology), child psychiatry, adult and child psychoanalysis, social psychology, and in the underpinning research in these fields and practices connected to the disciplines – child psychology; child and adolescent psychiatry and psychotherapy – has an established history going back more than half a century. Anna Freud's and Melanie Klein's pioneering work applying psychoanalytic methods to children made a significant impact on a generation of psychoanalysts, such as Erik Erikson, as well as medically and psychoanalytically trained practitioners such as John Bowlby and Donald Winnicott, in addition to their own psychiatric and psychologically informed disciples such as Michael Rutter.

For instance, the contribution of Bowlby's attachment theory to a general understanding of how early life relationships can inflict lasting and significant damage on the psyche, hence producing troubled adults with a range of emotional and often therefore social problems, has been significant and has been cited as a prominent psychosocial approach for two generations. Similarly the psychoanalyst and polymath Erikson, whose writings this book finds enormously helpful, offers a psychosocially informed way of understanding human development that is both rich and structured. Erikson's life stage model (discussed in the following chapter) offers a nuanced insight into how individuals are forged by their own internal psychological processes and also how this impacts on their specific and general relationships with the outside world. For example, Erikson's sixth stage in his classification of the life cycle 'intimacy versus isolation', focuses on building intimate relationships with others as a key 'task' of this phase of early adulthood: friendships, love, sex, groups and isolation as the counterpoint against which this takes place. He considers rituals such as marriage and group affiliation, and intimacy from the couple bond through to comradeship in conflict. The internal capacity established in earlier life to, for example, trust, is central to his discussion.

Erikson's work has psychosocial concerns at its core and indeed in some of his work (e.g. *Childhood and Society*, 1995 [1950]) he also draws on literature and myth, for example, to look at the cultural context of identity. This aspect moves his work far nearer to the contemporary use of the notion of psychosocial in the sense this book is applying it; though structural sociology or the structured approach to the wider social context of a person's life, such as class or gender as well as culture, is rarely apparent in such work. And indeed this is a point that can be made about much of the psychosocial work developing from within child and adolescent, and indeed adult, psychoanalysis and psychiatry: the focus on the psyche/identity of the individual is usually primarily relational and in the social context of relationships and families rather than the broader social context. It is social in the sense of highly important social institutions such as the family, but without the contextualizing social issues of, for example, culture and class. Social inequalities, power and repression, agency and determinism – those broad issues that sociology in the main has brought to the understanding of identity – are mostly missing in these approaches. Nonetheless all the mainly psychoanalytic authors cited above add a great deal in building psychosocial theory and can be found extensively in the following chapters to help us discuss the lifecourse psychosocially.

Psychosocial theory from psychology

Clearly psychology is a vast field of study, not amenable to a brief summary in such a volume as this. However, given a loose definition of the discipline as something like 'addressing questions of the nature of people', it is hardly surprising that contemporary psychosocial thinkers are just as likely to have emerged from psychology (and social psychology) as from sociology and psychoanalysis.

The revolution in psychology in the 1970s, when, in common with much modernist thought, the impact of postmodern ideas (questioning the validity of the scientific method and the likelihood of achieving certainty; disposing with 'knowability' and 'truth' as possibilities in themselves) put the cat among the pigeons. Out of this impasse emerged a new generation of 'critical psychologists', many of whom used the French and American post-structural and postmodern theorists to revitalize discussions of the human subject, identity, the body and the epistemologies surrounding knowledge of these.

However, much of the psychological establishment, in academic and practice contexts, remains unchallenged by this. Positivist psychology, for instance, applied in things like personality ('psychometric') tests as part of job application processes, has burgeoned, despite criticism from within the field itself.

The discipline of social psychology, as the name clearly identifies, has at its core a concern to locate the individual in their social context, and as such has produced a body of work that contributes a great deal to psychosocial studies.

Thinking about the individual and individual identity in the context of, for example, the institutions they inhabit, and the way these impact on individuals and are internalized, are central to the text. The work of Erving Goffman, for example, particularly in relation to contexts in which individuals' capacity to control the performative aspects of identity are encroached on by their contexts (as in being 'stigmatized', and as in the impact of being contained in 'total institutions' such as prisons) is extremely helpful for understanding psychosocial suffering.

Goffman's work pre-dates the addition of post-structural thinking to psychology, and unlike writers such as Frosh and Hollway, never developed in relation to thinking through, for example, the notion of language as the dominant structural force in the creation and maintenance of the human self (Frosh *et al.*, 2003; Hollway, 1998). However, its enduring capacity to focus our attention on an issue such as 'shame' ensures its continued relevance to thinking about emotion and identity in social contexts. Where it is less useful as psychosocial material is in its lack of engagement with issues of structural power.

Critical social psychology now: Steve Brown and Paul Stenner

These radical theorists are currently advocating a new approach to psychology as a discipline generally. They describe the 'traditional' arm of psychology as 'rigidly posing very narrowly defined questions which concern very specific facets of personhood that can be made to show up in laboratory settings or in the transcribed record of a tape-recorded interaction' (2009: 4).

They argue against a psychology that:

- oversimplifies how we understand people
- decontextualizes people from their life worlds and experiences
- demonstrates a reductive sense of certainty and direction.

They argue for a psychology that:

- engages with the 'fine and subtle accounts of the psychological in art, literature, music, theatre and in journalism, broadcasting and public debate' (*ibid.*).
- can be found everywhere there is human experience
- is not separated off from its 'surroundings' (e.g. time, place, culture, meaning, inter-relationships etc).

Box 1.3 describes a version of psychosocial theory without the psychoanalysis, the possibility and efficacy of which is an ongoing discussion in psychosocial networks

Brown and Stenner's broad sweep thinking that is multi-disciplinary, interpretative, contextual and open to suggestion reflects precisely the same ethos as the psychosocial theory put forward by such contemporary writers as C. Fred Alford and Lynne Layton (though strictly speaking from the disciplinary base of political science), Lynn Froggett from social policy, Rosalin Minsky from humanities, and many others, who embrace interdisciplinarity in the psychosocial, though they would argue psychoanalysis is central to this.

Psychosocial theory from sociology and social theory

Similarly to psychology, the 1960s and 1970s saw fundamental upheavals in the definition and discipline of sociology. We noted above the impact and refocusing of social theory brought about by the Frankfurt school (see Box 1.4), but other 'revolutions' were also underway. The critique of the possibility of finding truth, and the ways in which you might do that, impacted on not only research methods but how to think about the social. The ideas and interests generated by other kinds of social changes – for example, feminism, multiculturalism, 'gay' rights, challenged the traditional interests of (men's) working practices, and the undifferentiated white working class.

Box 1.4

The Frankfurt School

The Frankfurt school were a group of influential thinkers and writers working in Frankfurt in the 1920s–30s, and because of the impact of Hitler and the Second World War, later in America. The group is usually defined as Max Horkheimer, T.W. Adorno, Herbert Marcuse, Leo Lowenthal and Erich Fromm.

Their common 'project' was integrating psychoanalytical theory with forms of social theory to better understand the human subject in a social context, and to apply this to research and practice. They also formulated theories relating to the political and economic dimensions of cultural consumption and the transmission of culture. 'Critical theorists' and 'cultural critical theorists' have been other terms applied to the group.

The relationship between Freudian thinking and Marxist thinking, used in the service of understanding the atrocities of the mid twentieth century, produced seminal analyses of the human psyche in context. Marxism and psychoanalysis also formed the basis of an intense intellectual scrutiny of mass and elite cultural products such as film, photography and eventually TV. For a fuller discussion of the work of Erich Fromm see Chapter 7.

In the tradition of critical theory and the cultural range of interests developed within sociology and borrowed from Humanities and the arts, new fusions emerged. For example, the Birmingham Centre for Contemporary Social Studies, clearly building on Frankfurt, connected up sociology with literature and the arts, and made not just film and fashion but everyday social practices such as watching TV and doing housework valid academic areas of study. The massive social concern with identity in an increasingly multi-racial and multi-sexual world was reflected in this and indeed swathes of sociological work. Post-structural concerns with discourse and practices and new theories of power became the tools of analysis. Identity concerns became instantiated in areas such as the body, gender, post-colonial theory, and 'queer' theory, and psychosocial theory can be seen as a further iteration and example of this, building on the work and forging a new approach.

Sociologists concerned with the emotional/affective world of the human subject are cited a great deal in the following chapters, and used to build contemporary psychosocial theory. The big questions of 'who am I; what am I; how did I get to be like this; and can I change', have been addressed by some of the key social thinkers in Europe, the UK and the USA. George Herbert Mead and Erich Fromm are early examples, but Anthony Giddens and Pierre Bourdieu, Michel Foucault, Zygmunt Bauman and Stuart Hall, Franz Fanon and Judith Butler wrote extensively about how we come to be the individuals we are in the contexts (linguistic, 'material' and experiential) in which we live. This work has stimulated psychosocial thinking in its key concern of 'inside to outside and outside to inside', and indeed it may be helpful to think of these approaches as on a continuum with recent and contemporary identity theorists.

In the same way as we noted above, that to draw on psychology for psychosocial analysis we often needed to import theory for understanding the social context, we and the psychosocial turn in sociology also needed to theorize the internal psychic world of the individual into our sociology.

Psychosocial theory in applied contexts

Another aspect of psychosocial theory which is fundamental for many academics and writers participating in the development of this approach is its strength as a tool of analysis and understanding in forms of socially/personally 'therapeutic' practices. We looked at one aspect of psychosocial theory's roots in practice above (in relation to child psychiatry). But the language is tricky here, given the range of practitioners drawing on these notions come from diverse settings from conflict resolution in the community through to individual psychotherapy, with some social workers, counsellors, community workers, environmentalists, family therapists, organizational consultants and group workers using and developing the area. Are they 'helping practices'? 'Socially useful' practices? 'Therapeutic practices'? Perhaps, 'practices for developing social and personal potential' sums up the field best.

Developing appropriate theory that can help with how we work with people struggling in various kinds of ways in their lives is inevitably a complex process. Part of the difficulty here has been perceived as existing in the relationship between theoretical social science subjects and the nature of welfare work.

For many people who have only a passing knowledge of such work, it can easily all be seen as simply a matter of 'common sense'. But what constitutes 'common sense' is 'never really agreed on sense' and furthermore, what is common sense to some people is not for everyone. Think of the two sayings – 'a trouble shared is a trouble halved' and 'least said soonest mended'. Common sense suggests both are right, but they are totally contradictory ways of understanding the world.

As such, formal structured knowledge is needed to understand anything as complicated as a person/people with a problem. But complex social theory, if it seems unrelated to welfare practices in practice, can be just as unhelpful as over-simplification. Within welfare education there are academics who are formerly and currently sociologists, social policy writers and psychologists, who necessarily draw on their own disciplines and educational learning for constructing teaching and publishing. A disjuncture between academics/lecturers and students can be the outcome. Fook, for example, illustrates such a stance from her background. Describing her experience of social work academia she comments,

> What I found was … a world in which it seemed that male academic theorising sociologists tried to teach female practising social workers better social work by converting them to a world of theory (Pease and Fook, 1999: 5).

Equally there was a matching critique from social science theorists that practitioners were 'a-political'. Welfare work was heavily criticized for its perceived exclusion of any interest in power or inequality, and was seen to be too concerned with what is in people's heads to the exclusion of their material situation or concerns: an old but ongoing critique (Langan and Lee, 1989). Interestingly, psychosocial theory being developed in the field of social work (e.g. Trevithick, 2003; Walker, 2003, 2004; Ferguson, 2005; Frost, 2008) for the most part effectively dissolve the theory/practice and individual/social binaries.

The problems and differences between social theory and applied theory for welfare work, tend to receive more attention than the, equally evident, congruence and mutual interests. There has always been important common ground. Psychosocial theory takes this further.

Box 1.5

Psychosocial theory, agency and reflexivity: Paul Hoggett (2001)

Hoggett's early twenty-first-century work on welfare (mentioned above) is concerned with issues such as agency, powerlessness and reflection. This is helpful for understanding, for example, violent situations such as domestic violence.

Hoggett creates a schema: a grid which places subjects along twin axes: vertically, reflexive to non reflexive; horizontally, self as object to self as agent, through which one can look at dimensions of violence and 'victim-hood' in an explanatory (and practically) useful way.

This helpfully acknowledges that behaviour is both action and the subject's meaningful comprehension in relation to this – reflection. Behaviours such as unpremeditated violence (as well as acts of unpremeditated bravery) are by definition non-reflexive, but also demonstrate agency.

Hoggett explores how domestic violence is an expression of men's agency, but their accounts of this, often construing themselves as the victim, or denying the severity or importance of the action, demonstrate very limited reflexivity. Female partners can also be understood as 'not to blame' without recourse to the notion of passive victim-hood. She (and those subject to other kinds of power-related violence, such as racism) is positioned schematically as 'the non-reflexive object' which compels the reader to consider the complex *processes* of inaction, rather than assuming that not acting is nothing.

Hoggett explores how being subject to domination in any form, from personal through to structural, by a parent or by a whole culture or class, becomes internalized. This 'violence' he argues, 'violates our personal space', and limits our capacity to be able to look at what we are experiencing. Humiliation and shame can render people silent and unprotesting, because, as Hoggett explains 'when … we are attacked we do not necessarily resist, we might equally see this as our fate, our desert' (Hoggett, 2001: 49).

These nuanced accounts, drawing on a politics and ethics as well as subjective experience, offer a level of understanding which, incorporated into practice, allows for the possibility of welfare work which can help to move both partners on. It gives a 'rich' understanding of the subject (Frost, 2006: 19–20).

Psychosocial theory and the theorist

In the same ways as the developing psychosocial research methods outlined by Hollway and Jefferson (2000; 2012) and being applied by a range of researchers now (e.g. Mayo *et al.*, 2007) insist on examining the inter-subjective relationship between interviewer and interviewee, the psychosocial approach locates the knower in a relationship with the known. In other words, how we are looking at the subject (what it means to be a child in a working-class family, a black older person in a traditional family, etc.) and perhaps even *why* we are looking at it – is also a product of what is in our heads, hearts and lives as people constructing knowledge. The researchers and theorists who are building the psychosocial knowledge base here are also implicated.

We are not pretending to be objective or all knowing, but accepting that our personal experiences and leanings, our class backgrounds and psychic worlds, impact on our perceptions and discussions, our choices as to what counts and how we write about it. Thinking psychosocially, this is inevitable. And as writers we have tried to stay reflexively conscious of this, individually and together. The book, then, is partly a reflection of, and partly another contribution to the building of, psychosocial theory for understanding the life worlds and lifecourses of contemporary people.

Conclusion

This chapter has concerned itself with what we currently take psychosocial theory to mean. It gives an example of a psychosocial scenario to both demonstrate the elements of the approach, and begin to extrapolate them. We then spend some time looking at the development of the body of work using psychosocial theory historically and in the UK now. We then pay some attention to the disciplines and fields in which psychosocial developments have and are taking place: in child psychiatry and psychoanalysis, research, psychology, sociology and welfare practice. Finally we comment on the centrality of the position of the theorist in relation to the theory. In the next chapter we examine psychosocial accounts of what gets put into place in the life worlds of infants, and how.

2

How people begin: 'the child as father to the man'

Introduction

The aim of this chapter is to provide a psychosocial introduction to the earliest stages of the lifecourse, the stage that for many of the theorists we draw on, and indeed for many lay people for centuries (hence the Shakespeare reference in the title) crucially lays down the parameters of who and how we can be for the rest our lives. The debate now, both in the academic journal and in the pub, tends to focus on *how* early experiences and upbringing impact on our lives, and issues such as what factors have most influence: that babyhood and early life is fundamental to all later being is mostly taken for granted.

Here we explore both babyhood and early childhood psychosocially. As we explored in Chapter 1, this means that although we will draw on, for example, child development theory as seen within the professional and academic discourse of psychology, and socialization and other sociological perspectives, we are primarily concerned with the integration of disciplines to give us psychosocial perspectives. Usefully here, much of the mid twentieth-century theoretical writing on child development, from John Bowlby to Erik Erikson, was informed by just such a 'psychosocial' approach as this text is concerned with. We also hope to blend together some of the more sociological, structural and 'social' knowledge and analysis of the social conditions in which childhood emerges (as well as the ways in which 'society' and 'cultures' shape and influence the individual and family), with the more psychological and psycho-analytically influenced theories that explore the emotionally driven dimension of children's minds and worlds, inner reflections on the mind and the psyche that have major influences on the child's development.

The chapter provides a range of approaches to thinking psychosocially about becoming a person, and as such provides grounding for much of the rest of the text. Issues such as resilience, 'ill-being', violence, love, 'well being' and so on, we go on to argue, have their foundations in the earliest experiences people have. Much of the theory here will be linked into arguments in later chapters and as we will see throughout the book, many theories of adult identity and relationships, of their internal worlds and their capacity for pain and joy, are predicated on the 'events' and life worlds which form them in the early months and years of life.

For example, from different traditions, the sociologist Pierre Bourdieu, and the psychoanalyst Lorenzer both work with notions of the whole life-world of the individual; that is to say, what people can perceive and how they can be, is based on the internalization of their social interactions. For Lorenzer, this means something perhaps most easily conceptualized as the context – the 'scenario' is 'hard wired' or 'imprinted' into people's psychic development at a very young age. Everything the baby is 'in' – mixtures of senses, emotions, smells and sounds – all jumbled up and a piece – is absorbed. Desire, anger, integration, shame, confidence, the capacity for concern, anxiety and defences all take root in the individual's mental repertoire long before they reach school age.

For Bourdieu (see Box 2.6 below) this 'imprinting' is more to do with internalizing social ways of being – the nuances of tone, thought and action, how to *be* in the context of family norms themselves saturated with their class and cultural imperatives. All of this constitutes for Bourdieu the person's 'habitus', that which facilitates and impedes ways of thinking, relating and being, as surely as poor diet, under-nourishment and a lack of physical care or its opposite will make a lasting impact on the development of the body.

Structural sociologists and physiological psychoanalysts reach a similar psychosocial conclusion – that the baby's context permeates their internal world and forms them as people. This and other ways of psychosocially theorizing babies and small children is the meat of the chapter.

First, then, the chapter looks at key psychoanalytic theorists of the nineteenth and twentieth century, and outlines how they conceptualize the development of a child's inner landscape. From this, we look at the psychosocial theorists whose work was built on psychoanalytic foundations, but who applied this to their practice with babies and children, in particular Erikson, Bowlby and Winnicott. The chapter then turns its attention to the social development of babies, through ideas and critiques of socialization, and the ways in which the baby and its social context become integrated and merged. Finally, the need for all these multiple, inter-woven and complex processes to understand how babies can develop in the world is emphasized, drawing on research and policy which reiterates the use of psychosocial perspectives to gain a full picture of the development of babies and its impact on the rest of their lives.

Thinking about babies: the theoretical context

An aim of this chapter is to provide an introduction to the perspectives and theories that constitute psychosocial thinking on development and particularly early childhood development. During the early years a child develops a sense of who they are, and they recognize a concrete world beyond themselves and the object of their attention, albeit seen from their internal perspective. This process of the child becoming integrated into its surroundings – part of the social world – encompasses the enormous changes the baby undergoes as an undifferentiated pre-linguistic newborn becomes a speaking, conceptually sophisticated and social being.

Borrowing here for a moment a 'social constructionist' approach to get some helpful background to this discussion (see Chapters 4 and 5 for more on social constructionism), how this process of *becoming* is thought about from society to society, and what is seen as important and/or ordinary (such as how and when certain kinds of changes should take place) is always defined by sets of cultural beliefs. We cannot separate out the child's 'socializing' process from the specificity of any particular society or cultural norms. Also, these can reveal a variety of definitions and theories about what is 'normal' development, each of which are socially and culturally constructed; that is to say, they are historically significant and change over time. As such many beliefs and ideas about growth and development are the result of pre-existing socio-cultural discourses and ideologies about the nature of childhood, beliefs that gradually and sometimes imperceptibly evolved from the thinking of previous generations. How societies think about and speak about babyhood and child development is both historically and culturally specific and always undergoing change.

In the 'developed' West only really in the twentieth century did psychologists and to some extent medical doctors become the experts on child development. For example, prior to this philosophers and scientists, theologians, politicians and intellectuals were involved in creating the rich and often contradictory field of knowledge in Western societies about what babies and young children were and what they needed. Three important sets of ideas that evolved are:

1 The discourse of the young child as naturally wild and untamed (the state of nature), and so development is focused on the socialization of children within society, or the state that they would reach under the 'social contract' (Thomas Hobbes, 1588–1699).
2 The discourse of the young child as a 'tabula rasa' (a blank slate) with no innate knowledge, and so development is about providing the right conditions for development and nurturing their more natural tendencies (John Locke, 1632–1704).
3 The discourse of the young child as naturally innocent, and so development is fostered by protecting innocence and giving the child the freedom to play and learn (Jean Jacques Rousseau, 1712–1778).

Today these differing ideas about young children and early education continue, and many of the debates about young children in our society encapsulate the spirit of those earliest discourses. For example, debates about the focus of formal childcare in families and communities continue to raise issues about the 'right' approach, whether nurturing or 'taming' to enable children access to the right kind of developing environment.

Psychoanalytic approaches to babies

The examples from philosophical perspectives above are a good reminder that all thinkers, as well as all parents, use whatever ideas they have to hand to try and understand babies and children. Even given the wealth of material that says it is to do with babies, trying to find theorists who actually try to consider what babies are like, what is going on inside them and what their environments/relationships have to do with this, is not easy.

At the latter part of the nineteenth century and the early decades of the twentieth century psychoanalysis was making attempts to understand infants and young babies (for their own sakes eventually, but initially so as to make sense of adults). Sigmund Freud and later Melanie Klein (see Box 2.1) were early theorists mapping the territory, putting into the arena ideas which Anna Freud, Donald Winnicott and eventually people like Bowlby, below, used in their work with infants, children and parents.

The 'life stage theories' of the twentieth century, which we highlight below, are helpful in trying to get an overall picture of how people move through the lifecourse, with reference to what is happening to their identity and their expression of it. But the starting point of this – the world from a newly born baby's perspective – can be hard to read from them. Anyone who has ever spent time with newly borns may remember the shock at the totality and extremity of the transition from contentment to discontent, expressed with every bodily gesture and expression, voice and movement, everything the baby can express with, as misery engulfs the baby's being, and as contentment does too when the baby is warm, fed and comforted.

Box 2.1

Kleinian newly borns

Melanie Klein's key interest was in the psychic dimension; that is to say, the internal thoughts and feelings and sensations (all jumbled up in newly borns) of babies and children. Right from birth, driven by aggressive and sexual instincts, babies experience a powerful and multi-stranded *phantasy* life. Her focus was on the baby's relationship with the mother, a position developed by the object relation theorists (see below).

Newly born babies are unable to distinguish between what is outside themselves and what is inside, or what is fantasy and what is reality. A good warm comfortable feeling is initially experienced as within them, or a bad empty feeling, with no notion that this connects to mothers, or food, or any external person or event. What Klein calls the *paranoid/schizoid* position is when the baby projects the aggressive rage – the bad feelings inside it, onto the mother – the basis of the defence mechanisms of projection and splitting away from the good internal feelings but eventually has to recognize that these feelings emanate from the same source; the mother is experienced as both good and bad (conceptualized as the good breast and the bad breast).

The capacity to tolerate ambivalence, to accept that both good and bad can exist in the same person – the *depressive position* as Klein called it – grows from this stage.

The defences of projection and splitting – separating off what we think is bad and ascribing it to someone else (e.g. like scapegoating in groups; like sentences that start with, 'well I was quite happy with x until she/he made me feel bad about it') – continue through our lives, though if negotiated as a baby, to a lesser rather than an overwhelming extent. The capacity to tolerate ambivalence, to accept that imperfect is fine, that hate goes with love, also continues, and where this has been unable to embed, may produce adults who fear their anger may cause damage to those they care about.

Box 2.2

Freudian newly borns

Freud's highly complex and dynamic theorizing of the mind pays less specific concern to newly born babies than Klein's view. The Freudian baby also has unconscious and undifferentiated drives towards both sex and towards destruction/death, though the former was in the ascendency. The early drives became known as the 'id' in Freud's formulation of the mind.

The id, similar to Freud's thinking about the unconscious, contains *phantasy* material, much as Klein's baby but with less focus on destructiveness and aggression, and unbridled drives, until the psyche next develops the ego. The ego is reality entering the mind – consciousness through thinking processes like language and ideas, putting boundaries on the id – matching the real and possible against the instinct or drive. The super-ego (which develops in young children usually past the baby stage), operating unconsciously and consciously, functions as something like 'conscience' – the internalized authority figure and model – repressing and permitting.

From these interactions the kinds of anxieties and defensive structures each person differently constructs are established. For example, consider the repression of certain kinds of feelings/drives, such as anger.

The two foundational psychoanalytic writers outlined above start to edge us towards thinking about baby development psychosocially. Their work was enormously influential in much of the thinking (and indeed some practice) in child development and child psychotherapy in the twentieth century. Many of these pioneers worked with, were psychoanalysed by, and certainly heavily influenced by Freud and Klein, and took this work to the clinic (like Anna Freud), the hospital (like Bowlby), the community (like Rutter, later in the century) and even, like Winnicott (below), the media, to reach the broader public.

Life-stage theories

Another important conceptual development from these pioneers was a stage theory approach to not just child development but to the lifecourse in general. For example, Freud's work above, on the mind, shows the structure developing in incremental stages from the id, to the id and ego, and then id, ego and super-ego. Freud's account of the development of psycho-sexual stages (oral, anal, Oedipal, latency, adolescence) is also a fundamental account of children's phased development.

The underlying notion is that babies and children's development occurs in a series of stages, sequentially arranged in a predetermined order, which all children pass through; these are universal stages. This is not simply a psychoanalytic approach; for example, Jean Piaget's psychological model of cognitive development is seen as the 'classic' stage model of child development and has been of considerable and durable influence in education theory. However, where psychoanalytically trained and Freudian influences developed the work in relation to research and practice with children, something usefully psychosocial emerges. Erikson's psychosocial stage approach (see Box 2.3) offers a sophisticated and schematic analysis to development throughout the lifecourse.

> **Box 2.3**
>
> **Erik Erikson (1902–94): 'from womb to tomb'**
>
> Trained originally in the psychoanalytic tradition, Erikson shared many of Freud's basic assumptions about development, although we can see that there was less of an emphasis on the sexual drive (*per* Freud) and more emphasis on the emergence and formation of a stable identity that could be carried through the lifecourse. As such his theory and approach was an elaboration of Freud's psychosexual stages of development, and included stages that individuals go through right through adulthood and later life. As Richard Stevens (2008) comments, 'Erikson also succeeds in broadening the scope of his theory to take in not just frustrations and satisfactions but the whole pattern of a person's experience of life. He tries to indicate both the influence of friends, family and acquaintances and the part played by the wider culture'.
>
> Erik Erikson's focus was on psychosocial transitions in life, the stages of personality development characterized not only by sexual and other biological forms of development, but also by age-related social crises and key social events. These crises, which were to be overcome, involved major overarching themes of identity and generativity. These 'psychosocial' stages were influenced by common cultural demands and expectations for children of a certain age (e.g. toilet training or sleep patterns) as well as internal processes and changes. For Erikson each child moves through a sequence of tasks centred on a particular facet of identity and the construction of identity. At the heart of these is a conflict in relation to the self, other people and/or life.
>
> Erikson's Psychosocial Stages of Development: trust vs mistrust (0–1); autonomy vs shame (2–3), initiative vs guilt (4–6); industry vs inferiority (7–12); identity vs role confusion (13–19); intimacy vs isolation (20–34); generativity vs stagnation (35–65); ego integrity vs despair (65 onwards).

Thinking, then, about the baby's development, in the very first stage it is argued that the identity issue centres on establishing *basic trust versus mistrust*, out of which emerges hope, which is only established through the quality of interaction with significant others such as parental figures. In other words, from the quality of care (responsiveness of parents to the baby's needs etc.) grows an unconscious attitude that the world can be trusted to satisfy need, or an essentially pessimistic view develops that one is likely to be unsatisfied and let down. In the second year of life the conflict at the heart of identity development is *autonomy versus shame and doubt*. At this stage small children establish a sense that they can be competent in their world – for example, build a tower, brush their teeth – and not to experience shame at failure and doubt in their beginning abilities (and the role of the parent is crucial in supporting this).

For Erikson the early years are particularly important but identity is viewed as a fluid and ongoing construct and continues to form through further developmental stages in later life. The approach of Erikson's emphasizes that developmental stages are guided both by biological maturation (near universal) and cultural expectations (specific and relative). Importantly, his approach is also a psychoanalytic theory, based on years of reformulating Freudian psychosexual stages, but primarily concerned with ego development and 'ordinary' 'healthy' development, rather than, like much psychoanalytic work, concerned to explore psychic struggles or problematic development.

Erikson's work is helpful, then, for understanding baby and young child development psychosocially. By connecting up the internal and external worlds, and foregrounding relationships and emotional processes, we can start to understand what distresses and encourages, what is helpful and what is damaging, in the psyche of growing baby or young child. However, life stage theories are not without their critics.

Two key critiques of theories of baby development

One key problem that has been noted of much European psychology on child development is that it is Eurocentric and, more importantly, ethnocentric (see Robinson, 2007). Research studies exploring child development have also mostly been carried out in Western societies. In many ways there is the problem with the universalizing features of this point of view – that people's similarities, rather than their differences, are emphasized in developing a theory of development. Culture has not really been a significant feature of child development psychology. Therefore it has been important to see the ways in which babies, childhood and child development have been socially constructed.

A range of cultural practices surround how we manage and stimulate babies and children, from the use of comforters to the rights and wrongs about how we separate babies from their parents during sleep times. Many of these practices are different cross-culturally and form our ideas about what it means to have a 'good baby' – interestingly, in particular Western Eurocentric ideologies the notion of having a 'good baby' is judged on whether it is sleeping well through the night and is generally docile when needed! (see Selwyn, 2000).

In addition, ideas about what might be considered to be 'good enough' parenting and the assessment of that parenting will be largely influenced by cultural expectations, and so we would argue that it is important to be aware of and to recognize variation in cultural practice. Those variations might be related to the contexts in which childcare takes place, the behaviours that are taken-for-granted or 'common-sense', or to the developmental goals that particular families aspire to (Boushell *et al.*, 2000).

Life-stage theories of human development, (applying to babies, children and in some the whole of life) as briefly discussed above (e.g. Erikson) have also been the subject of some thought-provoking analysis. There is an identified difficulty with thinking about 'universal' life stages. As Woodward states,

> ... developmental psychology has traditionally projected a standardised image of childhood, especially through the emphasis on describing universal stages of psychological growth within what are assumed to be normal childhood environments. (Woodhead, 1999: 3)

Life-stage views of child development suggest that there are 'normal' stages of development that each child must successfully negotiate in order to develop and have a happy adulthood, as we saw with Woodhead's quotation. Many child development theorists adopt such an approach although there are significant and sometimes subtle differences as to what stages this might include. Psychosocially, we also need to keep in mind to what extent does the social and cultural context surrounding the individual's life impact on our ideas (and theirs) about what is normal and what are the expectations?

Rutter and Rutter (1993) have suggested that the problem with many of the stage-related theories of development is that their biopsychosocial model is one that is overly inclusive of a range of factors but that frequently they over-emphasize the role of society and the social environment, although Freud particularly and even Erikson are usually criticized for the opposite of this. Stage theories are therefore contentious and it would be difficult to easily disentangle what are the different effects of biology, of psyche and society.

However, thinking inclusively and psychosocially, there seems to be little need to undertake such a reductive exercise. What we most need to keep in mind is that babies' and children's development is a complex and multifactorial process, in which their physical and emotional environment, physical/biological 'givens' and growth, psychic landscape, social and cultural influences all have an impact on who they are and who they can become.

Perhaps even more influential than life-stage theories, and certainly extremely popular still/again in understanding children (and adults) psychological difficulties, is the burgeoning body of theory on attachment.

Attachment theories

At its core the theme of attachment encompasses a whole range of perspectives from twentieth-century object relations thinkers, attachment theory, purely psychological work on primates, through to contemporary discussions of the need for social relations to sustain mental well-being. Attachment is not really a single theory but what we might call a conceptual framework that helps us to think about how deep-seated human security attachments develop, strengthen or weaken.

In its initial theorizing, what attachment was most concerned with was the impact of babies being 'connected' to primary care givers – often, but by no means exclusively, their mothers. Primarily, attachment refers to the notion that the infant can develop a strong emotional bond with a caretaker, to help develop and strengthen their feelings of security. In referring to attachment as a particular approach to children's development the key figure is John Bowlby. For Bowlby, attachment is allied to a biological process and response which arises from the child's desire to seek security from an attachment figure, which as stated is a response to wider evolutionary need (i.e. adaption to self-preservation) (see Bowlby, 1982 [1969]). Bowlby recognized that attachments can form at any stage of the life cycle (from birth to later life), although few match the intensity and significance of earlier child-parent, infant-carer attachments.

Mary Ainsworth, along with Bowlby, was also very influential in the work on attachment theory (Ainsworth *et al.*, 1978). Attachment theory has its roots in psychoanalytic thought, especially in exploring the earliest relationship between the mother and the child. Attachment is based on securing an 'affectional bond' – a safe place from which to gain security and from which the child can explore the world. How we might conceptualize what is a 'safe place' is a moot point, and we need to consider that this may be somewhat socially and culturally variable. However, from these earliest attachments the child begins to develop the 'internal working model' (see Box 2.4).

Box 2.4

'Internal working model'

During the 1940s and 1950s John Bowlby (1907–90) developed a body of work on the long-term impact on children of either being separated from their parents for long periods of time (especially refugees and war orphans such as Jewish children rescued both during and after the war, as well as war evacuees from London) or having suffered periods of emotional difficulties or adversity during childhood (Bowlby, 1951). The World Health Organization (WHO) commissioned him at the time to write a report on the mental health of homeless children in post-war Europe, which gave Bowlby the opportunity to explore more widely the effects of maternal separation and deprivation on young children.

Bowlby argued that a child's attachment to his or her mother is underpinned by an instinctual behavioural system and that this in turn is influenced by the 'internal working models' that the child develops of the social world. These working models are based on the child's experience with their caregiver (see Bowlby, 1958, 1982 [1969]), and which Bowlby perceived as the mental representation or model of what to expect from the figure of attachment. The child forms a series of questions about that attachment, such as, are they a safe base? By the time the child is five years of age the internal model is firmly established and is unlikely to change much. These mental models were thought by Bowlby to determine the ability of a child to use the caregiver as protection against the challenging life events and situations (how they perceived threats and how they handled such threats), and so they act as a template for how they make sense of new situations.

In addition such models help in the development of a range of social skills and the influence of the model lasts well into later childhood and beyond. It is suggested that young children who easily seek and accept support from their parents or carers are considered secure in their attachments; secure children over time show a variety of social and emotional advantages over those who are insecure (Cassidy and Shaver, 1999).

For Bowlby children that are separated from their primary caregiver displayed similar types of reactions over time, and that breaking from that attachment bond ultimately led to great distress for the child and was inextricably linked to later mental health difficulties. For Bowlby, the separation anxieties were real anxieties located in the real world and were not, *per* Kleinian psychoanalytic views, subjugated phantasies or expressions of unconscious desires and motivations. The attachment figure did not have to be a mother – more a 'mothering' figure – indeed Bowlby's conclusion was that the key to successful and healthy development was that,

> For the moment it is sufficient to say that what is believed to be essential for mental health is that the infant and young child should experience a warm, intimate and continuous relationship with his mother (or permanent mother-substitute) in which both find satisfaction and enjoyment ... a state of affairs in which the child does not have this relationship is termed 'maternal deprivation'. (Bowlby, 1951: 11)

But, Bowlby seemed unambiguous in his initial formulations of these issues where the father played 'second fiddle' (1951) in merely supporting the mother in those relationships with the child; later he suggested that multiple attachments could be formed.

In addition, he suggested that attachment difficulties were often transmitted from one generation to the next, and so we can see Bowlby's work was influential in those developing theories to account for intergenerational deprivation and poverty – the 'wicked issues' of contemporary social life. He had an awareness of the interactional elements of the child's early life: the biological and psychosocial. As such, Bowlby also emphasized the role of social networks – a person's connectedness – on economic as well as health factors in the development of well-functioning mother-child relationships, and later research underlines that poverty, maternal depression and or marital discord damage a mother's capacity to facilitate nurturing attachments (Lyons-Ruth and Jacobvitz, 1999). In this sense Bowlby's theory closely reflects our notion of a psychosocial approach set out above. At its heart is a theory about relationships and connections, the personal and interpersonal nature of those relationships, and how an individual (the child) makes psychosocial progress through life.

From attachment to independence

As we can see above, Bowlby and the attachment theorists concentrated particularly on babies as connected beings; that is to say, babies in relation to their carers, usually their mothers. But the understanding of babies not as separate beings, as we saw with Klein and Freud above, but as part of a relationship, was also primarily the concern of a school of psychoanalysts called object relations theorists.

What differentiated these theorists from those steeped in Freudian principles is the notion that sexuality and the aggressive drives are less important as motivational forces, and that human relationships in their variety are the main developmental drivers. The importance of the relational to, for example, human health and well-being, is a psychosocial theme we will return to later in the book. Essentially, people have basic needs for contact and connection and meaningful interaction at an interpersonal level with others, and throughout life. That children and adults thrive and 'do well' when connected to other humans, and struggle when isolated seems to underpin a swathe of contemporary research and theorizing in relation to a whole range of issues from changing schools to retiring. These themes, from attachment theory, from Erikson's stages and from Winnicott, below, arguing that self is forged in these early childhood years and is formed in the child's relationship to the mother, or the primary care giver (object), highlight the function of reliable, stable and loving care in the positive development of babies (and eventually adults). The tolerance of strong emotions is part of this. None of these theorists argue that development is all sweetness and light for baby or carer, but there are internal and interpersonal struggles, that can be managed with differing consequences across a range of spectra, such as insecurity/security, optimism/pessimism, and trust/mistrust.

As we saw above, for Klein destructive drives are a fundamental part of the human subject (this is not just a consequence of the social environment). For Winnicott and the later object relationists, destructiveness is part of the love impulse. A modern psychosocial writer such as Hoggett draws on these ideas to think about the concept of the 'struggle of development' (2000: 14); the struggle is aimed at both ourselves and others. Importantly, object relationists such as Winnicott reformulate positively Klein's idea of 'the depressive position' (above) as 'the development of the capacity for concern' (for the mother), hence moving away from interpreting the workings of the internal world as essentially traumatic and inward facing, to something about relations with the 'other' (the 'object' in this terminology), the overall interest in which defined the school of psychoanalysis founded by him and similar thinkers.

We have sound examples of how and why small babies and parents firmly attach to each other, and as Bowlby's and Ainsworth's work above suggests, how babies and eventually the adults they will become would be damaged without such closeness. However, we also need to understand that babies and young children are compelled to physically and psychologically move from their parent's arms to the world. Autonomy, as we saw in Erikson's stages, is also important for a child to develop. Babies need to be able to survive distance and absence of the care-giver, even if only in small measures. But as we have argued psychosocially, the parent is not just an external figure in a world peopled with such, he or she is a part of the psychic space of the baby – built in – and so autonomy involves a highly complex process of both holding on to and letting go.

Thinking about connection and separation, the psychoanalyst and paediatrician, Donald Winnicott is very useful for psychosocial approaches (Box 2.5).

Box 2.5

Donald Winnicott (1896–1971)

Donald Winnicott was both psychoanalytically and medically trained, and his early experience connected him to the work of, for example, Melanie Klein. Like Bowlby, he worked with refugee children during the Second World War, work which influenced his thinking on children's psychological and social needs.

Winnicott mostly worked with mothers and babies, and wrote, lectured and broadcast on the subject for the middle and late decades of the twentieth century, offering humane, sensible and forgiving concepts on child care such as 'good enough parenting'. Central to his work is the importance of the relationship between the baby and its mother, and the 'intersubjective' (between the two) relationship.

For Winnicott the primary need is for the mother to offer an emotional 'environment' for the baby, in which all kinds of overwhelming feelings or fears, as well as the range of good feelings can be made safe ('held' and 'contained') by consistent loving responses. He advocated the need for babies of such safe emotional environments to grow and 'experiment' in, and need for support (the father's/society's role) for 'the ordinary good mother' as he addressed the care giver. The mother needs to be attentive but not overwhelming.

Winnicott's work has been enormously influential, and concepts such as 'true self and false self' (in which as babies we take on the mother's version of who we are as if it were 'really' us), and his cross-disciplinary writing around play, imagination and creativity have reached a substantial international audience and are still popular.

In relation to a psychosocial view of baby development, a further concept from Winnicott is particularly helpful: that of the 'third area' of human living: an area that is neither located in the individual (the intimate and personal) nor outside in the external world (the social and depersonal), but is an area that exists betwixt and between. This third area is the area of transitional space filled with transitional objects that infants develop attachment to. Winnicott (1953) suggested that many infants and young children move on from their attachment to mothers and primary care givers by the use of 'transitional objects'. These are 'bridges' between the mother and the immediate environment, physically and psychologically. The mother is seen by Winnicott as such an 'object' of attachment (at first) but later these transitional objects are ways of deflecting attachment into objects that allow for some degree of secure separation from the mother. Such objects include blankets, teddy bears, dummies and other comforters. They are real objects but also symbolic objects, which again is a 'third' space – between 'me' and 'other', between real and unreal. For Winnicott the transitional object is the crucial first step into culture and play – that the object represents a transition to the social world and a step away from the security of care-giver attachment. The baby can, through transitional spaces and places, integrate with the social world in a psychic and physical sense. The 'becoming social' is the theme of our next section on babies becoming people.

Babies becoming social beings

Each of the theorists we have discussed above is concerned with identity – what a baby is, is like and can be – and now we move on to concern ourselves with social identity and being in the world. As Hoggett phrases it, 'Each baby which arrives in this world brings with it a nascent appreciation of the politics of group life' (Hoggett, 2000: 158). Winnicott's work, above, as we saw, is helpful in trying to understand how babies bridge the gap between the psychic world and the social world, in a very practical and observational way. However, how we can understand babies becoming social – how the social world impacts on their development and how they become integrated into (e.g. learn the ways of being in) their families, cultures and society – is not only assisted by these psychosocial theorists but is an area in which psychosocial theory can to some extent draw on the work of 'identity sociologists' from a range of perspectives.

However, it is worth noting here, that much more in sociology than the psychodynamic theories outlined above, becoming a person/developing an identity is conceptualized as a complex and extended process, with the theories tending to focus far more on childhood from 4 or 5 years, than on infancy. Psychosocial theorists interested in babies and young children have been able to draw on a range of sociological approaches. Structural sociology's concern with social stratification, unequal power and inequalities, has been able to underpin psychodynamic theorizing about the psychic damage caused when the experience of living in undervalued, stigmatized and oppressed contexts become internalized as 'subaltern identities'. Functionalists and symbolic interactionists have been able to offer a clear focus on how babies become social beings. However, psychoanalytic theory is still predominant in theorizing infancy. This chapter reflects this by drawing more on psychodynamic theory, but also exploring, now, what these two branches of sociology add to our understanding.

What is interesting, psychosocially, is what sociology and social psychology explores in relation to how babies become *identified* with their worlds: a concept also developed in the next chapter. Socialization theory offers a coherent and accepted account prevalent since the early twentieth century. Traditional sociological thinking has taken a social learning approach and placed the process of socialization at the heart of explaining how an infant is made 'social', and how the norms and values of a social system at large become ingrained into the child's way of thinking, feeling and doing. The concepts of 'primary and secondary' socialization are core. Primary is usually conceptualized as that 'learning to be' initially acquired from the immediate social group, standardly a family unit – including how to be a boy or girl, how to be a daughter or son; how to eat, speak, and all the cultural nuances of the particular kind of family this takes place in.

Secondary socialization is theorized as the kind of 'learning' about how things are done, with friends, in school (later at work) and from the media and wider social structures, including how to behave in ways your world finds acceptable in the playground and classroom and community. This learning/becoming in both stages of socialization is neither an unconscious, in the psychoanalytic sense outlined above, nor conscious, in the sense of 'oh yes I must remember girls have to do…' process but some-where between the two. We could probably explain in some way what is expected, we know things are expected, but mostly we internalize 'how to be' and pay it little specific everyday attention. This would also be true in the concept of 'role'.

A further conceptual building block for understanding how people (all through life) become stitched into their particular cultures and societies is that of 'role' and 'role play', which compartmentalizes understanding society in to understanding the specific ways of being and behaving people need to learn in order to 'perform' (the theatrical metaphor is inherent here) in it. These encompass, for example, gender roles, culture roles, age roles; being a pupil in school, a mate in the playground, a son in the home, and eventually occupational roles and parenting roles: a manager, a father or mother. This process is begun in very young children, who in their play, role theory would argue, copy adults' behaviours, for example nurse their dolls like parents do babies. Mead, for example, (see below) argued this is the foundational process for building identities: learning to imitate the other and learning to see themselves from the outside – being someone else.

But even in its earlier twentieth-century beginnings, neither socializa-tion nor role theory was unproblematically conceptualized as society imposing fixed notions of 'how to be' on passive and only receptive babies and children. Even by the 1960s the notion that individuals have choices and freedoms in how they play their social roles was embedded in social theory (e.g. Turner, 1962), including the key idea of choosing the extent to which one conforms or deviates from role expectations.

Similarly, socialization's key notion, that developing a self is all about what the world imposes on babies, has given way to thinking about an interactive mutually constituted process, where the baby is not passive or overly determined. More 'recent' developments in this area have focused on the autonomy of children and childhood (see James *et al.*, 1998; James and James, 2004) arguing that children should be seen as active social agents. Socialization does not repress children's individu-ality; socialization may provide children (and babies) with the knowledge and skills needed – the tools to actively be – in any given society and context, through the family, the school or peers. Socialization theory therefore suggests the baby or child is in the process of 'becoming' and it is not yet 'being' (James and James, 2004: 27). We will return to this in relation to older children in the following chapter.

However, it is also worth mentioning that the notion that learning roles and being socialized does impose limits and constraints on how people can be, has also been a prevalent theme in structural sociology with a great deal of work on, for example, gender roles looking at how what it is to be a girl or a boy is imposed, via language, gesture, expectation, encouragement and so on from birth, including an unequal place in the power structures of patriarchal capitalism. Similarly on class, for example, and being socialized into 'one's place' in the social hierarchy, a point returned to below. This also resonates with Bourdieu's work on habitus, which in its initial conceptualization suggests identities are highly culturally determined.

Box 2.6

Pierre Bourdieu (1930–2002): habitus

Bourdieu was a pre-eminent French social theorist, whose work encompasses anthropological practice, primary research, philosophy and as well as building theory for education, issues of culture and taste, and in relation to habitus, the issue of social reproduction. All of Bourdieu's work centrally concerns itself with issues of social justice and inequality.

Habitus means the internalized and embodied life world which dictates how we can be – what we can think, how we sit or walk, ways of eating, what we think is funny. Because this habitus develops from birth within a family within a culture, then what is absorbed is culturally specific. For example, class attitudes and what Bourdieu calls 'dispositions': in other words, fields of, for example, physical activity, or emotional understanding, or expectations. The individual absorbs a habitus – ways of being – unconsciously, and this also then unconsciously dictates how the child (and later, adult) will behave, think and act.

Individuals therefore internalize not only 'how we do it here' but also 'what we can conceptualize here': what can be desired/wanted and aspired to. This is highly significant, for example, in addressing issues such as the education system's failure to offer working-class children more 'middle-class' opportunities (see Chapter 4).

Bourdieu's early writing about habitus was immensely influential, connecting into perhaps more well-known notions such as 'social capital' (discussed in Chapter 7). His initial formulation of the concept suggested an identity that was almost entirely fixed and unchanging. Later on in his writing Bourdieu conceded that the habitus could be impacted on in later life, and in his autobiographical work discussed the (his) experience of a 'habitus cleevè – a split habitus – to understand the impact of his class change from working-class childhood to becoming a revered middle-class intellectual.

Bourdieu's social structural account, concerned with the reproduction and transmission of social structures such as class, as manifest in unconscious identity, embodiment and language, is different from the more individually focused accounts of developing identity offered by the symbolic interactionists. The relationship between developing an identity ('self', being the preferred twentieth-century term) and the capacity to create and interpret meaning was the particular focus of this grouping of sociologists and social psychologists (see Chapter 1). The body of work has been at the heart of social constructionist thinking from as far back as the 1920s and still highly influential today through the work of British sociologists like Anthony Giddens.

Box 2.7

Symbolic interactionism

With nearly a century's trajectory, symbolic interactionism is associated with the most renown sociologists of a particular era: George Mead from the Chicago school, writing in the 1920s and 30s; Erving Goffman, a later Chicago school theorist, writing famous and highly influential texts such as *Asylums* and *The Presentation of self in everyday life* in the 1950s and 1960s; Anthony Giddens, an influential and prolific British sociologist writing social identity theory from the 1980s to the present.

The symbolic interactionist school gave the developing discipline of sociology a primary concern with how meaning is made and used – in other words, how within different cultures and times, 'objective' phenomena are understood differently: what meanings are ascribed to them. Symbols are used to convey and interpret meaning. Social constructionism (see Chapters 4 and 5) begins from this understanding.

Symbolic interactionists have also always concerned themselves in how babies and young children come to develop their social identities – in other words, how they learn to see themselves through the eyes of others and internalize what society thinks of them; indeed George Mead's work was pioneering in this. Goffman's famous statement: 'I am what I think you think I am' summarizes the position, though too deterministically – this is not such a neat elision.

Current symbolic interactionists like Giddens are also interested in how people 'mesh' with their societies, how they filter through the presented/available ways of being and becoming they see in their world (under conditions of globalization that is to some extent 'the world') and make choices using this information to produce their social identity ('reflexive identification').

As we noted in the last chapter, symbolic interactionism, then, has some similar concerns to psychosocial thinking – the interweaving of the external and internal worlds, but also some noticeable disagreements, in the sense that the processes of rational choice and agency usually at the heart of this work provides a very different internal landscape to the accounts of determining psychic structuring (e.g. damage inflicted in infancy may well impact on the rest of a person's life).

However, for understanding the baby, these sociological/social psychological theorists would agree that somehow 'society' gets into the child's way of being and becoming, so that at the minimum they are able to understand and fit in with the expectations of the family and culture(s) of which they are a part. Whether we see them as taking roles or adopting a habitus, becoming gendered, 'classed' and encultured, and becoming a user of the language through which these aspects are organized and made meaningful are active processes from birth. The relationship between society and the individual – how and to what extent each influence the other – is at the heart of contemporary sociology (e.g. Giddens' Structuration Theory, Bourdieu's concept of habitus (see above) and Hoggett's psychosocial version) and will be returned to in later chapters of the book.

Babies developing in adverse surroundings

Practitioners and theorists of baby and child development have long recognized that where families are struggling with a whole range of social problems, the emotional (and indeed cognitive) development of the baby will be affected, and that this impact (like the absence of attachment, and the absence of safe emotional environments) continues as part of the identity of this newly forming person. The complex relationship between maternal/family poverty, a range of other social difficulties, and poor development for young children and into later life, has accrued a great deal of research evidence.

For example, in 2010 the (USA) Urban Institute published the results of extensive national research on poor mothers, depression and baby care. The link between poverty and depression as well as other forms of ill health) was striking, meaning that below the federal poverty line, 1 in 9 infants is living with a mother with severe depression, in more than half with a mother with mild-moderate depression. The other risk factors were the mothers' exposure to domestic violence, high rates of drug and alcohol abuse, the absence of the father:

> For 16 percent of infants living in poverty with severely depressed mothers, their mothers report having been physically abused between the 9- and 24 month interviews – eight times the share of their peers with non-depressed mothers. Further, for 14 percent of infants living in poverty with severely depressed mothers, their mothers report binge drinking in the last month, compared with 6 percent of infants living in poverty whose mothers are not depressed. (Vericker *et al.*, 2010)

The impact of this is profound. Given what we have learnt from Winnicott and Bowlby, above, providing nurturing environments that focus on the baby's needs are likely to be very hard for a depressed and/or struggling mother to focus on.

And in the UK in 2010 came the report of what has become known as 'The Field Review', which again emphasized that the upbringing of under 3 year olds impacted into all areas of their lives, and for that upbringing to be successful it required:

> … the things that matter most are a healthy pregnancy; good maternal mental health; secure bonding with the child; love and responsiveness of parents along with clear boundaries, as well as opportunities for a child's cognitive, language and social and emotional development. Good services matter too. (Field, 2010: 5)

However, the context of the review, and indeed the context of families being able to meet these needs set out above, is still poverty, albeit not as inevitably or completely determining of a child's life chances. Field comments from the offset:

> I have increasingly come to view poverty as a much more subtle enemy than purely lack of money, and I have similarly become increasingly concerned about how the poverty that parents endure is all too often visited on their children to the degree that they continue to be poor as they enter adulthood. (Field, 2010: 12)

Love, responsiveness, bonding and boundaries, then, as well as (and, we could argue psychosocially, often because of) the health, mental health and financial security of families, set out in babyhood the capacities to learn, thrive, form relationships and make 'successful lives'. Even the government is thinking psychosocially!

Conclusion

This chapter has set out to consider how babies develop as emotional, relational and social beings. It has been concerned to think through the interaction of babies and their contexts: in other words, how relationships with primary carers, usually mothers, provide environments where levels of psychic well-being – perhaps resilience is a useful term here (see Chapter 6 for a full discussion) – will be established for the lifecourse itself. Perspectives on how this development takes place are discussed, and the chapter offers theories from Freud and Klein, Erikson and Winnicott, Bowlby and Ainsworth to look at psychic landscapes and their importance to identity development. Key sociological perspectives on understanding how babies develop as social beings are also offered, particularly a rather qualified version of socialization, role theory, drawing on the work of the symbolic interactionists Mead, Goffman and Giddens and of more structural sociological accounts of how the baby absorbs its life world, referencing the work of Bourdieu. Finally, the range of contemporary understanding of babies as psychosocial beings is demonstrated by large-scale United States and English research informing government policy initiatives. In the next chapter some of these key themes are developed as we consider children and young people.

3

How people become: agency and identification

Introduction

In the last chapter we considered the baby stage of the lifecourse, and looked at what psychosocial theory could usefully tell us about how babies start to develop. We particularly focused on psychoanalytic and psychodynamic frameworks of explanation, because in the psychosocial theory this book presents, what happens in infancy and early childhood creates the internal/psychic world of the person, which will determine much of what they can be and do through to the end of their lives. That is not to suggest that nothing ever changes, but that a great deal is put in place which can be hard to change.

In reality, of course, babyhood and childhood slide into each other, and the age at which small children start to do this or think that varies enormously from culture to culture, and individual to individual.

This chapter will also attempt initially to continue with some of the themes begun in the last chapter. It begins with revisiting the development of the psychic landscape, using Freud and also Lacan to look at emerging gender identity, and some critiques of this work. Identification as a key issue in children's 'becoming' is discussed here. Psychosocial life-stage theories of childhood, from Erikson, are considered and attachment theory briefly revisited. Drawing on a range of social theories which can be used to build psychosocial thinking, for example, the 'new sociology of childhood' mentioned in the previous chapter (James *et al.*, 1998; James and James, 2004) themes of the child in the body and the child in friendship contexts will be introduced further into the chapter. Finally, the child in the family is given some thought, with the family seen as less of a 'nurturing environment' and more as a social and psychodynamic space. A discussion of education – the child and the school – can be located in Chapter 5, which looks psychosocially at how people are occupied, from school through employment to retirement. Similarly to the last chapter, this one is not intended to be a complete account of child development, but a discussion of some key psychosocial themes in the life stage of childhood.

As with all the chapters in this book the issue of children's lifecourse is being approached here 'in context'. The starting point for the writers is that which constitutes childhood is only possible to understand when the child is considered dynamically and as inseparable from the social and emotional spaces they develop within. A child's development is both a highly personal, but also a completely social set of stages and events, though not occurring in neat lines and predictable orders. Children's transitions to adulthood seem to be more circular and messy than phased, complete and 'neat'.

Psychoanalytical thinking about entry into the world

Even though the chapter does not consider school itself, 'school age' is quite a handy way of conceptualizing the age group and life stage of the 'child' this chapter is concerned with. What this gives us a starting point here is the transition made at the age of 4 or 5 in many European and Western countries, when children first go to school. The 'environment' of children before this is often mostly the mother and the intimate family. Of course the reality of mothers' and some fathers' working patterns, beliefs about the efficacy of children's pre-school education, different national policies on starting school and so on means that a child's move to independence, into a world other than the home, is by no means a fixed point but for many a gradual transition. So, too, the psychoanalytic stage with which it equates, during which the psychic separation from the mother is a key focus: the Freudian Oedipal phase (see Box 3.1).

For Freud, the Oedipal phase offers a way of understanding the young child's drive to 'leap out of its mother's arms', as it were, and adopt the 'appropriate' gender identification and separation. Up until this point gender and sexuality are unfixed, but after this gendering is more established. Freud argued that a differential process completes the Oedipal phase, offering a different kind of relationship to 'independence' in boys and in girls. We discuss this further in relation to gender and adult 'dependence' in relationships in the next chapter.

Box 3.1

The Oedipal phase

In thinking about small children, the Oedipal phase offers an explanatory schema for understanding emotional separation from the nurturing environment, and identification with the mother, to the separating out of a distinct gendered identity in the world.

Drawing on the cultural references of a different age, Freud takes the mythical figure of King Oedipus, as written by Sophocles, who inadvertently killed his father and married his mother, to discuss the intense love of the mother experienced by a small boy.

This encompasses moving through his sense of his father as his rival, a wish to be rid of the father, and eventually, because of fear of the father's power (to castrate him) his abandonment of his claims to the mother and his identification with the father, and with masculinity more generally.

Freud's language in formulating this phase is true to the passion, vengefulness, carnality and cruelty of its Greek tragedy origins which has rendered it unacceptable and even vaguely silly to some modern audiences, but the passion with which small children can attempt to claim the sole attention of one parent and completely reject the other is an ordinary observable experience in parenting,

The idea of changing identification from the mother to the father and hence solidifying masculine identity all seems helpful to understand a crucial phase in a child's development.

Lacan's development of Freud's thinking in relation to this is also useful, in the sense that even though he unapologetically deploys the sexualized language of the original – the notion of castration, the loss of the penis, (though recast as the symbolic 'phallus') – he connects the phase to the entry into masculine culture and language. As a post-structural thinker, language for him is *the* central construct. Language is determining of all social phenomena and relationships, it is not an explanatory tool, but that which constructs, for example, agency, power and human subjectivity (identity); it does not just reflect thoughts, it makes things, and makes things happen. Therefore the entry into language is the entry into the pre-existing order of how and what can be said – the 'symbolic' rules (Lacan names this stage 'the symbolic' – see Box 3.2) that order culture and society, given all is language. Therefore completing the Oedipal phase is the demarcation of adult 'becoming': of taking one's place and having the capacity to operate in the adult masculine world.

> ### Box 3.2
>
> **Jacques Lacan (1901–81)**
>
> Jacques Lacan was a French medically trained psychoanalyst significant as both post-Freudian (building on Freud's work) and post-structuralist, privileging language as the key determinant in human existence.
>
> In one sense Lacan is a 'life-stage theorist', as he uses the notion of infant/child negotiating 'the mirror phase' as a necessary development stage in identity formation. However, his further demarcations of 'stages' function more as 'orders of experience' than conventional life stages, in the sense that the 'imaginary', the 'symbolic' and 'the real' are the psychic realms – the way the psyche is structured – which individuals continue to inhabit simultaneously.
>
> - The imaginary: the 'realm' of the baby's fantasy world: a first psychic 'environment' where parental psychic expectations of what this baby are are already in place and the baby inhabits a space of demands, disintegrated longings and disorganized biological activity. The mirror phase creates some kind of ordering of the identity – falsely.
> - The mirror phase: how babies internalize an image of themselves which is distorted. Although it sees what seems in the mirror to be a whole and complete self this is a fiction. The baby's identity comprises multiple and contradictory drives and disjointed affects, and from the mirror stage also comprises parental (mother's) expectations as they reflect to the child some version of themselves which includes parental hopes, dreams and fantasies. 'Our' identity can only ever be partial, conflicted and mistaken.
> - The symbolic: the post-Oedipal phase of entry into the use of language as the carrier of all society and culture's meanings, as a resource and the key to operating in the (masculine) world (see below).
> - The real: that which is comprised of the unspoken and unspeakable. Something hard to define and primitive, which is always underneath the symbolic, and to some extent threatens the order of the symbolic. This is nearer chaos and longing.
>
> Even more than Freud, Lacan's work is complex, contradictory and metaphorical. However, its focus on language, identification, desire and culture has firmly embedded it in cultural studies and cultural analysis more generally, and currently Lacanian psychoanalytic practice is becoming a dominant training and form in much of Europe (Frosh, 2012; Maguire, 2004; Minsky, 1998).

Freud and Lacan take this Oedipal/symbolic phase as a masculine turning away, if only partially, from the mother, acquiring gender/language and entry into the masculine world. Both approached the female passage through this stage as a rather different process and as unsatisfactory and incomplete in aspects, a discussion continued in a substantial body of psychoanalytical feminist writing. We will come to this below. However, because much of this writing has drawn on a slightly more psychosocial than psychoanalytical paradigm, it may be worth briefly highlighting the extent to which this phase, undertaken probably between about 3 and 5 years, can be seen psychosocially.

Psychosocial thinking with Oedipus

Lacan's account of the entry into the symbolic (through the Oedipal situation), because of the connection into discourse/language (not just literally words but the structures they construct, of ways of being, essentially everything we call identity and society) is fundamentally a psychosocial account. It identifies the child becoming social, finding a place in the social world that already exists; and also internalizing the tools of that world to make their own interventions in it. Moreover, it forces the child to internalize some of the rules of desire and power for society – who you may and may not love, who you must give way to – and by implication that *there are* rules about all of this. Becoming masculine and feminine is absolutely at the root of who we can be in the world, and gendering a complex psychosocial process. Frosh (2012) is worth quoting at length here:

> Socially, the structure of the Oedipus complex reflects the constraining force of society, which is in essence opposed to the expression of the child's omnipotent, unbridled desires: for society to function, laws and regulations have to be imposed. Desire has to be channelled into a productive form, and some outside structure that is greater than the individual always makes this so. The oedipal father is a representation of what society allows in terms of the expression of desire and through this also of sexual difference... (2012: 82)

Girls also become gendered through an Oedipal stage of sorts, whereby understanding that they are without the penis/phallus (understood symbolically or not), and cannot therefore have masculine power is fundamental. Lacan was conscious of the masculine, symbolized as the phallus, as synonymous with power, in that language is the regime in which masculine power is constantly ascribed and re-ascribed, and that to be female was to experience lack/exclusion in this. Freud, similarly, argued that to be female was to 'lack', though not understood through language but through individual unconscious affect, and experienced as 'penis envy'. This has posed a variety of difficulties for many practitioners of psychoanalysis, as well as social theorists, some of whom align themselves to feminist thinking.

In the next chapter we consider Chodorow's splendid and complex psychosocial reworking of the Oedipus complex, essentially explaining that women are allowed to go on identifying with the mother: they have no penis and cannot fully identify with the masculine. Not having to switch identification from their safe and known 'nurturing environment' as boys do, girls are not in fact more damaged at this stage, but more supported, than boys, and internalize safety (durability) as well as need in relation to relationships. Boys on the other hand have to give up the safe and known (in other words their 'safe' relationship is severed) and identify with the often 'unavailable' (given contemporary parenting arrangements) father.

Post-structural feminists (some Lacanians themselves) have been interested in rather different debates around Oedipal gendering, as one would expect, particularly around language and Lacan's 'phallogocentrism'. This is a concept not dissimilar to patriarchal capitalism in that it analyses dominant masculine power, but the structural element is language not economics.

Discourses (i.e. meanings: all aspects of language) are essentially part of 'the rule of the father', as bearers of masculine power and masculine principles. Entry into language therefore must mean for both sexes entry into a world in which masculinity, or at least masculinized principles and ideas, forms and structures, is privileged. Whether one is male or female, the hierarchy is the same.

Lacan's lack of a considered and reasonable account of femininity, which did not just position women as lacking, powerless, envious and without a language, was challenged by a strong grouping of French and European analysts and theorists, for example Luce Irigaray (1977) mainly in relation to female language and female desire. More recent theorists such as Maguire (2004) have suggested that in fact female identity is built round multiple identifications, and is shifting and unfixed: that gender identity is not completed at this early phase, but continues and includes identifications across gender boundaries as the child develops into a woman.

Lacanian versions of Oedipal gendering and masculine power are particularly interesting if one starts to explore what that might mean socially for children. Many girls want to be, or are at least are comfortable being, 'tom-boys'. However, the idea that boys might want to be seen as even the slightest bit girlie is mostly unthinkable/unpronounceable – there is no socially comfortable discourse of a boy playing as a girl. Experiments in gender and children's play show that toys become categorized as 'boys', girls and (possibly) 'neutral'. Girls will play with boys' toys and 'neutral' toys, but boys play very little with girls' toys and not very frequently neutral ones (Idle *et al.*, 1993). How can this be understood? Maguire's suggestion that girls' gender identifications are less fixed in childhood may be useful. Or in relation to power, masculine language and order might preclude alignment with lower status femininity. Or perhaps all girls as well as all boys have 'a male in the head' (or in the psyche) as Holland *et al*. (1998) suggested in their research that explored how it was *masculine* discourses/ideas of teenage girls' sexuality policed and controlled what they felt able to do and be.

Identification

Even more important here for thinking about children 'growing up' is the issue of identification itself. The Oedipal phase discussed above suggests that 'identification' is a process of rejecting or accepting an identification with a same or opposite sex parent, and then gender identification, at least, is straightforwardly sorted; less with girls though, where it is a bit more confused and incomplete. But the notion of 'identification': who or what we want to be, desire to be like, emulate – this range of ideas – is in itself helpful for thinking about children as 'becoming' adults, and is a term that also works comfortably between psychoanalysis, and recent sociology.

Identification suggests an active engagement with becoming, more than just, for example, the implied copying of 'role modelling' or the enforced shaping of 'socialization', but something more like actively wanting/desiring something or to be like someone, making some links/leaps in terms of fantasy and imagination, making attempts to emulate and incorporate aspects of the 'object' into the self, some evaluation, some change. New sociology of childhood theorists also outline an active process involved in children 'becoming', particularly critiquing traditional socialization theory, arguing that even quite small children are active participants in the process of taking on an identity. They have agency in this – they engage with it, with differing mixtures of acceptance and rejection. That this may also be a group not purely individual process – group identification – is discussed towards the end of the chapter.

Identification, then, is a concept resonating with psychoanalytical ideas of 'projecting' ourselves into the 'other'/the world (imagining 'being in their shoes') 'introjecting' experiences, fantasies, images of the other/the world and making them part of oneself, and social ideas of actively choosing models (heroes and celebrities as well as the bigger kids in the playground, siblings and parents) to emulate, building a growing idea of self as childhood progresses. In other words it understands how the world gets into a child, and how the internal world of the child impacts on the world in a dynamic process which explains much about how children become adults.

In recent decades cultural studies has made good use of the concept to explore desire and identification in relation to engagement with cultural products and social practices in consumer societies. This is also claimed to be part of the 'growing up' scenario for children and young people: what Langman (1992), called 'shopping for subjectivity'. It is a psychosocial concept of considerable explanatory and exploratory value in thinking through how identity connects to desire, is both unconsciously and actively produced, and how we can understand when our children tell us fervently who they want to be (or be like) when they grow up.

Psychodynamic life stages through childhood

In terms of the kinds of 'life-stage' models of human (psychic) development established by Freud and built on by theorists such as Erikson, the whole period of childhood tends to become focused on infancy and then once the Oedipal phase is finished, adolescence.

Box 3.3

From 6 to 12 psychosocially: Erikson and Freud

Traditional psychoanalysis leaves us rather high and dry in understanding mid-childhood: the middle years of perhaps 6 or 7 to about 12, receive relatively little attention. Freud called this stage 'latency': which can be conceptualized as a kind of inactive, under the surface state, perhaps taking a metaphorical deep breath before the supposed turmoil of adolescence.

Erikson, as we saw in Chapter 2, theorized each life stage as predicated on an essential psychic conflict requiring resolution before moving on. He outlines two central dilemmas in the period between 6 years and the end of adolescence: that of 'industry versus inferiority', and 'identity versus identity diffusion' (Erikson, 1963).

Industry versus inferiority:

As children move from play (baby 'work') to schoolwork they have to develop competence at certain kinds of tasks in the context of consciousness of their abilities in relation to others. They need to acquire at this stage a sense of their own capacities and capabilities via some successes in their activities, avoiding the danger of feeling a more than occasional sense of failure or internalizing unrealistic aims.

Identity versus identity diffusion:

Erikson's next stage is also very useful for thinking about adolescents in their social context. At adolescence, he conceptualizes, the psychic conflict inherent is to do with the development of identity. What is needed is space to find out who one can be: relationships that reflect back trial identities, situations in which possible identities can be tried out and so on. What needs to be avoided is taking on identities that do not fit – trying to become who they are not.

In terms of thinking about, for example, issues such as the importance of the group to young people, of being accepted and also of finding meaning, Erikson's work is helpful. As always his internal stages are also about the outside context of developing, and the outside context connects to inner developments.

Where the more post-structurally inclined theorists would disagree is in relation to the idea that there is a true identity pre-existing group membership that might be compromised, but instead focusing on how identity forms in relation to the group.

For psychoanalytic theorists from both the Freudian school and their rival object relations theorists such as Klein and Winnicott, psychic vulnerability and/or strengths and even 'clinical' problems may have already been laid down before the completion of the Oedipal phase at somewhere between 3 and 5 years. A propensity to difficulties such as separation anxiety (see below), depressive tendencies or even major psychiatric disorders will be established by 'latency' – also referred to as 'middle-childhood'. The internal structure – the unconscious elements – of the personality is determined. As Bateman *et al.* describe,

> By the time of entering middle childhood the child has come to adopt his own ways of integrating internal and external pressures and the conflicts they engender. He has begun to deploy a characteristic range of coping strategies and defences ... Development does not stop here; but whether early crises have been resolved for good or for ill, towards or away from the establishment of sufficient trust, autonomy and initiative, will determine an individual's attitude and response to subsequence challenges. (Bateman *et al.*, 2010: 52–3)

Within psychoanalytical understandings of identity, by this latency period universal features such as anxiety, conflict, ambivalence, emotional drives, defences and desires will have been established in person-specific patterns and forming individual psychic structures, as the product of the rich phantasy life of the infant/child and perhaps relationships, primarily with the mother, and 'events' in the real world.

Children and attachment

A further psychodynamic 'lens' through which children's development and well-being can be viewed is that of attachment theory. As we discussed in the previous chapter, the notion of attachment here originally relates to the mother and baby bond. However, it is worth just noting in relation to the life stage of childhood that attachment as a concept tends to be used more broadly in contemporary theory and practice. Holmes offers a definitive example:

> '*Attachment*' is an overall term which refers to the state and quality of an individual's attachments. These can be divided into secure and insecure attachment. Like many psychodynamic terms, 'attachment' carries experiential and theoretical overtones. To feel attached is to feel safe and secure. By contrast, an insecurely attached person may have a mixture of feelings towards their attachment figure: intense love and dependency fear of rejection, irritability and vigilance. (Holmes, 1993: 67; his italics)

Put simply, what Bowlby states is that the need for attachment constitutes a basic drive within humans (and some animals) not within a specific category of life stages but as a primary motivational system itself. Attaining such 'attachment', or the various limitations, failures or damage to such a state, impacts fundamentally on the development of the individual, through childhood and into adulthood (Bowlby, 1982 [1969]). For children, then, friendship groupings, teachers (especially in primary school where the educative and caring functions of adults often become a little blurred in the class teacher. 'Miss' and 'Mum' may overlap sometimes in the internal landscape of the child), siblings: all may be attachment figures.

Attachment theory connects to theories of 'resilience' discussed below, and for attachment theorists this is the basis of a person's well-being. In practice, for example, attachment theory can offer a framework for understanding why an issue such as group inclusion is fundamental to children's mental health and happiness, which in turn helps us understand the overwhelming importance children place on having friends and being part of the group (see Chapter 6 for discussion of fundamental issues of human well-being). It may offer a way of conceptualizing how the child's experience of severance and loss involved in, for example, moving schools (or starting school and leaving Mum or Dad behind) can be traumatic. Losing established relationships, changing friends and friendship groups, or losing position in a social group, may be experienced at a psychic level as generative of high levels of anxiety, fears of abandonment and quite primitive terror reflecting earlier attachment phenomena. In relation to understanding children's struggles and how they negotiate them, this is helpful.

Children and resilience

Another theoretical perspective for thinking through how children grow and develop is the key concept prevalent now in much child development literature: how they develop 'resiliently'. In other words, what kinds of factors in children's lives contribute to happiness, health, the capacity to learn, make friends, take satisfaction in their world, feel good about themselves and importantly, imagine and work towards a future. One could equally express this as freedom from a range of factors that do not facilitate this growth, such as fear, addictions, violence and crime. We discuss resilience in some depth in Chapter 6, and only sketch in some key points here.

Resilience and vulnerability has been a popular way of theorizing well-being for some years, within psychology and within much applied welfare thinking in, for example, social work (Cairns, 2002; Gilligan, 2009). However, it has also been criticized for focusing too much on individual psychology, placing too much emphasis on internal characteristics such as personality/traits, and for not including the person's social world. Sociologists might argue that living in poverty or being subject to racism, for example, are equally important to how you can manage in the world. Other ways of thinking about 'alrightness', such as 'cultural capital' (also discussed in Chapter 6) meaning something similar to 'status in your/the world', they might argue are more useful.

However, resilience is another concept like 'identification' that has readily lent itself to psychosocial thinking. The psychosocial approach insists we think about the internal and emotional landscape entwined with the social world, using psychology and sociology together, not separately. From 6 to 16 years, the horizons of the child broaden out and a whole range of relationships and situations become significant. The idea that the proportions in which children struggle or thrive depend simply on their parent's conscious or unconscious influence, or on the personality type of the child or what events happen to him or her are less than adequate. When psychosocial theorists and practitioners, from child psychiatry and psychology, for example, and indeed social researchers, consider the factors which impact on children's mental well-being (usually referred to as 'psychosocial stressors', or 'resilience and vulnerability factors'), they consider a range of influences and situations, in a complex interaction with each other.

Box 3.4

Resilient and 'vulnerable' children

Resilience:

- The presence, and strength, of friendships and significant relationships; sociable and popular with peers
- A non-dysfunctional family, offering support
- Having had a secure attachment experience
- A good school experience

- One supportive adult
- Available help for difficulties: with behavioural problems; for vulnerable parents
- Problem-solving skills, reflective rather than impulsive, flexible
- Attractive
- Gender: being female, but also boys who are emotionally expressive and perceptive; girls who are autonomous and independent.

Vulnerability:
- Contextual and community factors such as racism
- Troubles with and loss of friends and/or friendship groups
- Characteristics of the child, such as disability, an 'unusual temperament', being 'different'
- Lack of attachment network or any community supports
- Family dysfunction (which has many possible features)
- Parent's lack of emotional support
- Parental psychiatric disorder
- 'Daily hassles'
- Life events which pose a threat, for example, loss, abuse and neglect.

(Goodyer *et al.*, 1990; Rutter, 1999; Henderson, 2007).

It may be worth noting that girls seem to show more resilience factors than boys. Mayall (2002: 158) points out that by year 5 (aged 10–11) girls are speaking for themselves and others, and looking after themselves and each other; boys on the other hand were mostly unwilling to ask for help or seek help for each other.

Growing up in the body

For children the idea of getting big or growing up covers a whole range of meanings. Thoughts about increased physical size and becoming an adult (or at least a 'big boy' or 'big girl') are very connected up, so that 'when I am big' speaks for a whole range of hopes, dreams and identifications for the future, not just the physical. 'Big' seems to give responsibilities and possibilities: physical strength and dexterity link to admiration and respect.

Box 3.5

The body: the 'new' sociology of childhood

The body has been a key topic of sociological and cultural studies for three decades, and has generated a quite phenomenal body of theory (see Turner, 1984; Frost, 2001;

Riley *et al.*, 2008). The publication in 1998 of James *et al.*'s definitive collection of sociological writings about children and the body marked a new and continuing focus of this work (*Theorizing Childhood*).

As is the hallmark of all their writing on children – and central to ideas labelled 'the new sociology of childhood' – it is a way of thinking about children that is far more participative and with far more self-determination than was traditional. The editors and authors in the volume were concerned to focus on the body as a vehicle for children's own agency and individuality: in other words the body as part of being a person in the world.

This involves giving consideration to the body not just as a biological container for the self, but looking at the ways in which the body and identity tie up, and the body and how it is perceived by the outside world as well as the child themselves, and how this is internalized and externalized, also connects to this.

When trying to get some purchase on how it is to be a child; that is to say, how does it feel differently from being myself as an adult, then one useful starting place is the body. Adults can more or less take their bodies for granted: they are more or less stable, although we recognize that there are different trajectories (people diet, get fat, have cosmetic surgery, age, get fit, become pregnant, and so on). But some basic markers such as height, shoe size, physical type and so on are put in place in childhood and are fairly enduring. However, for children the body is constantly changing and those changes are implicated in what the child can do, how they are seen, and what they can be and what they dream they can be.

Body size impinges far more on self-identity than most adults can remember or relate to. Excitement, as well as fear, about the future, who you are in relation to parents and other children, what you are capable of doing and expected to do, confidence and fears of failure: all of this is measured in (changing) body size and capacity. Those little pencil lines ascending walls in family homes, where childhoods have been marked out in centimetres or inches, symbolize a whole world of hopes and dreams as well as perhaps unconscious parental attempts to impose order and structure on change which is outside their control. And if writers such as James *et al.* (1998) are correct, and children's interest in their own bodily change is insistent, because of the body/time ('growing up') dimension, it seems reasonable to deduce that these changes into adult territory are exciting and/or even terrifying, but certainly massively absorbing and preoccupying.

As the body is tied up with your sense of identity as a child, so is what that body looks like – the child's appearance. Appearance has become of central importance to how we are perceived and how we feel about ourselves in a consumer capitalist world and has been discussed broadly in sociological, cultural studies and psychoanalytical theory, some from explicitly feminist perspectives and some not (e.g. Hakim, 2011; Frost, 2001; Weitz, 1998). Acceptability and group inclusion (being seen as 'cool', for example) connect to appearance and looking 'good' in older children in particular. This seems to mean primarily being tall, fit and strong for boys, and slim and 'attractive' for girls. Younger children may also be part of this system and the range of consumer products (e.g. clothes ranges, magazines) now available for the younger age groups may be indicative of and partly implicated in children's consciousness about looks. Given the relationship between 'connectedness', in other words being part of friendship groups, receiving 'recognition' and esteem from others (see Chapter 6) and psychic well-being, then appearance becomes a psychosocial issue. A great deal is at stake in being 'attractive' to your peers. Research quite unequivocally demonstrates the connection between being the wrong shape and size (e.g. 'the fat kid') and social exclusion from other children and young people (Zeller *et al.*, 2008). No wonder adults are panicking about children's weight.

Box 3.6

Children's weight: a 'moral panic'?

Department of Health (DoH) figures for 2006–7 suggest that the proportion of 10–11 year olds either overweight or obese is 31.6 per cent, a blanket figure which includes what would once have been ordinarily dismissed as 'puppy fat' through to children seriously physically disabled by size.

Whatever such figures reveal or disguise, childhood obesity at present shows all the signs of a 'moral panic' in the sociological sense as theorized by the late Stan Cohen in the 1970s (1973). What is meant by a moral panic is a massive exaggeration of the scale of a problem which becomes seen as a threat to society.

Escalated by coverage in the media (media 'amplification'), the involvement of 'experts', politicians etc., such a problem gets identified with a group and 'talked up', so that a small number of incidences of a particular phenomena is seen as a crisis or a 'national scandal': the obese, then, currently (in the past 'teenage mothers', 'muggers', 'rioters' etc.).

Kline's (2005) analysis of two broadsheet newspapers (*The Guardian* and *The Observer*) between 2000 and 2004 showed that the number of stories annually about the risks of childhood obesity went up from 2 to 202.

By 2008, the notion of an 'epidemic' of childhood obesity had become common parlance, broadsheet journals carry items predicting one million obese children by 2012 (*The Guardian*, 16 August 2008), with a quarter of all boys becoming seriously obese (Rogers, quoted in www.timesonline, 16 August 2008).

The Local Government Association – the 'council' – are reported as recommending taking fat (hence 'neglected') children into care (www.timesonline, 16 August 2008).

The issue of the body and its appearance is implicated in, and also has implications for, the issue of being acceptable to the group. Being friends and keeping friends provides forms of attachment, offers identifications and recognition and is, as we saw above, strongly implicated in the resilience – the ongoing positive psychic development – of the 'school age' child.

Being in the group

It is not a coincidence that much of what theorists of all persuasions say about older children and young people focuses on them in groups, from Erikson's concerns around keeping individuality and being acceptable in a group, to much of the study of young people in sociological/cultural studies concerning itself with youth 'cultures': gangs, 'tribes' and groups.

Thinking, then, initially about boys and groups: boys seem to have to contend with a struggle in relation to the body, and acceptability. For example, the boys featured in Prendergast and Forrest's work (1997) tended to group around having physically mature bodies, and within these groups commandeered space and place (i.e. exercised power relations) with the big boy groups very much in control. 'Respect', capability, pride, safety – a whole range of dimensions of being – connect up to group membership. Smaller boys' groups sat in the wings more, learning and ready to become the new big boys and exercising the kinds of dominance that they were subject to. Strength, size and physical dexterity are the hegemonic defining features of Western masculinity, and as such those against which boys measure themselves and are measured (Connell, 1995; Frost, 2003). The masculine task of acquiring the expected elements of strength and physical capacity, very much what defines 'how boys should be' and how boys get respect, is differentially available to different groups of boys, though at the age we are discussing, the importance of the physical to social capital, group status and so on may be quite fundamental. After studying their interviewees – urbanites in the 11–14 age range – Frosh *et al.* identified 'canonical narratives of masculinity' (in other words what is believed by the boys that boys need to be) as 'hardness, sporting prowess, coolness, casual treatment of school work and being adept at "cussing", dominance and control' (Frosh *et al.*, 2002: 77).

Being in a group, and the type of group, links to status and seems crucial to boy identity, inseparable from who you can be and in what way you can be. The notion of 'identity' can be thought of here as being significantly tied into group membership. Being outside of any group for boys becomes a position without status: insecure and subject to possible humiliation and bullying. Prendergast and Forrest describe how it is to be a 'loner' particularly well,

> ... the victims of bullying, teased by bigger boys and objects of pity and embarrassment to girls. Without a group they have no way to fight back. The avenues of bullying others, getting a good reputation – being good at sport or having a close group of friends – had all been closed. (Prendergast and Forrest, 1997: 164)

Their bodies and its capacities give children their cultural and social capital. No wonder its growth and development is a source of anxiety and concern, and a major preoccupation for children of all ages. Being bullied, being teased, being rejected and excluded: psychic damage on a broad scale, with the body and its appearance as a central broker.

As this chapter has very much reinforced, gendering becomes more differential in childhood, and therefore how girls and boys are able to perceive themselves (differently) is marked. The notion that girls 'natural habitat/'primary identification context is the group, has not always been taken for granted, though youth studies writers in the late twentieth century critique the focus on masculine behaviour, and the invisibility or misunderstanding of girls' friendship and group behaviours in the available literature, and do much to investigate girls as collective subjects, not just 'best friends' (Griffin, 1985; Blackman, 1995; Hey, 1997). Within those group contexts, girls' relationships exist across a wide range of contradictory and complimentary dimensions: identification, emotional and social investment through to indifference, again with embodiment important.

In ethnographic studies of girls in friendship networks, groupings constructed and reconstructed gendered identities, within systems and structures of desire (and identification) of, for example, a particular girl's friendship and/or the pleasures of being in, and identified with, a particular group. The 'investments' in such relationships are powerful, producing identity satisfactions and conversely painful rejections and exclusions. Power works in micro and social ways, so that gender relations (exclusion from the masculine) and class relations intersect with the social relations between the girls, creating marginality and acceptability and the 'rules of engagement' across choices of friends, and the norms within and across different groups. Identifications were made both against and with other girls. And as Hey's research, for example, underlines:

> The microcultural politics of girls' heterosociality were steeped in co-appraisals. Girls insisted on making each other into acceptable selves, in

suitable appearances and dispositions (variously caring, nice, kind, attractive, confiding but not to close) positions and predispositions which went right to the heart of how girls were supposed to perform their roles as each other's friends. (Hey, 1997: 130)

Friendships groups (peer groups, gangs – the whole range of group relations children are merged in) play a significant part in children being and children becoming. Identification with (seeking to merge with and become like) is a crucial part of friendship grouping practices, experienced at both profound and mundane levels. Friendships and group memberships are negotiated, exist within internal and external power relations, and involve exclusions and evictions, recognition and invisibility. Connections to others, as this book shows across various ages and stages, are a profoundly psychosocial experience, with profound psychic consequences.

Box 3.7

The intersection of language, the body and agency in children's play

Majorie Goodwin's book, *The Hidden Life of Girls: Games of Stance, Status and Exclusion* (2006), is a three-year ethnographic study of playground games of girls in a middle school in Los Angeles in early 2000s. It offers a useful psychosocial analysis of identity and identification in girls' groups.

Goodwin demonstrates girls actively constructing their social worlds through the language of the playground, both formal and informal: 'the specific practices through which they construct their local social order' (2006: 3). Social groupings are spaces in which identities are actively negotiated through talk, and roles are achieved in this negotiation, not given.

Class particularly, as well as ethnicity and gender, impact on the formation of groups and identities: 'Differences among children at Hanley were most overtly articulated in terms of class among preadolescent children' (2006: 250).

Relational aggression, degradation rituals and victimization formed part of the repertoire of the verbal practices of inclusion and exclusion in the life of girls recorded here: 'clique members ... openly humiliated the social outcast to her face ... issued imperatives and insulted her through deprecating references to her social and economic situation and status as someone who lacked friends, in personal insults and stories' (2006: 251).

The internalization of the experience of relational aggression/exclusion (bullying – see Chapter 8) can usefully be understood as 'the hidden injuries of class' as Goodwin comments, and interwoven with those, the hidden injuries of broken attachment, failure of recognition, loneliness and degradation.

Being in the family

So far this chapter has looked only briefly at children in their families in relation to resilience and some of the factors which impact on it, for example whether or not they receive support from parents. For most children, other than those in the UK looked after by the state, their family is still the immediate emotional and geographical location of their lives. Some key relationships are with parents and siblings, even though some children will experience the break-up of their family and some are living in 'blended' families.

Typically child development texts have tended to think of childhood as a developmental progression away from the influence of/connection with the family and the home, towards friends, school and the outside world, although of course the family is not a hermetically sealed system for even very young children. It is probably equally important to keep in mind that for some children and at some times the family may be of higher priority, psychologically and temporally: for example, if the child undertakes caring functions for an ill or mentally ill parent, where families are breaking or have broken up, or if there is abuse within the family.

Children may have relatively few opportunities to 'grow away from' their families if the family is exceptionally 'tight knit' for religious, economic or cultural reasons (though the family itself may offer a broad range of social and development opportunities), or in extreme circumstances it has a belief that the outside world is to be avoided where possible because it is unsafe, critical, or hostile. 'Distressed families' – through poverty, disability and illness, addiction and abuse – may make very high demands on their children. Families, then, can be systems of support or demand, stressors and spaces in which distress can be alleviated.

How much the notion of 'parents' and 'other family' are conflated in this idea of 'family' is itself interesting. Parental 'distress' would seem to mostly have the highest impact on childhood, if only because if siblings or wider family are suffering, disruptive or in need, a parent's role in at least mediating this for other children in the family becomes crucial. Parents will be returned to below, after some very brief thinking about siblings.

The study of siblings, such as sibling order as a measure of personality, the roles and relationships of siblings and the importance and quality of relationships with siblings for identity development and intimacy, has traditionally received most attention in psychology, with some more recent studies emerging in gender sociology, youth sociology and the sociology of emotions.

The concepts of 'influence' have tended to be one of the main foci of the research and study in the area of siblings: how they do, the extent to which they do and in what circumstances they do. This is not always straightforward, however. Whiteman, for example, conducting contemporary research into the subject of how siblings impact on each other, suggests that 'older siblings serve as models, advisors, caregivers to their younger sisters and brothers' (Whiteman *et al.*, 2007: 642) but also that younger siblings may not always identify with the older one, but try to be different from them – to 'disidentify' from them and occupy different roles and spaces in the family. That is to say, the sibling strategy is to occupy a different 'space' and identity within the context of the family.

However, from the perspective of the children's world, the research suggests that influence is of less interest than how to live everyday life around your siblings, and that issues of negotiation, camaraderie and reciprocity, intersecting with the structural hierarchy of age and birth order that impact on everyday interactions between siblings are more preoccupying concerns. McIntosh and Punch (2009) tellingly title work from their child-centred research on siblings aged 5–17 ' "Barter", "deals", "bribes" and "threats": exploring sibling interactions', and claim that birth order is not a guarantee of power within sibling groups, that the situation is more fluid and negotiable than that, though age does impact on the capacity to influence outcomes between brothers and sisters and indeed with parents.

In Frost and Hoggett's (2004) transition research there seemed little doubt that having an older sibling at your new school was valued highly by the children, who spoke tellingly of feeling safer if their sibling was established there. This seemed to have symbolic value as cultural capital, as well as offering real protection or at least the potential for this. At a certain stage in, particularly male, childhoods, given the rigid hierarchy of age, simply having access to an older brother and their mates gives kudos and reassurance, even if the reality is pretty much being told to leave them alone. In the status game of boy groups (see above), even being said 'hello' to by a 'year 11' provides a little advantage.

Parenting as a stage in adult life, along with singles, forming and unforming couples and making and breaking families, will be considered in the next chapter. Here it may be worth considering what evidence there is of the impact of parents on children's lives, and from the child's perspective, how this is experienced. This cannot of course be disentangled from other aspects of children's lives.

Thinking about the various themes in this chapter – how children grow, whether they are healthy or ill, their bodies and their weight, how they think about life, their attachments and insecurities, aspects of their 'resilience', their aspirations, successes and not, their class and geographical location, their poverty or wealth, and their identities – all of these themes implicate parents quite profoundly. This is not the same as saying that these things are only produced or caused by parents or it is their 'fault' (see 'how babies develop' in the last chapter), but that parents, by virtue of their capacity to act directly in the world in a way that children cannot always, are invariably part of these scenarios. Not just social theorists but psychoanalytical thinkers equally, perhaps even more strongly, emphasize this connection. As we discussed previously, object relations theory and attachment theory, for example, position the relationship with the primary carer as fundamental to psychic growth and development, impacting into adulthood.

The significance of parents in children's lives varies hugely across this age range here. However, blanket 'parental determinism', if we can call it that, and its opposite, have certainly been challenged in the last two decades, and the work of James *et al.* (see above) are far more promoting of children actively engaging in the intergenerational influence/impact scenario.

Parental income certainly has a broad impact. Childhood poverty can be seen as problematic because not only does it impact on early development (see the ending section from the Field report in the last chapter) but because of the ways in which it limits how children can progress through to adulthood and establish their stake in society. Whether they experience social inclusion or exclusion may be based on this. Part of their informal and formal learning may be, for example, what Shropshire and Middleton (1999, cited in Ridge 2002) described as 'learning to be poor' – 'controlling their expectations and reducing their aspirations in the face of their family's severely constrained economic circumstances'.

Thinking psychosocially, we also need to understand childhood poverty in relation to the lived experience of being a child in the here and now. Being poor is likely to mean being unable to join in and fit in with groups, particularly in consumer capitalist societies such as the UK. Roker uses the expression 'exclusion from the norms and customs of children's society' (1998: 5). That exclusion and isolation from friendship groups inflicts severe psychic damage on children was argued above: having friends and being part of a group (connected to a social network) are determining features in terms of mental well-being and resilience.

Making and keeping friends relates to financial circumstances. Being able to go to clubs and groups and after-school activities, having friends round to watch films (DVDs), communicating online, and in the slightly older age group being able to go shopping on Saturdays and trying each other's clothes and make-up, playing music, seeing bands and going to festivals with and without parents, all involve economic as well as social and cultural capital. Social isolation and loneliness are the other side of this, the lack of group membership, and the stronger possibility of being bullied and excluded.

Conclusion

This chapter has outlined some fundamental psychosocial thinking in relation to children's being and becoming. One of the key concepts, in that it allows for an active engagement with the process, as well as an unconscious element to development, is that of identification which we outlined as something linked to desire and imagining, as well as emulating and reproducing. Older siblings, 'the big boys in the playground', stars, teachers, even parents, might be identified with, but for many children friends and friendship groups provide much of the material for 'becoming'. The chapter also critically considered younger children's being and becoming through the psychoanalytical gender identification of the Oedipal phase, and the critiques that exist particularly around the theorization of girls in this work. The psychosocial juxtaposition of concepts such as resilience and identification filter through some of the chapter's later thinking about the context of children's developing lives, within their bodies, their groups and their families. In the next chapter we will turn our attention to how these kinds of family and group relationships, as well as more intimate relationships, form the basis of not only children's but adults' lives.

4

How people connect: love, marriage and the family

Introduction

Emotional attachments, as we saw in previous chapters, when understood psychosocially, form the basis of how we 'become' as people from the beginning of our lives and relate to our ways of seeing and being in the world. Connecting with (e.g. falling in love) and being with others is partly what makes us social beings but this fundamental experience also alters what it is to be individual (the individual psyche), and the nature of personal and social identity. What this means for our choices of partners, how we experience the family, parenting, friendships and so on are the fundamental themes being explored here.

This chapter considers a key psychosocial theme: love, marriage and the family. Forming relationships, friendships, falling in love, connecting to others through intimacy, are clearly aspects of becoming an adult and a defining feature of making that important transition of childhood to adulthood, but the theme explored here is wider than the lifecourse issue. We also consider the wider aspects of those connections in terms of being in families and becoming a parent. In discussions of the lifecourse in more traditional psychology texts, one of the key themes that arise in the understanding of the transition from childhood is increasing independence and the ability to form new connections to others in relationships, and we highlight the complexities surrounding the issue of independence here. Moreover, our chapter considers psychosocially how love, marriage and the family are pursued in contemporary Western society.

Romance, dating, love, emotional intimacy, sex – that whole complex area of emotional life about which so much is written, sung and painted, and in relation to which so much time is spent in practice and so little on social research or theory – will also feature as a central theme of this chapter. In our psychosocial thinking about love, marriage and the family we are also as concerned with the inter-dependence or 'connectedness' in social life that such themes give rise to. Paradoxically both independence and connection define what we might call emergent adulthood: the latter particularly in the sense of connecting to another key person, such as forming a couple.

At this stage it is worth just commenting on an issue of terminology in this chapter: 'dependence' as a term, even if technically the opposite of independence, seems to have become rather devalued and often used critically, seen as a 'bad thing', and to be avoided if possible, interestingly enough in relationships particularly. That will also be discussed, but for now the slightly mechanical term 'connectedness' is used as the contrast to both 'aloneness' and 'independence'. Both in lived experience and in how we theorize the lives of adults, there seem to be contradictions about independence and connectedness, and this is our starting place.

In this chapter we are going to look at some of the theories that constitute or inform psychosocial thinking in this area. As we discussed in Chapter 1, psychosocial theory borrows from psychoanalysis, sociology, psychology and humanities subjects to try to offer a holistic and contextual way of thinking about people. One of the aims of this chapter is to integrate theory from social constructionism and psychoanalysis to consider how social connections, both in a personal and more general sense, are established and maintained. We will use this intermingling to think about how we can theorize how people 'connect' in adult identity generally, and we will look specifically at social constructionist, 'life-stage' and psychoanalytical gender theories. We offer an example of what 'social constructionism' helps to explain, and relate it to the example of independence by way of illustration.

To suggest ways of understanding the meanings of gender, relationships, families and parenting to adult life worlds, we consider how these are experienced and how they can be understood. Psychosocial life-stage theories are outlined, before considering the broad area of psychosocial gender theory. In the latter part of the chapter we go on to look at some forms of 'connections' – love, family, children, work – their ebb and flow through the decades of adulthood in contemporary Western societies.

Dependence and independence: emerging adulthood

Traditional life-stage theories, highlighted in previous chapters, write about the forms that connectedness takes in emergent adulthood, but do not always theorize developments through the lifecourse. The perspective taken often assumes that a process of connectedness ends once some independence is achieved in a person's life. This is one of the criticisms of them, that they neglect developments in identity that happen throughout the lifecourse (not just in establishing adult identity), underpinned as they are by an approach that suggests, 'when you get to adulthood you are more or less developed'.

However, in all the stage theories of identity development, it is important to keep in mind that psychic development and any difficulties and distortions – the internal psychic landscape which each person establishes as a baby and young child individually – continues into adulthood. The extent to which reparation takes place is a controversial debate in psychosocial theory, with the traditional psychoanalytical position that really only through analysis can psychic change happen, being questioned. A cautious optimism that certain kinds of powerful relationships and experience can be reparative or indeed cause adult psychic damage is the more usual stance for contemporary psychosocial thinkers.

Erikson's life stages: intimacy and relationships

For Erikson it was seen as crucial that individuals develop and nurture close, intimate and lasting relationships to others. As we will see in Chapter 9 on older age, Erik Erikson is the exception to the usual life-stage theorists, in that his schema does include developments into and during adulthood and these are significantly focused on the concern with intimacy and relationships through the lifecourse: how they are handled and how we connect to others. Although it is best to keep this in perspective given that the first five stages of his eight stages of psychological development were argued to occur before this stage. The latter lifecourse period for him has three broad phases: intimacy vs isolation (19 to 40 years); generativity vs stagnation (40 to 65); and finally ego integrity vs despair (65 to death). The phases we are concerned with here are the first two, but focus specifically on the application to family and relationships and the ways that adults connect to each other through intimacy.

In young adulthood the key events are love relationships. For young adults facing 'intimacy vs isolation', what we could see as 'attachment' – that is to say, making intimate relationships as friendships and lovers – is the developmental task, and to do this without compromising one's identity. Here Erikson places the most emphasis on the young adult forming close personal connections and ultimately ones that will last as long-term commitment (from age 30 onwards). Erikson sees this more as searching for a shared identity, a person to 'lose oneself' in, success at this stage represented as feelings of accomplishment and usefulness. The opposite of this he defines as isolation and the lack of a capacity to form intimate relationships because of self-absorption or fear of rejection and the pain that implies. Love emerges out of overcoming this struggle between intimacy and isolation, and the integration into society's expectations and rituals of sexual experience and relationships: marriages and partnering.

For Erikson generativity vs stagnation is the tension that characterizes middle adulthood, which we can also consider in relation to the issue of connectedness and intimacy. This stage emphasizes the expression of loving connections through more than just sexual contact, and hence the longer-term nature of the intimacy. Connected to the notion of 'needing to be needed', the task here is to shape and support the next generation – to bring up children with the maturity to give without return. He argues that not to do this leads to stagnation; when knowledge and ideas cannot be passed on, they cease to develop. The successful outcome of the conflict here can be summarized as 'caring'. As always Erikson considers how this stage 'locks' the person into the society and institutions they inhabit, and makes much of the teaching, handing down and shaping the next generation that goes on in a whole range of formal and informal ways: religions as well as schools, families and community mores (Stevens, 2008).

Psychoanalytical gender theory: independence and connection

Psychosocial approaches to becoming and identity, as well as independence and connectedness, have also paid attention to gender differences, which have a significant influence on the lifecourse. As we saw in the last chapter psychoanalysts such as Freud struggled to theorize how boys and girls differently achieve adult identity, an idea mostly ignored by mid-twentieth-century theorists. The new wave of French psychoanalysts and feminist psychoanalysts from the 1970s, however, returned to the question of gender – partly as a response to Lacan as outlined previously – that had never entirely gone away (Cixous, 1976). The notion of independence as a marker of 'full adulthood' is quite crucial to the differences argued.

Freud, for example, suggested that women are emotionally damaged from early childhood by the relatively less intense love felt for them than their brothers, by their mothers, for complex reasons but connected to the differences in negotiating the Oedipal phase as outlined in Chapter 3. Maguire explains this thus: 'the mother could not adore her daughter as she did her son since the girl could not provide her with masculinity by proxy' (2004: 58). Boys are 'adored' more, and girls as a consequence of this will always need the compensation of – will become *dependent* on – love and affection from other people to shore up their damaged sense of self-worth. Men are free to love as and when they choose, but women need to be loved: independence as a (preferred) male quality, women as lacking this.

Psychosocially, the 'problem' of female dependence – as part of how women may be seen and may see themselves – has been interestingly explored. Writers such as Nancy Chodorow (see Box 4.1) refocus Freudian material, and take 'connectedness' in relationships, and its acceptance and rejection, failure or success, as the key personality variable, not dependence and independence as such. Chodorow's explanation suggesting that, psychosocially, women's identities become more tied into the reaching out and maintaining of connections with others, and a man's more tied into aspirations of autonomy and independence, is helpful for understanding the process of gendered adulthood.

Box 4.1

Nancy Chodorow and gendered adulthood

Chodorow is a feminist writer, with a sociological and psychoanalytic background. In *The Reproduction of Mothering* (1978) Chodorow argues that because of the continuity in the way women mother their daughters, but the discontinuity in the way they mother their sons (a boy must break with this mother–son identification and form one with his less involved and more distant father to be able to grow up a man), 'women mother daughters who value connection, while men unconsciously fear and devalue connectedness' (Lawlor, 2008: 95). *The Reproduction of Mothering* (1978) is an influential text in social science and psychoanalysis, and an important text for this book, as it shows the intimate links between the psyche and culture, between psychoanalysis and sociological thinking.

As we have stated, the notion of independence as the core marker of adult identity needs to be approached with caution. In reality it is limited as a way of understanding when maturity is achieved and how it is achieved. For women, working-class men and some different ethnic groups, independence may not be desirable, sought, nor permissible. How independence is defined may differ according to the society one is a part of; it is therefore socially constructed. In Western societies for women adulthood is marked far more by the establishment and maintenance of bonds and intimacy connections with others. Leaving home only occurs within systems such as marriage in many cultures in Europe and USA. Disability, mental illness etc., or caring for those who have such struggles, may additionally entirely change expectations and patterns of independence and connections and of staying or going.

Relationships, love and, sometimes, marriage

Here we are going to look at what is paradoxically another standard indicator of adulthood and the opposite of going it alone: that of connecting to another key person – forming a couple. How can we think about love psychosocially? Important here too is the social construction of love, but also as we see below the 'under the surface' dynamics of such relationships. Gender differences, as we theorized above, have relevance as well as the expectations of certain cultural norms and the availability of certain narratives.

As we discussed in Chapter 1 psychosocial theory is underpinned by psychoanalysis and social theory, social theory frequently drawn from structural sociology and also social constructionism as alluded to in the last chapters. As we have shown, many practices and human concepts are said to be socially constructed: childhood, age, gender, sexuality, addiction, schizophrenia, money, pain and, of course, love. Social constructionism asks the question, 'how do certain sets of beliefs become seen as "natural", right, or taken for granted?' A social construction is a concept or practice that may appear to be natural and common sense, but in reality is an invention or artefact of a particular culture or society; it is contextually bound. It is also said to be historically particular; that is, it arises at a particular moment in time and is subject to change as society undergoes social transformation. For example, had we been a different kind of society (in terms of values, norms and ideology), then would the ideas that we hold about what love is, have existed? What it means to love someone or to be in love is contingent on factors that are social and cultural in origin, and these are characterized by enormous variation (Beall and Sternberg, 1995).

Love and intimacy in consumer societies

Love and intimacy has enormous influence both on the nature of our social organization and the inner narrative of our lives. For instance, in many contemporary Western cultures 'falling in love' is the foundation stone of social and economic organization, including child-rearing and economic consumption and most of informal education, as well as health and social care activity. The context of our own families and the dynamics and patterns within them has an impact on love: our emotional capacities and thinking, though not necessarily consciously. Psychoanalytic thinking about this common and complex notion would focus on how our internal worlds contain the capacity to form this kind of 'transference relationship'. Erikson talks of adolescent love as 'an attempt to arrive at a definition of one's identity by projecting one's diffuse self-image on another and seeing it thus reflected and gradually clarified' (1968: 132). The idea that 'feeling loved' connects to having an idealized version of our selves reflected back at us, as adults as well as young people, is one way of thinking about the psychodynamics of this emotion. The paradox here is that this intensely social relationship is also seen as our most intimate and private.

In the very individualized societies of late consumer capitalism (see Anthony Giddens, 'the pure relationship', in Box 4.2), being in a loving couple is constructed as a most private and intimate relationship, offering the potential for individuals to find personal recognition and self-fulfilment, intimacy and understanding, that post-war generations have come to see as fundamental for emotional well-being (another contemporary way of thinking about being 'alright', see Chapter 6). But it was not always that way, and many societies across the world see Western ideas about romantic love as unusual. More significantly the idea of love is often quite separate from the social organization of marriage: it can be seen as a transfer or rights (economic, sexual, property) or a contract between individuals and groups (e.g. through systems of bridewealth more common in tribal and agricultural societies) (Keesing, 1981).

The expectations of what 'adult' love has to contribute to each individual's sense of their own happiness, whether heterosexual or homosexual are both very high and very broad. The sociologist Anthony Giddens (Box 4.2) has offered an account of how we can understand 'romantic love' as the dominant form of 'intimate relationship' in the twenty-first century, compared to pragmatic and companionable love of traditional marriages, and compared to passionate, disruptive affairs and sexual love.

Box 4.2

Anthony Giddens (1991; 1992): 'the pure relationship'

In contemporary Western society individuals themselves forge a distinct identity, which has advantages but also the disadvantages of insecurity and constantly needing to keep remaking this. Giddens has explored how this can be seen in the area of modern relationships.

For Giddens marriage used to be a contract, and this was often initiated by the family, but with the division of labour that emerged – men as bread-winners (sphere of work) and women as tied to children (sphere of the domestic) – the reward became that of the pure relationship.

The pure relationship is not financial, status-based or traditional; the reward is intimacy between those involved. The pure relationship is '...sought only for what the relationship can bring to the partners involved' (Giddens, 1991: 90). The 'pure relationship' can act as a source of trust and support, but the individuals involved are also vulnerable, as they can 'fall out of love'. For Giddens we live in a turbulent, ever-changing and difficult world, and this turbulence is also reflected in the intimate features of our lives.

An addendum to this might be that 'falling out of love' has very recently replaced infidelity as the leading cause of divorce (*The Guardian*, 31 August 2011). Thus, intimacy can be psychically more troubling than it is rewarding.

As with all Giddens' work his ideas about intimacy has at its heart the idea of the individual as having a significant capacity for free choice and individual agency. This perspective certainly contains a sense of optimism, or at least a degree of positiveness, about the state of modern relationships, gender equality and the feminization of intimacy ('romantic' as opposed to, say, sexual love, evidencing this). It offers a useful analysis of the variety and flexibility of the modern romantic relationship, in terms of the form of living, partnership and family it connects to.

In the UK and USA today many groups of people live outside the twentieth-century norm of a married heterosexual couple and their children in a household together. Gay couples, couples who live in different dwellings, reconstituted families, groups of friends, singletons: Giddens is right that there is now a plethora of mostly acceptable ways of 'doing intimacy' to choose from, and evidence suggests that sexual identities, particularly for women, may shift over time (Patterson, 2000). Moreover, what we might consider some of the key features of heterosexual relationships are integrated into lesbian and gay families in ways that have not always been possible, partly aided by the acceptance of either gay marriage and/or civil partnerships for lesbian and gay couples in countries such as Denmark (the first country to recognize this), Norway, Sweden and the Netherlands (the first country to recognize marriage amongst same-sex couples). In the UK same-sex couples in civil partnerships hold similar rights to heterosexual married couples and they are sanctioned with differing legal status in other parts of the world.

In thinking about the 'pure relationship', it could be argued that gay and lesbian relationships display forms of intimacy, connection, love and equality, that have features that are both similar to and different from heterosexual couples. They may exhibit other ways of 'doing families'; that is to say, families as a source of psychosocial identity (Biblarz and Savci, 2010). In some ways they may be more aligned with the idea of the pure relationship as they by definition reject some of the more 'traditional' assumptions of power balances in conventional heterosexual relationships based on gender and expectations of gender roles, although balance of power may not necessarily be equal in any relationship (Patterson, 2000). Such expectations about who does the domestic tasks and who cares for the children, for example, may not feature so strongly in lesbian and gay relationships; and yet, overall research reports more egalitarian divisions of labour between lesbian and gay couples either with or without children (Patterson, 2000; Biblarz and Savci, 2010). Giddens argues that pure relationships rely on mutual trust: 'trust tended to be geared to established positions ... personal ties in the pure relationship require novel forms of trust – precisely that trust which is built through intimacy with the other' (1991: 96). We could argue, as Weeks *et al.* (2004) have done, that mutual trust and a shared responsibility and openness for negotiation are a key characteristic of gay and lesbian relationships and more readily illustrate the pure relationship.

However, there are counter-views to this theme, that some gay relationships are stereotyped as adopting a more egalitarian ideology. For example, some of the themes raised by Giddens in relation to gay relationships are discussed in Worth *et al.*'s (2002) research study on gay men's views on gay relationships, love, trust and intimacy in New Zealand. Their research study was based on in-depth interviews with gay men and the findings showed that their talk of the relationships was similar to Giddens' ideas about the dominance of romantic love, but that their views on monogamy did not represent a radical transformation of intimacy:

> ... these stories seem to belie a belief in the growth of more democratic relationships based on mutual self-disclosure ... Rather than breaking with traditional forms of intimate relations, most of these gay couples struggle with the same jealousies and fears common among heterosexual couples. (Worth *et al.*, 2002: 248)

Staying in, and leaving, relationships

When we view the coming together of people for 'emotional connectedness' through psychosocial lenses, there are perhaps some useful critiques or discussions worth considering here. Despite so much apparent reflexivity and choice (evidenced in Giddens' work), huge numbers of people love and marry within the pattern of their social/cultural expectations and 'traditions' (i.e. it is normative); it is perhaps not so much thought through choices, but doing what is acceptable in your own world.

Giddens does recognize that within this new social arrangement under late-modernity that such continuation of tradition may endure: 'Some of these traditional characteristics of marriage persist, more pronounced amongst certain socioeconomic groups than others' (Giddens, 1991: 89).

As well as following tradition (i.e. Bourdieu's notion of 'habitus' explained in more depth in Chapter 2), 'choice' might be limited by a number of factors, such as the presence of children, which Giddens sees primarily as a source of 'inertial drag' on separation. Moreover, getting in and out of intimate relationships involves personal trauma and pain as well as economic hardship. The independent, modern notion of 'choosing to live alone' for example, might mask the hurt and loneliness (as well as potential stagnation) involved in not being able to find, or having lost, romantic love. Also, a feminist perspective on inequalities in marriage and divorce may still be pertinent. And importantly too, their internal unconscious worlds may drive people towards attraction and commitments that are not necessarily understood, acknowledged, recognized or taken into account.

It is also worth considering that if Giddens is correct, then the dominant form of relationship may be rather problematic: such reflexive decision making seems not to produce enduring relationships, though 'commitment' is seen as a dominant feature of the pure relationship. There is a gap between the form of relationship that Giddens argues is dominant, and the capacity of that form of relationship to endure, to provide long-term emotional, familial (e.g. child-rearing) and economic stability. In other words romantic love is maybe the most common form of intimacy in Western cultures, but it lacks the capacity, in isolation, to sustain the demands of parenting, income generation and psychological support expected from long-term relationships.

In the UK far fewer people stay together than in the past, and far more people live alone in one-person households, though this partly reflects the numbers of women who outlive their partners. Of the 25,000,000 households in 2009, 15 per cent under and 15 per cent over pension age comprise single people (30 per cent in total), with a larger proportion of men in the 16–44 age group, contrasted with a larger proportion of women over 65 (Office of National Statistics, 2009: 14–17). In 1961 only 11 per cent and in 1971 only 18 per cent (in total) of households were single occupancy. There seems to be a falling trend in marrying, and a rise in cohabiting. In 2006 there were 237,000 marriages – the lowest since 1895. Only 38 per cent of people now marry before the age of 29 years. One in six people marry between 35 and 39 years (*ibid.*: 18–19). However, these statistics may not necessarily imply instability. The number of divorces is currently going down and has been for nearly two decades. It is now at its lowest point since 1977, at 144,000 in 2007 (*ibid.*: 20). Cohabiting, however, is well established as a real alternative, particularly for younger adults, almost one-quarter of all men and all women aged 16–59 are currently cohabiting (compared to 11 per cent and 13 per cent respectively in 1986) (*ibid.*: 21).

Psychosocially the forging of lasting intimate one-to-one relationships of cohabitation and marriage, heterosexual or homosexual, can be seen as the bringing together of internalized and often unconscious specific family histories and expectations, of needs met and unmet, located within a particular socio-cultural milieu. Likewise, 'falling in love' is understood as recognition (both conscious and unconscious) of patterns – a familiarity with the unfamiliar. Psychoanalytic theory provides rich material here. For example, one strand of psychotherapeutic thinking is that though it may not always be obvious, we choose people whose damage is similar to our own. At its most simplistic, for example, two very emotionally needy people, whose childhoods have left them craving love and care, may compete with, not sustain, each other, in relation to the supply and demand of nurture, support and kindness. It is precisely their similar needs which may lead to recognition; their early patterns of family lives in which love is withheld, withdrawn or unavailable, may render fulfilment and reciprocal satisfaction impossible.

Box 4.3

Henry Dicks (1967)

Dicks was a marital therapist from the 1950s who developed a three-part scheme about the rationale behind choice of romantic partner: cultural/material; personal similarities/likenesses/shared interests and ideas; and lastly unconscious connection.

Culturally, we are likely to choose partners from similar backgrounds with whom we share assumptions, knowledge values and priorities, for example, social class, religion, education, money, housing, race or culture.

We make conscious choices about the kind of person with what kinds of qualities and ideas, expectations and capacities. To a large extent we know we are doing this. There is also a level of unconscious attraction at work – desires and longings projections and fantasies etc. (Dicks, 1967).

What the social and psychoanalytical examples both suggest, and indeed much popular and academic social theory would support, is that a common struggle for marriage in consumer capitalist society, that which accounts for its failure to endure, is high expectations which cannot be realized. Unrealizable expectations may be the product of our own biographies. These expectations may unconsciously be the inevitable but unrealizable desire to wholly merge with and be made complete by another person, an impossible longing to revisit the 'oceanic feelings' of baby and mother merging (Freud, 1927). Equally, they are the outcome of ubiquitous global phenomena such as the media. The additional social factors in the media-oriented 'touched-up' world portrayed as possible, via various forms of screens and print, may also put enormous pressures on couple relationships. As we discussed in the previous chapter, mediated experience – that is to say, what people consciously and less consciously learn (and learn to desire) from the global media – plays as strong a part in identification as the direct experiences of everyday life (Thompson, 1995).

Generally, the demands of the economically driven social world – of consumer capitalism – are discussed in Elliot and Lemert's study of *The New Individualism* (2009). They make a fundamental point that, 'it [sex] has become that which capitalism has ruthlessly colonised for the selling of everything from movies to mobile phones' (2009: 115). Sex and relationships have become commodities, and as such are likely to be not satisfying and not lasting. Following sex and relationships in our book, often in reality but rarely in the fantasy/'romantic' versions, is the theme of parenting.

Being a parent

Perhaps the most enduring, intense, rewarding and frustrating connections and relationships people make are with their children and psychosocially there is a strong argument that the transition to parenthood is more the key marker of adulthood and adult identity. The fundamental transition parenting demands is that somebody else's needs have to be privileged. Self-absorption, as Erikson would put it, becomes less of an issue with the demands of another person's needs. Looking after another as well as oneself is a key change to a person's lived experience and social status, and these experiences and social status issues are likely to be different for men and women. The contemporary social and cultural context of this makes it a difficult and fraught transition to make. Understanding how people both become and are parents has similarities with love, relationships and marriage, as it draws on the external socio-cultural and family context in which it is taking place, but equally on the inner patterns, resources and struggles of the particular person and their couple relationship.

Good enough parenting

Parenting attracts an enormous range of commentary from social scientists from all persuasions. As much of the material in Chapter 2 directly and tacitly makes evident, what babies need in order to develop emotionally and psychically (nurturing environments, 'holding', secure attachments, etc.) must be provided for by the parent or parents. Being a parent is therefore a profoundly psychosocial issue.

Box 4.4

Winnicott: 'good enough mothering'

Winnicott (object relations psychoanalyst) coined the phrase 'the good enough mother' to describe parenting that can adapt to a baby's emotional needs, and provide empathetic nurturing and attention.

Mothers' emotional containment provides the space into which babies can draw together an identity from the mass of differential affects and contradictory impulses, which forms the psychic landscape of the very early stages of a baby's life.

Mothers do not need to be, indeed should not try to be, perfect, but offer a relationship characterized by a relaxed and undemanding attentiveness, allowing the child to, as it were, reach out and creatively make its identity growth through reciprocity and creative play, rather than have this imposed.

How the mother responds to the baby – with sensitivity and care – is what allows the baby to feel loved and important: a giver of happiness, and therefore builds in to its identity these qualities important for lifelong well-being. The mother must also tolerate the baby's rage, anger and destructive forces without retaliation or becoming damaged. Eventually the child must learn it is not omnipotent but still lovable.

The baby is mirrored by the mother, and finds its 'true self' in what the mother reflects, but does not impose (contrast with Lacan's version, see Chapter 2).

Winnicott, in tune with a range of object relations and some feminist psychoanalysts, finds an explanation for some men's internalized fear of and hostility towards women because of their early anxieties of disintegration and the power of the mother in preventing or failing to prevent this.

Drawing on Winnicott, then, what a parent needs to be in terms of affect and attitude, is relaxed but attentive, attuned and undemanding, loving and nurturing, able to put a baby's needs and the baby's pace first, not make their own demands or expectations, not fulfilling their own needs through the baby. Even at a 'good enough' level, this is perhaps a hard relationship to provide for contemporary parents if other aspects of their lives are a struggle. It seems to suggest a kind of maturity and capacity to give rather than take, and the undistracted time for reflection and attention, a relaxed attitude and confidence that a whole range of material and ideological factors in society may militate against parents sustaining.

Parenting in consumer societies

Contemporary sociologists have been particularly good at analysing the external social pressures parents come under that may undermine good enough parenting. Three major ideas here are, first, that parents are 'paranoid'. The media and so-called 'experts' have ruined their confidence through interference in relation to how they should parent and additionally 'talk up' risks and dangers so that parents are overly fearful for their children (see Furedi, 2001). Debates about the role of childcare and the risk this may pose to children are one aspect of this risk awareness and paranoid parenting culture according to sociological thinkers like Furedi, who tells us 'parental anxiety is nothing new'. For much of the twentieth century parents have been preoccupied by familiar parental anxieties about what stage of development their child had got to and whether that was 'normal' or not. Furedi explains how children's health was often the talk of parents of the 1920s and 1930s, by the 1990s that had turned to a more general talk of children's 'safety' and risk, and the capacity that parents have for 'good' parenting.

As well as concerns with safety and risk, the range of advice in how to care for babies and young children varies enormously in terms of both scope and claims to expertise. As well as enormously popular websites and internet forums such as Mumsnet.com a range of books and magazines have emerged with titles that emphasize the importance of 'success' in negotiating parenthood (Selwyn, 2000). Of concern is the fact that 'Parenting books and magazines do not reflect the reality of many people's lives' (*ibid*.: 37). They show a stereotypical view of parenting and of young children that does not aim to show diversity and/or complexity in parenting and childhood experiences. Furedi's ideas concern the very modern idea about risk in society (Beck, 1992) and how this is managed by parents.

Box 4.5

'Risk society'

Sociologists such as Anthony Giddens (1991), Ulrich Beck (1992) and Scott Lash (amongst others) have written extensively about the concept and reality of risk in the contemporary West. Beck and Giddens suggest that risk has become one of the central and most pervasive concepts in late modern society. The world is overshadowed by anxiety and uncertainty about the future and about the role of technology and science. Although more complex than this summary suggests we can say that 'risk society' incorporates a number of key sociological changes:

1   There are globalized risks that are universal and omnipresent.

2 Science does not provide all the answers and ordinary 'lay' people challenge the expert-led scientific view. Reflexivity guides individual action in the absence of incontrovertible evidence.

3 'Individualization ... means that each person's biography is removed from given determinations and placed in his or her own hands' (Beck, 1992: 135). As such it is up to the individual to shape their own biographies as traditional institutions are no longer prominent.

Secondly, families are 'market led' and are subject to the same material forces in society that may threaten or change the nature of areas of institutional life. Here the dominant idea amongst sociologists is that consumer capitalism damages family life, so that owning material goods is put before spending time with your children etc. The spread of personal consumer devices such as smartphones and tablet computers is seen as potentially changing aspects of parenting and family life. This is often a stereotype used in relation to families with two working parents. However a counter-view – that working may mean families have well-resourced leisure time to 'play' together – is rarely put forward (Ciscel and Heath, 2001).

A third theme is that of 'child-centredness', the notion that children are put at the centre of the project called 'family life', the reason and focus of other kinds of activities, and that their needs are privileged in various ways. This, it is sometimes argued, may connect to a loss of hierarchical power within the family, almost a friendship model of parenting.

In the UK, data from the most recent 'Social Trends' demonstrates that of the 25 million households in GB, 11 per cent are those of lone parents, 36 per cent are couples with children. There are 8.32 million children being brought up in married couple households, 1.66 million by cohabiting couples, 2.81 million in female single parent households and 240,000 by single parent men. This has some cultural variations (Office of National Statistics, 2009). For instance, statistics suggest that Indians, Pakistanis, Bangladeshis and African-Asians were the ethnic groups most likely to be married and have the strongest familial bonds (Modood *et al.*, 1997, cited in Giddens, 2009). Fifty-two per cent of families with a single parent are living below the poverty line (Office of National Statistics, 2010). The most significant change here is the number of children brought up in cohabiting relationships (from 10 per cent in the 1970s to over 40 per cent in more recent years), and people are more accepting of the notion that cohabiting may be the basis of successful parenting.

In the UK, then, we are still more likely to parent as part of a hetero-sexual couple, though for many women, and particularly black women, single parenting is also a strong possibility. Financial resources may also be more of a struggle for women parenting alone, and going out to work as well as parenting is a necessity. In thinking about gay and lesbian par-enting, it is useful to note that there may be a diversity of family arrange-ments, depending on whether the children were born or adopted in the context of the gay and lesbian relationship or whether they were part of a heterosexual family that dissolved after one or both parents came out as gay or lesbian (Patterson, 2000).

Other external socio-cultural factors such as ethnicity, social class, religion, will impact on the diversity of experience for gay and lesbian parents. For example, Susan Golombok is well known for wide-ranging studies of same-sex parents, primarily lesbian parents, and her research has shown the diversity of the lived experience of parenting within les-bian families, and not just between lesbian and heterosexual couples. Her research has also highlighted that children are not disadvantaged by growing up in fatherless families, but that the presence of a second parent is important (Golombok and Badger, 2010).

Then to more psychoanalytic accounts, which might also focus on anx-iety and parenting, looking at the high level of fears parents experience in relation to their children both consciously – seeing the world in which their children move as a highly dangerous place (unsafe world vs safe home), realistically or not, as mentioned above – and unconsciously, as anxiety. So, for example, in thinking about risk Beck's view (1992) is that risks are about the physical risks presented by a globalized world, but Furedi takes a more psychosocial view in some ways by suggesting that such global risks and uncertainties have an effect in terms of their lived experience; that is to say, there are risks to the emotional health of indi-viduals, they lead towards the individual feeling in a state of vulnerability. Indeed, the kind of couple who get together to unconsciously fulfil unmet needs for nurturing may find it hard to offer the nurturing needed, or men may resent that the woman's attention, care support and nurture has, at least temporarily, to be focused elsewhere.

Box 4.6

Why becoming a mother might be hard

Here we highlight some of the ways that parenting – being a mother or a father – might be difficult in contemporary society, taking into account some of the psychoso-cial themes above. Half a century ago Winnicott psychosocially argued there were 18 reasons why a normal mother might hate her baby; here are four contemporary ones:

1 *Feeling a failure.* In the West there is an idealized view of what mothers should be like, partly drawn from myth and legend, Victorian fantasies of the hearth goddess, popular culture and the media. This says mothers should be gentle, generous, putting their children first (certainly before themselves) hard working, multi-skilled, etc. Nobody could live up to this, but women carry this version in their heads: a central psychosocial issue in that they internalize the dominant image and experience anxiety when not living up to it. They are never able to reproduce their internalized version of 'a good mother', though the extent to which mothers may feel this may depend on social class (and habitus), and the normative aspects underpinning it. Feeling a failure does not accord well with feeling good about mothering, and may connect to anxiety, or even withdrawal and denial.

2 *Doing looks.* Added to this if they live in affluent areas of society they are also required to be 'yummy'; in other words to recapture the standard of appearance (slimness and good looks) that society expects of women before they have children. The kinds of identities that go with late consumer capitalism – individualized, appearance driven, reflexive, self-oriented – may find the demands of a baby hard to absorb.

3 *Because you're worth it!* The notion of 'self-actualization' – the putting yourself first, advocated and analysed in popular and academic social science – grinds to a halt with the adjustments brought about by parenting; self-actualization appears the preserve of the childless.

4 *Lack of support.* The structures that traditionally supported families, such as communities and churches, may have weakened as cultures have become more individualized, rendering parents more isolated and less confident. For women this may also mean less access to confident and experienced women as supportive guides and models of mothering. Hill (1989) spoke about the importance placed on the role of wider social networks for young children and particularly those under five years of age, networks that are clearly influenced at first by the activities of the parents. Young children may indeed come into contact with a very wide range of other figures that come to have some influence on their connection with sociality and more broadly society, whether it be more distant relatives, friends, neighbours and their children, babysitters, live-in tenants, and so on.

Box 4.7

Why 'fathering' might have become hard

How have expectations changed for fathers? How might we understand this changing role psychosocially?

1 *Expectations.* 'Fathering' a child, as a slang term, has only ever implied conceiving a child, not becoming a father in the sense of care or an ongoing relationship. The former tells us quite a bit about the myths and fictions, but it does not offer men any guidance on how to be a father; it is not at all clear what the expecta-

tions of twenty-first- century fatherhood are. There is uncertainty and lack of clarity over what is expected and what to expect.

2   *Roles.* Connected to expectations is the idea of role. The clear-cut role of the major bread-winner, supporting a wife who worked little if at all outside the home, is a receding social model now in the West. The external expectations of men might be the same but then it may be hard to maintain a strong male image and ego, change nappies, push the buggy, and sort out the domestic sphere, whilst the woman (also) works.

3   *Authority.* Authority and hierarchy within households is very different now from two generations ago, and it may be unclear how a father is expected to behave. Certainly the release from 'you wait until your father gets home' authoritarian role may be a relief, but then what is men's role in relation to the rules, boundary setting and regulations (bed times, in and out times, homework, etc.) within families? Are all family members to be just good friends, with nobody taking authority?

4   *Separation.* Additionally, as the statistic in the text suggests, a substantial number of fathers are not living in the same household as their children. The negotiation, compromises, emotional wrangles etc. which may accompany the role of the occasional or access parent are a source of struggle and one which some men do not manage to continue, and contact with the child is broken.

Conclusion

In this chapter we have offered some introductory comments on how the transition from childhood to adulthood is seen in contemporary society. The chapter introduced the theoretical 'canvass' of social constructionism by way of looking at independence, and then considered the issue of independence from gendered psychoanalytical perspectives. Forming partnerships and relationships is then addressed in the chapter, offering some views on free choice or traditionally determined ways of forming families. Parenting is then discussed again, acknowledging unconscious as well as gender dimensions.

5

How people are occupied: school, work and after

Introduction

Being occupied and engaged in the world is of central importance to individuals in modern societies. As individuals we are occupied in various and diverse ways, the type and nature of the forms of occupation influenced by the lifecourse. In early life schooling and generally education takes an all-encompassing influence in an individual's life. Furthermore, the way we define adulthood and adult identity is frequently in relation to paid employment and the ushering of independence this implies, and the issue of employment and work more generally does not go away until late old age, where being 'occupied' remains a crucial but less well-defined theme. We examine some of these central issues against the backdrop of consumerism in modern societies and how this has influenced how people perceive the idea of being occupied through the lifecourse.

In this chapter, then, we look at the different ways in which people are engaged in activity through the lifecourse, and how we can approach these issues psychosocially. We think about what it means for children to be occupied by their education, the issue of identity development and the risks and opportunities that brings, and the establishing of independence usually following a period of post-school education. We explore the issue of work and the main ideas about being occupied in the middle period of life, but that continue into late life decisions. As such, work and its role in identity formation and sustaining are considered, with some focus on changing patterns of work, security and insecurity, work and health, and the notion of a life balance. We explore the psychosocial theme of work to try to make sense of what it is to do well in the world of adult identity. This is set against the backdrop of a broad thematic discussion about work, such as the income, status and satisfactions or struggles derived from it, and from which a sense of well-being can be said to arise. Lastly, we explore existing ideas about the occupying process in later life, retirement and the role of consumer societies in creating old age as an undervalued part of life.

We highlight the ways in which some aspects of the lifecourse associated with occupation have come to be seen as 'natural' or the right way to do things, but show how this is problematic and that we can use theory to make sense of how this comes to be seen as natural. In the UK the idea that children from largely middle-class families are seen to move away from home at the age of 18 in order to establish some independence, is viewed in light of what is seen as the norm in social groups and how this comes to be defined as right.

How children are occupied: education

The psychosocial development of school-aged children has been discussed in some depth in Chapter 3, paying close attention to group or individual identification. Here we are specifically focused on how schooling features in this, and of course group membership is equally relevant here. Psychosocially schooling provides a unique context for how children live out their emotional and inner lives, but it also partly shapes what is to come in terms of their future material advantage or disadvantage.

Along with family and friends, school forms the physical and symbolic hub around which life, for children, coheres. In psychoanalytic terms it also provides a rich environment of phantasies and projections, fears and anxieties, as many adults who continue to have nightmares about school can attest to. When Delamont (1991) took a Jungian 'lens' to children moving to secondary school, she found the archetypal 'bogey men' of demon head masters and perverted sports teachers, of malicious big boys prowling the school in packs to pick on isolated new kids and shove their heads down toilets, or worse, to be a virtually universal feature of children's imaginings – the projections of their anxieties and fears.

The education of children – how, what, why, where, by whom and in what way – has long been wrested from the hands of those trained to work in the field, and has become a deeply politicized, controversial and contentious area, constantly simmering in the media, the party political

---

Box 5.1

Karl Gustav Jung (1875–1961)

Jung and Freud worked closely together in the early years of intense psychoanalytic development in Vienna, before falling out publically and bitterly over theoretical issues, and unconscious rivalries.

Jung's psychoanalytical work focuses on different themes to Freud, with less central focus on sex and more on the relationship between the psyche and myths and culture. Jung sees dreams as a central source of access to these kinds of phenomena.

Jung's work seems overlaid with ideas we now would think of as almost anthropological, resonating with late nineteenth- and early twentieth-century intellectual alliances between psychology, the occult, literature, myth, religion and anthropology (e.g. Frazer's seminal work, *The Golden Bough*, 1922, first published in 1890).

Jung's work did much to lay down the foundation of thinking about 'types', of personality/character: e.g. the well-known characterization of people as 'extroverted or introverted', though not in the reductive way that such notions are often used.

A further important concept for Jung's work is the idea of archetypes – universal mythological and historical figures that all societies understand, for example 'the wise old man' found in fables and the fairy story. Collectively and individually such archetypes and symbols offer points of reference within the unconscious through the lifecourse and within cultural groups.

The idea that not only individuals but societies/cultures have an unconscious – the collective unconscious – within which they experience, transmit and carry ideas together, through these archetypes – is also a powerful but slightly mystical Jungian concept. It can also be understood as not unlike contemporary psychosocial notions such as 'collective states of denial' being used in relation to 'turning a blind eye' in, for example, organizations where staff abuse patients/clients, war and atrocities, or things like climate change (Cohen 2001; Weintrobe 2001).

Jung's 'analytical psychology' theory, and style of analytical practice, has been particularly linked to the artistic and 'creative', mystical and romantic rather than rational or scientific (Bateman *et al.*, 2010).

---

system, and in homes around the country. Emotional and financial investment in our children's education is enormous, and yet some would argue, very little changes despite this. Inequalities in educational outcomes for some social groups, such as children in working-class families and/or in poverty, are one such an example.

Whereas many of the markers of a successful lifestyle (and hence the internal feeling of self-respect or pride for some) in the developed West can be ensured by the incomes of two working parents, in relation to entrance to a 'good' school – a school with social kudos to express and reflect family lifestyle – it is the child's job. Via the passing of the appropriate exams, from SATS to selective entrance, for the first time confirmation of status becomes the responsibility of the child, although this may be not without considerable investment in time and money from parents. Children's educational attainment may also support the esteem of the family, and may be experienced as additional pressure on the child. The psychic injuries of class, of 'inhabiting' a sense of being unworthy, not good enough, second rate, or their alleviation, may be part of what is at stake here: very high stakes indeed.

For most children and families secondary school may seem to offer a potential range of changes and achievements and any child, regardless of background, would have as much chance as the next of moving successfully through the school to GCSEs, A levels and a choice from the full range of university places. However, research clearly demonstrates that this does not usually happen. Some sociologists of education, like Noyes, for example, take serious issue with the 'fresh start perspective' employed by secondary teachers (among others) which is, he argues, naïve. He suggests, using Bourdieu's notion of 'habitus' and (durable) 'dispositions' (see Chapter 2 for discussion of Bourdieu) that even with such a discontinuity, the strategies of children, their friends and teachers will relocate the children within the same social space (Noyes, 2003: 262). In other words, the expectations, demands and recognition of the teachers, the children and the parents can only be in relation to what ideas, knowledge and aspirations they carry. Teachers will expect what they know is likely – children will stay connected to the familiar, parents will hope for what their life-worlds encompass. Continuity of development, rather than changing track or the loose notion of 'opening out' or 'broadening of horizons' that is often employed, will ensue.

How do children experience school?

Secondary school may not be able to change a child's social class or economic position; economically and socially it cannot claim to open up a new future for many children. But what about children's actual experience of being engaged at school in childhood? Emotionally and in terms of the inner life of individuals, what do schools and the change of schools facilitate, restrict or simply change? One notion was explored earlier – the idea of stress and pressure: entry into and success within schools may place considerable levels of pressure on individual children, in the UK's highly assessed system. But what else is at work?

School transitions, including making the change from the arguably more gentle, 'motherly' atmosphere of primary school to the more competitive, anonymous and rigid world of the secondary school, take place within the external social context of class, gender and culture, but also within the more inner dimensions of the rational and the non-rational, across the worlds of conscious lived experience and fantasy life. The meanings children make of the experience (in the playground and in their phantasy life) and how that builds their developing identities is the key issue here.

One way of thinking about identity development here might be in relation to the dimension we used above in relation to class – that of continuity and change. As children develop and are brought into sharp focus by the break of school change, opportunities to 're-identify – to 'become a different person' – may be available and generate excitement and a sense of possibility; new friendship groups and (life) style choices, new subcultures and new kinds of person to be in the playground and the classroom all emerge.

However, these opportunities have positive and negative dimensions. The experience for some children may be that the kinds of eccentricities and dimensions of character and taste that were established in primary school or perhaps even barely noticed within their well-established friendship group will change and perhaps be entirely rejected as new group identifications take hold. This can be and frequently is interpreted by parents and other adults as 'peer group pressure', pre-empting a loss of individuality and conforming to stereotypical notions of gendered identity as survival strategies at 'big school' take hold. Having an occupying interest in racing pigeons or collecting stamps may be fine at primary school, but is likely to be replaced fairly quickly with a demonstrable interest in football, TV, games consoles, pop or rock music, watching 'soaps', clothes, make-up and personal style, if that all important label of 'cool' is to be applied.

It is possible that children express excitement about the *bigger* range of possibilities anticipated as available at secondary school in all kinds of ways and expressed as more, not less, choices: of subjects, friends, things to do, teachers and other ill-defined possibilities. Changes in tastes and interests, the kind of person children see themselves as being, may not necessarily be perceived as a restriction but part of the ongoing process of identification that constitutes 'growing up' (see Chapter 3), whereas the parent's (or other adults') perception of loss of the child's previous or 'real' identity may reflect mourning for their lost (more 'innocent') child and anxieties about separation and independence.

Young people themselves inhabit a psychic, symbolic and spatial experience that is both exciting and anxious, full of imagined possibilities of freedom, growing up, new friends and new challenges, but also with fears of loneliness, humiliation, rejection and failure: the ambivalence that from a psychosocial perspective sums up much of the human condition. School, then, and the relationships, opportunities and experiences it really and imaginarily encompasses, is a fundamental part of the material for building young identities.

Box 5.2

Lucey and Reay's (2002) transition research

Lucey and Reay's research in boroughs of London highlights the realities of the educational 'market place' at eleven years at both a social and psychodynamic level. The authors trace the transition process primarily to families' perusal of the local education market at the beginning of year 6 (age 11). They point out that despite the rhetoric of such 'free' choices, a whole range of restrictions, constraints and inequalities are built in from the very beginning of the process – for example, the existence of selective schools.

Expensive and time-consuming strategies, such as the engagement of private tutors, are mostly available to the relatively wealthy middle classes. Lucey and Reay also discuss the relationship between schools perceived as 'good' (in the schools' league tables) and living in a 'nice' area and consequently the respectively high house prices in London. Poorer middle-class families as well as working-class families were excluded from their choices by being outside of catchment areas for 'good' schools and being unable to afford to move into them.

Schools that are routinely demonized – in other words labelled as 'bad' schools – were nearly always the destiny of working-class children. For example, in their sample of 454 children Lucey and Reay discovered that a significant number (22 per cent) of mostly working-class children in their sample, ended up going to schools which were commonly understood as the schools that nobody wanted to go to (Lucey and Reay, 2002).

Being occupied in post-school education: constructing adult identities

The UK has a rather special position in relation to much of the rest of Europe when it comes to expectations of its young people, how they might be occupied and the form that might take. We expect for the most part they will leave the parental home whilst still in their late teens, and subsequently return as a visitor rather than a resident, albeit with class and gendered differences in expectations. The beliefs and expectations around this were highlighted in 1998 with the introduction of university fees. That this might threaten the usual UK situation, that young people will leave home for a different part of the country by choosing a university without necessarily taking geography and distance into account (which is seen as a good thing), was a major concern. Occupation, then, through the half-way house of advanced education, takes young adults out of family life for a potentially liminal phase of their lives.

However, in most European countries and for the majority of young Americans, the idea that young people are occupied in attending the local university whilst living with their families is the norm. Leaving home (for college) has not been seen everywhere as essential for making the transition to adulthood in the way it tends to be in the UK for some middle-class families. Independence, adulthood and post-18 education become a connected stage. This is not necessarily arguing for a right or a wrong way of understanding independence or how young people are engaged, just highlighting that there is nothing 'natural' or indeed more or less 'correct' in equating this form of engagement with physical departure from the home.

This idea, then, is important in the illustration of social constructionist perspectives, that what is defined as a norm or 'natural' is historically and socio-culturally situated and contingent; there is nothing 'natural' about equating adulthood and new forms of occupation post-schooling with leaving home. Social constructionism asks 'How do certain sets of beliefs become seen as "natural" or taken for granted?' We looked at examples of this in previous chapters, in relation to the idea of childhood (Chapter 2) and love (Chapter 4). Specifically, here, we look at how, in the UK, being engaged in post-schooling education has become linked with physically leaving home, and for whom this is true. A social constructionist lens raises some interesting issues, not only about what we think of as normal in terms of kinds of occupations, but also what defines occupation itself in emergent adulthood, and how we come to see this as 'normal'. Is it reflecting our own likeness, is it what is normal for the class or group of people who *get to say* what is normal – who write down the ideas and make the policies, for example? There are important questions about how we see what we see and how it comes to be defined as the norm.

Occupations have always been the springboard – the pivot on which such independence balances. For example, histories invariably continue to shape even 'new' ideas (see Michel Foucault, Box 5.3). We can trace upper- and middle-class boys 'leaving home' to take up new forms of being occupied back nearly a millennium. From probably earlier than the fourteenth century many aristocratic boys were sent to other households to become squires (trainee knights) instead of learning these skills at home, where they could equally well have done so. Apprenticeships in medieval and early modern trade guilds were similarly conducted and such formal educations as were available – not much more than Oxford and Cambridge and Scottish establishments from the fourteenth to nineteenth century – involved living away from home. The church and the military could also be live-in occupations into which the sons of well-off households could be entered. The establishment of the UK public school system (private, independent schools) from medieval times also required boys to live away from home. In the UK, universities developed from and within these existing and gendered practices and the notion that living away from home was more conducive to learning.

Box 5.3

Michel Foucault: history, discourse and ideas

Michel Foucault's (1926–84) primary concern in much of his writing is the nature and operation of power in the shaping of ideas, and over the years that he wrote his views changed, so that a straightforward summary of what we can learn from him in relation to power and change turns out to be rather complex.

Foucauldian analysis understands how the power within macro systems – for example, capitalism or patriarchy – infiltrates the thinking of individuals (insists that only certain ways of being are 'normal') and impacts on their personal agency through fear of ridicule, loss of reputation, loss of self-worth/self-esteem and being cast as socially unacceptable. These are risks and punishments that few people can ignore, and which fundamentally challenges any notions of 'free' choice.

'Discourse' is a useful Foucauldian concept to understand the history of ideas. Power is not seen so much as being totally monolithic and visible. Rather, ideas such as power being a force neither allowing nor just preventing, power being in all human interchanges and always in a relationship with resistance, pervade this material. Foucault also advances the central argument that everyone has some access to power in minor or major ways. Discourse denotes something like power that is linguistic – that is, the ways in which things are spoken about and defined. One example might be the medical power to define who or what is sane and mad: 'you have a personality disorder and are ill, but you are a vicious criminal and are wicked' (the 'medical discourse' of mental illness); or the power referred to above to define the norm of independence and adult identity. Power is intrinsic to these discourses and, as individuals, people are subject to the same discourses – the same ideas of the right way of doing things, thinking and understanding – as anyone else (Foucault, 1972, 1980; Hall, 2001).

Girls from poorer and more rural families are the other major group with a history of leaving home to work, though for different reasons – to go into service. At 12 years old – 14 by the early twentieth century – the major source of being occupied for girls was domestic service, which almost always meant entering and residing in the household of another person. Girls from rural areas might work on farms somewhere in their region, but prior to mass cheap transport most were expected to live in. However, work in the cities, and migration from the country to the city, was normal. Up until after the First World War in the UK, domestic service was the biggest employer of girls, indeed all the 14–20 age group. Unlike the trajectory for boys, which actually saw many more boys from all classes leave home to join the military because of the world wars in the twentieth century, for other than the small new class of university bound young women, and those who moved to the cities for work and a life in hostels for young women or 'digs', the majority of girls in the early and middle years of last century remained at home with their parents until they married. The 1960s and 70s saw the introduction of more universities, and generally more geographical and social mobility and some liberation of attitudes towards women, and leaving home for work and education became far more of a middle-class norm for both sexes.

History then leaks into the present, nothing comes in fresh, and how we think about the present is influenced by how the issues have always been thought about. For some groups, leaving home has come to be seen as normal and desirable for growing up; independence is therefore closely associated with the different ways of being occupied. In the UK today there are still social class differences about who leaves home. Regardless of whether it has come to be seen as desirable, it may not be equally available. Being engaged in apprenticeships and poorly paid jobs are more likely to involve staying in the parental home, though there is no particular reason to believe that all young people would choose to leave, money aside. According to Gill Jones it is working-class males who dominate in these statistics: as was historically the case, they are the last to leave home (2007). Office of National Statistics (ONS) figures released in 2009 suggest that despite 2.5 million young people in higher education, 1 in 4 males and 1 in 6 females between 20 and 24 years live at home with a parent (2007).

Given the various ways in which individuals may be occupied, one might want to question the notion that living in the parental home means young people lack independence and/or any form of significant kind of engagement. Young adults usually have a life they own separately from their family, as well as other ways of being occupied. Neighbourhood and networks, friends and perhaps intimate relationships, school or college, work, part-time jobs, clubs, interests, nearly all of these forms of occupation are developed and maintained by the young person acting independently. This independence and connectedness, as we discussed in the previous chapter, represents a life of their own: a life world, a set of occupations, relationships and emotional connections, geographies and spaces, institutions and organizations which is different from that of their parents – independent of their parents perhaps but not necessarily 'independent' in the sense of emotionally disconnected. Young adults, indeed all adults, life worlds and contexts are part of their identities too.

Thinking about being occupied post-schooling in the context of leaving home as unproblematically 'a good thing' because it brings independence neglects other meanings and views. As a conceptual framework for thinking about independence and in the context of adult identity and occupations, social constructionism helps us to think through issues critically from a range of angles, to question self-evident 'truths' and common sense and in particular to see that social norms and values are contextual and contingent (Rorty, 1989). And this is one of its uses for psychosocial thinking; it problematizes the notion of the 'natural' or 'normal'. In going to university (or the armed forces or away to work), what young people in the UK are being asked to do is leave behind a whole life world and deliberately and consciously create another, whilst simultaneously concentrating on studying. It is unsurprising that newly established peer mentor schemes and welcome sessions flourish in even the most traditional of institutions. And no wonder perhaps the notion of student counselling and the services provided in this field by most higher education establishments have flourished. If identity is indeed relational, then these kinds of total transitions may in the end be highly stressful.

How adults are occupied: work

Work, and the conditions under which people undertake this and the material and psychic rewards it provides, is highly significant to adult contemporary life. What are you going to do when you grow up? What are you going to be when you are grown up? – both these questions put to children are asking them about their jobs, as their markers of identity in the world. Later, questions like 'what do you do', are pervasive in defining the parameters of adult life. Work, particularly the income, status and satisfactions or struggles derived from it, is, along with family, the underpinning for most people of what they can have, do and be, and as such profoundly tied up with well-being. The relationship between under- and unemployment rates and depression is well established (Price *et al.*, 2002) as is the connection between relatively low-status menial work and poor health (Marmot *et al.*, 1991, 2010). The unconscious expectations and identity needs we take into work are also a field of enquiry of concern to psychosocial theory, along with structural inequalities in the work place, gender and 'emotional work'. Work plays a central role in how we can be and who we can be and whether we can feel alright about ourselves, and as such is a core component of 'well-being' (a theme we will explore in more detail in the following chapter) and of how we identify ourselves.

Work occupies a fantasy and lived space in adult lives (similar to relationships), and though one might still comment on gender differences here at certain life stages (approximately half of women cease to work when their babies are little, and 38 per cent of women with dependent children work part-time, as opposed to 4 per cent of men (www.statistics.gov.uk, accessed 22 September 2010) from leaving full-time education to retiring, work sets out many of the boundaries and possibilities of adult life.

Work frequently defines income, geographical location, status and sense of self, who you will meet socially and perhaps make friends with, even who you might marry. The extent to which work dominates all aspects of life (especially the number of hours dedicated to work) as opposed to hobbies and past-times, community involvement and even family life (other forms of being occupied), has been a prime concern of the late twentieth century, and 'quality of life' debates frequently centre on an assumption that people should be prised away from the 'long hours culture' to undertake a more socially engaged, family oriented and relaxed life style – assumed to lead to happier and better physical and mental health, and family and community life: greater well-being in other words.

Work implies a salary of course and some kind of meaningful use of our time, but what else does it have to do with? What does it mean psychosocially; how does it connect up to psychosocial well-being? Does it, for example in the case of a 'helping profession' such as social work, reinforce your idea of being a 'good' human being, of being helpful and kind, and/or being able to make/have close relationships, and/or have influence in other people's lives? What 'identity work' is going on? What kinds of resonances and identifications lead us to choose, if indeed we do choose, a certain kind of occupation and will it make us happy?

Work and 'doing well': choosing a job

Even though we frequently address young people as if they actively decide their future it seems unlikely that for everyone there is a rational decision-making process here. For many people 'identifying with' (see Chapter 3) is the building block of 'choosing' a career. Relatives and the people you experience in your daily world and perhaps even the celebrities depicted in the media present examples of different kinds of work and occupation (and indeed lifestyles connected to this) about which opinions are made, but also dreams, desires and ambitions (positive and negative) are likely to be triggered. This of course may be limited. If we think back to Bourdieu's idea of a habitus (Chapter 2), or even a basic notion of role modelling, it questions whether all children access such dreams and ambitions, if their life worlds are dominated by people experiencing unemployment or poorly paid and socially unvalued working lives. Is it possible to fantasize being a barrister or a professor or a newspaper editor, if none have ever entered your world or your consciousness? The role of the media as providing realistic ambition, rather than desire/fantasies, is quite uncertain, and although conscious use of role models is sometimes introduced the evidence that this works is slim.

The opportunities to achieve the kinds of educational qualifications that lead to real choice in employment are also of course 'classed', as we have seen. Living in a struggling housing estate in a poor part of town, going to a struggling state school, leaving without the qualifications for university is not going to allow you access to top jobs, or even a social milieu in which your ambitions and connections can be expanded. It is perhaps also not so much, in relation to 'top' professions like law, of 'choosing' but of being allowed in. You may have to pass a 'knife and fork test' (i.e. can you perform upper-class manners, at table and more generally) as well as extremely difficult exams, and also have the contacts to acquire a place in a chambers and tutelage arrangements. 'Becoming' and doing well needs both identification (a vision of what there is to become) as well as the mechanisms of connectedness (socially and personally) for achieving it.

In addition, jobs in the media, the arts and sport – 'celebrity' jobs – have acquired social capital as evidenced by the droves of young people prepared to work as unpaid interns in music, photography, fashion, journalism, film-making etc. The highest prestige with the young, and with the highest risks of failure, exerts a powerful pull, and ultimately for most the disappointments of not making it up the star system. Again, desire and identification sets the process in motion. This is a good point to think about the ongoing impact of work and being occupied, as well as people's relationship to it, as well as the consequence for what work signifies about doing 'well' in the world.

What do adults get from work?

As the above might lead us to expect, the percentage of people who enter the same kinds of work as their families is still high. Not necessarily in the direct sense of going into the family business, but of occupational choices and the capacity of the family to support them (financially and emotionally). Even those who are perceived as outstandingly talented or exceptionally gifted in a field usually turn out to have family backgrounds of similar talents and encouragement, support, 'hot-housing', or even direct teaching/coaching (like the Williams sisters in tennis). Following in family footsteps is likely to mean as adults a continuity of experience, and an identity fit within the family, friendship group and even perhaps community, where certain interests and ways of being, knowledge and social position, economic position and the standard of life this produces, are familiar and known. What we can get from work is a secure identity and sense of personal fulfilment and well-being, though commentators have argued that one of the major social changes over the last generation is that there are now few 'jobs for life', and this kind of continuity has been broken up by the demise of industrial capitalism and traditional patterns of work – apprenticed after school, or trained young, for life-time professions. Working to short contracts, the service industry, rapidly changing knowledge bases and the global economy all impact on how and what you can work at.

Even if a career or job is chosen that is radically different from one's family, and the circumstances of work also differ, the capacity of work to determine economic standard and lifestyle as well as well-being, partially answers the conundrum of what we gain from being occupied by work. Certainly in countries like the UK, the benefits system reflects a world-view that many people would not 'bother' to work at all if it were not for the money. This is under-evidenced and certainly contradicts the recent battle in the UK for the right not to be forced to retire. Work, thinking functionally, is for economics and lifestyle, as the lynchpin of contemporary consumer capitalism. However, it also serves the significant function in the ongoing project of identity construction and reconstruction through the whole period of adult life.

'What do you do' almost invariably means what is your (paid) job, even if the person questioned thinks keeping bees or being in the Labour Party or caring for children is a far more significant piece of information. However, equally for many, what they 'do' does say an enormous amount about what they are like, and not all of it evident at a conscious level. What we have discussed above demonstrates how social and identification factors are important, but also too are unconscious factors. We have used an example below to demonstrate what we mean.

Psychosocial occupation choices

Just to return to our example above from the 'helping professions', it might be useful to think about the 'under the surface' of job choice. Interviewing prospective social work students leads one to assume that all candidates want to be social workers to help other people. On one level, of course, this is (hopefully) true, but only tells part of the story. How did some people get this sense that it is up to them personally to help people directly as a job (rather than, say, choosing a very well-paid job and giving a lot to charity, or informally looking after the old lady in the street who can't do her shopping any more), and how will this withstand the nature of the work? Social workers come from varied class backgrounds: from high-status families with a public service ethic; from working-class achievers through the education system, where they may feel this is a way to 'pay back'; from personal experience of being 'looked after' (in care); from struggling with life perhaps through drugs, alcohol or early life experiences. Mixed motivations are also evident, ranging from the political and personal, such as helping the individual 'fight' authority and/or championing those who are marginalized.

Unconscious motivations undoubtedly also play a part in the choice to be needed by people whose lives are seemingly more of a struggle than ours. The workers' own deprivation can be sidestepped because in relation to many of the service users they work with, they are highly competent, undamaged, successful, and giving instead of needy. The worker can feel like a good, useful and competent person – helpers being helped by helping.

The above example suggests mental well-being may be the product of such a choice. It certainly is not meant to imply that those who become occupied by social work have worse mental struggles – more or less unconscious unmet needs, unrealistic expectations and emotional entanglement – than other adults do. There is a relationship between unconscious factors such as unmet needs and/or defences and all adult experiences including work, if examined psychosocially. So, for example, although slightly stereotyping, one could equally argue that all forms of 'standing up at the front' (teaching, acting, being a barrister, a politician, a TV presenter, a rock star) provide an audience and the power to impose one's ideas and self. What an audience provides is (perhaps) attention, admiration and applause; hence these are professions for egoists and narcissists, whose identities require high degrees of validation/adoration.

The relationship between donning a uniform and working in controlled and controlling environments with the power to impose order, whilst being subject to rigid boundaries and intense depersonalization might also be examined in similar ways. Christopher Bollas's (1987) concept of 'normotic personality' examines these kinds of identity needs. However, none of this implies that these are the 'wrong' reasons for undertaking a particular form of work: where unconscious needs or expectations are met by work and the work place, then egoists, for example, will probably make useful and fulfilled university lecturers!

In the media and in social science the notion of a 'crisis of masculinity' has been represented for the last two or three decades (Clare, 2000; Connell, 1995; Messerschmidt, 1997), within which a factor given much credence is the notion of the decline – almost disappearance – of working-class male labour: the kind of 'hard graft' that offered self-respect, and perhaps the envy of men more generally, where values such as physical strength and male camaraderie were seen to be involved. However, this hard-working hard-living masculine world hardly exists, since the loss of the mining and heavy engineering and manufacturing industries ('de-industrialization') and also most land-based employment, in the UK and to some extent most Western industrialized nations. It is not there for men to draw on, nor to pass down to their sons, as discovered by Jimenez and Walkerdine's (2011) study (see Box 5.4).

Box 5.4

Being under-occupied in South Wales: Jimenez and Walkerdine
A version of working-class but respected masculine employment may be hard to find. For instance, in their study on the impact of unemployment in a traditional ex-mining town in South Wales, Jimenez and Walkerdine found that some of the young men, influenced as they were by their father's working-class masculine ethic, did not want to work in service-related jobs, which they saw as feminine. The young men did not therefore make the transition to other employment.

The young men mourned the loss of the manufacturing industry and steelworks, as well as the forms of being occupied and ordered reality that it fostered. Having to do service work it was felt would bring shame and embarrassment to the young men, having to consider forms of work that did not fit with the working-class masculinity (see also Chapter 7 for a fuller discussion of this in relation to loss and shame).

Certainly the service industry, and the men who work in shops, wait at table, clean cars (serve the rich, or richer, in other words) are not subject to the same respect from film-makers, writers or indeed the public, and then may find respect for themselves harder to establish. Jobs in construction, building trades, farming and fishing, and some small amounts of manufacturing, only account for approximately 15 per cent of UK employment.

For women, the traditional caring sector has enlarged, so that health and public sector jobs generally have increased. The service sector is seen as closer to female gender expectations, though there may also be issues of lack of respect and recognition for women. If salaries can be taken as some kind of crude measure of how certain categories of workers are valued (flawed as a measure, but indicative) then child care, cleaning, hotel and catering work –unskilled labour – and even the degree-level professions of nursing, social work and primary school teaching are all highly gendered, poorly paid and mainly female. Women in the UK still earn averagely less than men, and are under-represented in management jobs, on boards and in the 'top' professions. Power, status and wealth (= respect?) are still substantially gendered as well as 'classed'.

Psychosocially, then, what is interesting here is how society's valuation of certain kinds of employment impacts on the person undertaking this work. The overall approach suggests that the 'outside gets in, and the inside gets out': people's own values and those around them are intertwined. Certainly workers may be able to tap into other systems of respect and recognition than work (forms of establishing well-being), but work for many is fundamental. We need our job, via immediate managers and also things like promotion, pay and awards to make us feel a valuable and worthwhile person, certainly if it is not available elsewhere. Well-being may largely depend on this.

The link between unemployment and increased rates of depression and suicide, for example, may be just one indicator of this (see Chapter 7 for discussion of depression). Poorer physical health in those in the lowest paid and least respected professions may also indicate the strength of these differences and why it matters. Issues such as 'recognition' and 'resilience' in the workplace will be discussed in the next chapters.

Work and later life: being occupied in consumer society

Debates about being occupied in society and how this relates to the later-life period have broadly taken one of two perspectives: either that individuals entering later life gradually retreat (or disengage) from certain kinds of occupations and activities, or that they do not necessarily disengage completely but that they change the nature of those activities; we will highlight both perspectives more comprehensively below. Typically, late-adulthood marks out the age cohort between broadly 50 and 70. The role of consumer societies in creating old age as an undervalued part of life, and the impact this has on individual's confidence and esteem will also be looked at.

Disengagement and activity theory

The functionalist social gerontology theory mostly developed by sociologists was about how to best theorize older people's place in society, given the changes to social roles following retirement. These are characterized as modernist theories whereby the narrative about later life is that following retirement the individual disengages from society, which is often inevitable and desirable (Cummings and Henry, 1961).

Box 5.5

Being alone and being connected: structural-functionalist disengagement theory

The functionalist social gerontology theory (Cummings and Henry, 1961) emphasized that not everyone disengages but that this is a gradual withdrawal process from society. It is suggested that older adults lessen their preoccupation with others, lessening emotional ties, and show less interest in society in general.

The functionalist disengagement theory takes the view that ageing narrows a person's social sphere, which results in withdrawing from and relinquishing social roles, increasing passivity.

In more sociological terms disengagement theory belongs to a structural functionalist view of society and ageing, as the process of ageing leads towards a phasing out of older people from particular social roles that are best fulfilled by people of 'working age'. It is therefore important that people prepare for their key disengagement (death) so that the ordinary functioning and social order in society does not become disrupted. As such, the social ordering of change to social roles (social frailty) mimics the 'natural' order in which older people become biologically frail.

If ageing does narrow social spheres, as functionalist disengagement theory suggests, what then is inhabited by the individual is a reduced, or shrunken world, with less opportunity for friendship and love, for stimulation and creativity, for sources of happiness and indeed positive feelings generally – a depleted affective and intellectual landscape.

In contrast, some social gerontologists of a similar functionalist leaning have argued that the available occupations and roles for older adults have changed, and that most importantly older adults would want to continue to adopt the activities of their more youthful identities. This presents the view that elderly people want and need to remain active in a variety of social spheres, such as with relatives, friends and community groups, and they only become withdrawn unwillingly, as a result of ageism. This gives credence to the view that many individuals are seeking to continue their work beyond the conventional retirement age. Moreover, any lost or relinquished social occupations should be replaced with new ones, ones that may have community focus. Again, such a perspective in many ways fits with a structural-functionalist view, albeit a revised one, that suggests that society is changing and that such changes necessitate a change in occupation that older people play in society.

Activity theory also suggests that those who enter the 'third age' retain many of the activities and values that they adopted during middle age, thereby delaying any 'dependency' period of later life. As such, increasingly the boundaries between late-middle age and older age become blurred. Of course, the reality of activity theory depends largely on a range of factors, not least socio-economic security, existing social networks and cultural capital.

The lifestylization of occupation in retirement

Thinking also about the specific social context and the ageing identities produced within it, the specific zeitgeist of consumer capitalism is central here. It is suggested that the unevenness in which people experience retirement and the relative affluence of many retired people, has implications for patterns and experiences of consumption (Higgs *et al.*, 2009). These issues are also more significant if we take on board sociological writers such as Zygmunt Bauman who has argued that consumption rather than production has a greater impact on the formation of our identities. We must take into account that the retirees of today are those who were generationally a part of those who created the post-war consumer culture with which we are familiar. As such, 'older people today can no longer be considered a residual category of society marked out by their lack of participation in consumer society' (Higgs *et al.*, 2009: 108). The idea of a 'third age' of activity and leisure came out of this earlier participation in a consumer society.

More importantly, the changing relationship between work and identity, as well as the shifting nature of employment in society has meant that the meaning of retirement has shifted over time – what we might term the *lifestylization* of post-retirement has meant a move towards a more active notion of independence and identity making in late adulthood. As such, individuals nearing retirement today may have very different ideas about what is expected of that period from previous generations. The current generation of older people (born 1945–64) were part of a more general social shift into a culture of consumerism unlike previous generations:

> The once young consumers of the post-war period have grown older, all the while retaining their propensities to be active players in a society where the pursuit of lifestyle and identity is as likely to emerge out of the commodities purchased as it is out of the ascribed identities of employment. (Jones *et al.*, 2008: 49)

As such, active consumption is now very much a part of how we are occupied in later life, particularly in relation to health consumption given our current policy and emphasis in the UK – on user involvement, citizen participation, with the ideology of choice, participation and empowerment

> **Box 5.6**
>
> **Consumer society and the silver spender**
> Using a recent study examining consumption patterns in retired households in Britain between 1968 and 2005 Paul Higgs illustrated that older people were no longer a residual category of consumer but, rather, a consumerist force with considerable means. This brings to light the emerging role of the citizen-consumer. Higgs argues that individuals born in the 1940s and 1950s have acquired a wider range of consumerist habitus than those born earlier in the twentieth century. Third age is about lifestyle and a resistance to 'old age' identity (Higgs *et al.*, 2009).

central to this. Not just in relation to mainstream health-care markets (the commodification of services) but also use of complementary medicines and other vitamins and health foods, over the counter medicines, etc. (Willison and Andrews, 2004; McClean and Moore, 2013), much of which has been argued is due to late-modernity and shifting perceptions of what drives well-being throughout the lifecourse (Sointu, 2006). Consumption, in all its myriad forms, is therefore one of the key drivers behind diverse forms of being occupied in Western societies.

More significantly, such issues about consumption and identity highlight a theme that suggests we are increasingly occupied in our identity construction (our becoming). For sociologists such as Anthony Giddens the project of the self is the ongoing identity work of the lifecourse and this also drives what happens in later life. As Hockey and James suggest, Giddens' notion of the demise of tradition in high modernity suggests that nothing can be taken for granted and that there are no longer the same bonds to 'this is the way we do it' (Hockey and James, 2003: 112). To focus on tradition is to make choices; under late modernity we can no longer claim to be unaware of the choices. In *Modernity and Self Identity* (1991) Giddens argues that new mechanisms of self-identity emerge and it becomes a 'reflexively organised endeavour'. Whatever one's age, agency not tradition means that choices can be made: we can decide (reflexively organize) our identities and how our self is to be occupied.

Featherstone and Hepworth (1998) have argued that this reshaping of identity has had some positive effects in terms of later life in that it has led to the 'modernisation of ageing'. Part of this involves what they see as an extension of middle life into a complex of states of development and personal growth – new forms of ageing are replacing negative stereotypes. Giddens argues that what we witness today is the commodification of lifestyle in late-modern society (1991). Giddens suggests that people's consumption patterns are central to identity and the 'narratives of the self'. This is important, as this is not just about well-off older people –

an easy critique to make; this is a broader social transformation linked to how consumption provides important markers of self-identity not just indicating wealth or prestige of social position. Bauman refers to this process as the 'aestheticisation of consumption', and hints at the changes to a post-war golden age where state welfare is being replaced by a 'silver age' where the state is more aware of global competitiveness, the market and individual choice.

However, this theme about consumer choice and identity is not without a sustained psychosocial critique, which essentially suggests that ageing bodies with increasing limitations, and illness, loss, mourning and eventual death are the realities of the later period of our lives, and that we do not have choices about this. In later life we can shop for 'youth' with cosmetic surgery, private therapists and for distractions with cruises and adventures, but much of this activity is the psychic defence mechanism of 'denial', part of a mass turning away from the unpalatable knowledge that we must eventually lose our looks, our energy, our flexibility our importance/esteem and we will decline and die.

Conclusion

How we 'do' is often linked to what we 'do', and as individuals we are clearly occupied in myriad ways through the lifecourse. This chapter has addressed the ways in which schooling and education in early life has a psychosocial influence in an individual's life, examined against the backdrop of establishing independence in post-school education. We looked at how work as a form of being occupied can be understood psychosocially, and how these preoccupations continue into late life decisions. The psychosocial theme of work was therefore explored to make sense of what it is to do well as an adult and forge adult identity. We continued on to ideas about the occupying process involved in later life, taking into account retirement, and we examined these central issues against the backdrop of consumerism in modern societies.

6

How people thrive:
resilience and well-being

Introduction

The standard measures of health and well-being found in textbooks from
a medical or even broadly social science perspective may provide little
meaningful understanding of the day-to-day reality of what it means for
the individual to *be* well and *do* well. It may tell you something about the
chances of someone either becoming unwell, experiencing depression or
anxiety, or their capacity to cope, but what it is unlikely to tell you about
is the broader psychosocial issue of why do some people sink and others
swim, or perceive objectively similar life trajectories as failures or successes. Here we will try to consider the factors, therefore – both internal
and external – that make some people appear to do better and feel better,
and others struggle, and how can we make sense of this as we think about
individuals located within relational and social contexts.

As we understand it, wellness and well-being implies something
greater than the sum of its parts. Such terms offer a broader understanding of the person's life position and that people's sense of 'wellness' is
linked to not just being free of disease or ill-health, but a wider conceptualization that incorporates subjective and psychic (interior and below
the surface) as well as social (exterior) dimensions of well-being, as well
as the lived experience. As such, in a psychosocial sense, well-being is
more difficult to grasp immediately and make sense of, but it does incorporate a more useful holistic dimension about the ways in which people
thrive and flourish, which we will explore in this chapter. The next chapter will focus on the opposite issue – the ways in which people struggle
and feel bad: 'ill being'.

In the conventional textbook approach the most popular use of the term well-being is in its broader application to health, and that has been the policy emphasis also, although we should also note that 'health' may be only one aspect of what constitutes someone's well-being; the two terms are interrelated. Well-being therefore has become an umbrella term concerning all things 'self' and not just health, and has a more useful link to the psychosocial approach that we take in the book. The term well-being has emerged in recent years as a defining notion encapsulating multiple levels of both personal health and the experience of personal worth or value. The term well-being is complex and multifaceted as well as largely contested, and in this chapter we highlight a range of theories (such as capabilities, recognition and resilience) that have been used to make sense of this.

Continental philosophical thinkers like Nietzsche, Husserl and Heidegger, individuals who are considered influential figures for the Critical Theory school (see Chapter 1), saw that the issues of what makes us uniquely human – the existential issues such as the problems of suffering, loss, and so on – were the principal problems of philosophical thinking. This also led to a range of broadly psychological perspectives that suggested that periods of struggle and not 'doing well' in life are vitally important to self-development and wellness, and add 'richness' to life (Haworth and Hart, 2007). So well-being and wellness is not just about the promotion of positive emotions but whether the individual can be seen and see themselves to be fully functioning, reaching their potential, and so on.

Psychoanalysis of course, as we have seen in previous chapters, is all about well-being, though that which prevents it is the focus of most study. Freudian notions of 'the pleasure principle' and the Lacanian one of 'jouissance' (a rather less rational, more chaotic notion of pleasure/joy) have made some impact on the theory here. There are also some psychoanalytically derived notions such as the 'authentically' developed self – being able to be one's 'real', as opposed to 'false', self – that are particularly concerned to understand self-fulfilment. Jung, alluded to in Chapter 5, and more importantly Winnicott discussed in Chapters 2 and 4, demonstrate an optimistic and positive notion of becoming and being which implicates 'authenticity' of self – becoming a 'real' self, which has been more influential in thinking about well-being.

In this chapter, then, we consider how we can link up some of these ideas and consider how well-being can be psychosocially conceptualized. We start by looking at health and well-being briefly, then draw on some classic philosophy to orientate our ideas. We spend some time discussing the strengths and problems with key ideas from positive psychology before exploring some nuanced notions of, for example, 'good enough' well-being from object relations theorists. A critique of self-help and self-oriented 'methods' for fulfilment is offered by highlighting Giddens' work. A central section of the chapter considers the psychosocial notions of resilience and of relational well-being and friendship, though Honneth's work on recognition mainly falls in the next chapter in relation to 'ill-being'. At the end we look briefly at how individuals frequently describe their own well-being as connected to life-changing events. Primarily, then, this chapter considers how best we can understand well-being within a psychosocial framework and as such some cross-referencing with 'ill-being' in the next chapter will be used here; this chapter and the next should therefore be read together.

Health and well-being

'Well-being is a quality in demand in today's society' suggests Sointu (2005: 255), and feelings of well-being are 'regarded as a state of virtue' (Furedi, 2003: 31). We may consider why this is. Some of the questions we could ask ourselves and have been asked by others are, is well-being about happiness, is it about success or achievement, or is it in a psychosocial sense about how you are doing well in the world? In the broader context of the individual and their growth and development, is it also about equality and 'the good society'?

Over a half a century ago, in 1946, the World Health Organization (WHO) at the World Health Assembly came up with their definition of health that broadened the concept of health to include, as they saw it, the psychosocial dimension, taking into account subjective experience: 'Health is a state of complete physical, mental and social well-being and not merely the absence of disease or infirmity' (World Health Assembly, 1948). This is one of their most well-known and oft-cited statements, and the term 'psychosocial well-being' has since become popular in the study of mental health, for example, adopting the WHO definition.

The notion that 'complete ... well-being' is possible or perhaps even desirable is not one we are particularly subscribing to here. Nevertheless, the use of the term well-being by the WHO is important because it sets the context for what was the potential of human health rather than what was necessarily achieved (and measured) in any given society. How well this definition related to a more psychosocial concept of well-being is debatable, and we will explore other approaches later in the chapter.

Approaches to well-being have generally focused on the factors that allow individuals to achieve well-being and the potential those individuals have (at the psychic, emotional level as well as at the material, structural level) to make themselves feel well and act well. Well-being, then, can be seen as to do with human capacity (emotions and the affective qualities, as well as knowledge, health and the cognitive skills of an individual), culture and values (material), and social ecology (the community relationships). Well-being is a balance of the objective (measurable) aspects of income, employment and social environment with the subjective (and less obvious) feelings of happiness and contentment.

More psychosocial approaches adopt trans-disciplinary or post-disciplinary perspectives to the dynamic problem of well-being, attending to issues of bodily and emotional experience and subjectivity, and at the same time relating these experiences to rooted social relations and material circumstances. Our discussion represents a move away from more scientized and objective concepts to something approximating an experiential and subjective evaluation. As such, we could argue that the individualized dimension of well-being approximates more with changes to self-identity and the reflexive project of the self in late-modernity that we have so far discussed (Giddens, 1991). Indeed, Carlisle *et al.* talk about well-being as a 'collateral casualty of modernity' (2009: 1557), meaning that well-being as a concept is a product of the significant levels of social, cultural and political change to emerge in our late-modern times.

Philosophical roots of approaches to well-being

On one level there are, we would argue, well-established links between well-being, satisfaction, contentment and happiness; that is to say, in the context of an individual's growth and development, how well one's life is going in a subjective sense. The late eighteenth/early nineteenth-century philosopher Jeremy Bentham put forward the classic utilitarian view that happiness was the balance between the good and bad things happening in one's life, or rather the greatest happiness for the greatest number. Increasingly, as we shall see, in positive psychology (see Box 6.1) and popular self-help books that proliferate in bookshops and libraries in the UK there is an interest in helping one to evaluate the role of happiness (or, 'doing well') in one's life (and how to achieve it of course) and the relative notion of well-being.

In this way, well-being is a useful term that can be deployed instead of terms like mental health, as well as happiness, for it is about the individual's whole life – well-being can also be said to contain a 'holistic' message about the nature of individual and social health and fulfilment. Thus, it is a term that aims to give us a more holistic and broader understanding of someone's total health and happiness situation. For that reason alone it can prove to be a more useful term to help us understand the psychosocial dimensions of doing well, as it seeks to get beneath the surface to understand how internal psychic dynamics operate in a social context.

Furthermore, what this utilitarian idea (from Bentham) also tells us is that most popular psychology theories and ways of thinking about well-being take into account the *hedonic* view of doing well and happiness, that is, the view that one's purpose is to maximize pleasure and minimize pain and misery – this is in the dominant, ordinary sense of the term that happiness is suggestive of ebullience or *joie de vivre*. Many individuals strive for things and material pleasures that may give them a form of happiness; and thus frustration and strain can arise when these cannot be achieved (see Merton in Chapter 7 for a discussion of the implications of this for ill-being). For this approach 'hedonic' well-being is the raising of subjective levels of happiness (Carlisle *et al.*, 2009) and having access to as many 'pleasures' as possible, however they are defined.

Other approaches can be summarized by the eudemonic approach to well-being, which the early Greek philosopher Aristotle put forward to argue that not all pleasures are equal in terms of providing well-being. Here, well-being is not solely about subjective happiness. Moreover, human striving, suffering, effort and engagement in the pursuit of something in itself can be worthwhile and provide well-being (pleasure and happiness may therefore be one particular outcome) as well as leading to the realization of human potential (Ryan and Deci, 2001). Pleasure in this sense may not be the only outcome, and it is not uniformly good for people; indeed, in a collective sense one's individual happiness may be created at the expense of someone else's and we may understand that happiness and wellness is a relational concept.

Positive psychology

Some contemporary psychology, and certainly much popular and 'self-help' psychology which has grown in popularity in recent years, gives the impression that our identities are a process or a 'project' to be worked on, and that if done in the right way we can be happy and fulfilled (or 'self-actualized' to use Maslow's 1943 term). A better job, a better marriage, love-life or relationship, a more positive attitude, a different size and shape – we can make and remake our identity; our bodies, minds and selves are pretty much fluid and elastic. These self-help ideas push for a perfectionist model of self-improvement, and one of the problems with these ideas is that they are likely to make people feel worse if they fail to be happy, fulfilled or 'self actualized'.

Martin Seligman (1990), along with Mihaly Csikszentmihalyi, is considered to be the founder of the positive psychology movement, although it has its roots in much earlier thinking about the self and development (see Box 6.1). In some ways positive psychology, like the humanistic work of Maslow, takes a critical position on the disease-centric medical model of human faults and frailty – that as human beings we suffer from a range of disorders that need to be put right, and as a consequence we neglect the issue of trying to think up interventions that make people happier. For example, the positive psychology movement made a direct critique of the psychiatric movement and their standard classifications of mental illness, legitimized by their entry in the definitive United States reference manual for the profession, the DSM (Diagnostic and Statistical Manual of Mental Disorders, currently 4th edition) and/or the International Classification of Diseases (currently 10th edition, Chapter 5).

For the positive psychology adherents such as Seligman, well-being is seen as a positive characteristic that helps individuals to thrive and to flourish. This approach reinforces the view that individual well-being is founded on autonomous action – that individuals act autonomously to achieve happiness and that reducing 'dependency' is part of this (see Chapter 4 for a discussion of the problematic, gendered nature of the notion that 'dependency' is a negative quality or state).

Box 6.1

What is positive psychology?

Positive psychology is interested in human strengths and building on those, as opposed to thinking about weaknesses and deficiencies, as well as with making ordinary people more fulfilled and happy. For the positive psychologist happiness could mean a number of things: it could mean the Aristotelian notion of the good life, *eudemonia* and the strived-for life; it could mean the *pleasant life* or the life that brings happy emotions and pleasure (hedonic), though they recognize that has its drawbacks (not least that it could be genetic); and it could also denote the '*meaningful*' life, one that reduces the self to broader humanistic or spiritual/religious goals.

For one to be able to achieve the 'good life' or the productive satisfying life, it helps if the individuals can get to a state of flow (a concept put forward by Csikszentmihalyi, 1990) where time 'stops' for that person from the start to the end of the activity in question – an assumption here being that noticing time through to not noticing time constitutes another continuum across which happiness can be registered.

Similar to the normative assumptions of a traditional psychological approach where well-being and happiness is an outcome, positive psychologists also believe you can measure people's levels of happiness. For example, the Apple iPhone has an application that you can download called 'Mappiness' in which the aim is to chart people's feelings of happiness across time and place, generating charts that allow individuals to see how their own happiness changes over time and during the day.

The critiques of Seligman's perspective have been varied. Ehrenrich's *Smile or Die: How Positive Thinking Fooled America and the World* (2010) takes one particular view by providing a personal and political (a rather psychosocial) rebuttal of Seligman and the Positive Psychology movement, and in particular the notion that individual positive thinking (particularly in relation to how to overcome life-threatening illnesses like cancer) should somehow be held responsible for life outcomes – in other words and at the very extreme of this, that if we do not recover from severe illnesses it is because we personally have not applied a positive thinking approach. Ehrenreich also makes an important link between advocates of positive thinking and corporate profits: ill health and misery are often generated as part of capitalist profit systems (e.g. industrial food production, pollution etc. not our state of mind, but we have been persuaded/coerced into taking our state of mind as responsible).

The positive thinking thesis comes out of the notion of a 'me generation' (a generation that puts self-fulfilment as opposed to, for example, doing one's duty or self-sacrifice for others, at the top of its priorities) and also attracts challenges from within popular psychology itself. A theme has emerged which says 'too much of a good thing makes you miserable' (e.g. Oliver James's *Affluenza*, 2007, and *Britain on the Couch*, 2010), although much of this replays Seligman's take on the rounded dimension to positive well-being and the importance of striving and working hard to achieve personal well-being. The argument put forward here is that capitalism, as an economic process and condition, generates envy and unfulfilled desire; having everything is unsatisfying and/or unattainable.

One might also add that there is a cross-cultural critique of the positive psychology perspective, in that the positive psychology view takes a very Western, modern and ethnocentric perspective on the subject.

Psychoanalytical well-being

Within critical psychology, which, as discussed in Chapter 1, includes many psychosocial thinkers, the notion of 'identity crisis' as the product of living in the post-modern world has also been a core theme (Frosh, 1991), more similar to James and Ehrenrich's than positive psychology. Psychoanalysis has often been linked to the notion (emanating from Freud) that misery is the ordinary lot of humanity and that ordinarily human beings struggle psychically. To deny this fact is a denial of the full richness of life, which may include a range of personal struggles, difficulties and unhappiness. Interestingly, the sociology of identity also veers towards the pessimistic end of the spectrum, such as highlighting the fragmentation of identity in multi-cultural contexts.

The psychoanalytical version of what people are like highlights that anger, envy, hatred, rage, dependence, guilt – the whole gamut of emotions that society sees as bad and even shameful or pathological – are as ordinarily part of the make-up of humans, in different ways and in relation to different contexts, as the 'good' and acceptable emotions of love, affection, passion, generosity, care and gratitude. This suggests that internally people defend against 'bad' feelings swamping them and others (this is considered in relation to violence in Chapter 8). People 'cover up', trying not to be exposed as, for example, envious or ungrateful, ashamed and guilty. At one level these feelings are deeply personal, making people 'feel bad inside', but thinking psychosocially they are also fundamentally social: in whose eyes might a person feel diminished, whose observance will expose them as less than perfect? The social audience may be present – we are seen and caught out – or we carry the audience in our head, so we can feel ashamed with nobody actually watching as the social judgement is in-built and internalized – 'I am what I think you think I am' (see Goffman, 1990 [1959]; Giddens, 1991). Psychosocial writers such as Hoggett have suggested that we must not rule out the destructiveness and self-destructiveness that individuals and groups are capable of, that positive feelings may be replaced by negative emotional capabilities (2001) or indeed that destructiveness, hatred, anger etc. are also crucial emotions, though in need of containment and direction.

Both psychoanalytical and psychosocial 'versions' of what people are like suggests we all struggle in various ways (quite different from the positive psychology view that we can all be self-actualized, empowered and successful if we choose). Well-being might be described as something like the ability to live with acceptance of one's flawed and struggling self, but have the freedom of movement to change the destructive elements of self into something manageable.

The impossibility of reconciling our various kinds of ambivalence, the structured-in unachievable longing for completeness ('oceanic' feelings – see Chapter 3), the mistaken recognition of our identity at the very core of ourselves, as Lacan theorizes, set the notion of 'well-being' as nearer self-tolerance and some understanding of our imperfections and miseries, not the cure of them. However, as mentioned above, 'the pleasure principle', 'jouissance', becoming 'authentic' and living creatively are also explored by psychoanlytical thinkers concerned to understand the 'positives': people's life forces, their urge or striving for relationships, pleasures, desires and capacities to transform their worlds and so on. These aspects, too, are part of human identity, and indeed a frequent aim of psychoanalytic or psychotherapeutic treatment might be to reduce anxiety and immobility, allowing then for the experience of some possible change and movement. Not living without struggle, but also living with some joy, some pleasure, some energy and creativity.

The psychoanalytical and psychosocial view, that psychological struggles, senses of inadequacy, uncomfortable feelings such as envy and mourning, are ordinary and everyday, can paradoxically be as life enhancing as positive psychology's message that everyone can achieve personal happiness. This is, in one sense, the acceptance that the full richness of life needs 'light and shade' which includes struggle and unhappiness. But also in the sense that you are not therefore a failure, or ill, or inadequate if you have not been able to become the happy shinny person some say self-help psychology promotes. Struggling, getting things wrong, doing what you can, 'good enough ...': these are all fine – we all struggle – is the message. The aim, therefore, of much social intervention, such as welfare, to help people's growth and development is to allow people to create a sense of well-being that is not necessarily based around perfectionism of the self – to have well-being that is 'good enough' but open to change may be the goal.

Self-help psychology and its critique

Self-help is the popular and populist manifestation of positive psychology, projecting similar values in many instances as those discussed above, and overlapping as a phenomenon in many of its core concerns. It has been for the last couple of decades a growing industry and big business, as evidenced by the proliferation of self-help groups and networks as well as the books and gurus that drive its popularity. Writers and sociologists like Furedi (2003) see the danger of the self-help movement as the attempt to cast social problems as solely emotional, psychic-level problems about the individual. Furedi suggests that popular therapy and television type confessional stories also open up private troubles and experiences to public scrutiny and where all forms of adversity and mental ill-being is linked to lack of social esteem – major social problems are thereby recast as individual woes.

But on more than one level we can see how there is an important interplay between the private emotional aspects of human experience and the social conditions (environment) underpinning that experience. The 'pure' sociological view is therefore just as problematic and constricted by the boundaries of knowledge.

For Giddens there is a different risk, a danger that self-therapy and the process of self-actualization (such as outlined by Maslow below) and the project of the self becomes commodifed; that is to say, it is a commodity that is bought and sold like any other. As he states:

Not just lifestyles, but self-actualisation is packaged and distributed according to market criteria. Self help books, like *Self Therapy*, stand in a precarious position with regard to the commodified production of self-actualisation. In some ways such works break away from standardised, packaged consumption. Yet in so far as they become marketed as pre-packaged theorems about how to 'get on' in life, they become caught up in the very processes they nominally oppose. (Giddens, 1991: 198)

Giddens' point is that the process of packaging up self-help as an industry is paradoxical, as it is the industry-specific nature of the self-help business that self-help texts, with their advice on meaning in life, are trying to move away from. From this perspective, well-being may emerge as something that can be thought about in a commodified way, but it detracts from the original philosophy underpinning it.

For Giddens, self-therapy and the process of self-actualization are features of late-modernity (see the Introduction to this book) and are therefore open to anyone and everyone living under such socio-historical circumstances. Giddens argues that this leads to more empowerment and agency for individuals, where they are able to 'alter the material world and transform the conditions of their own actions' (1991: 138); such empowerment influences the person's ability to influence their own well-being and reflexively manage the 'panoramas of choice which confront the individual in day-to-day activity' (*ibid.*: 139). Self-therapy involves, then, the process of seeing how the self as the individual can approach the problem of living and happiness; *ergo sum*, it is not something which has anything much to do with society and the structural conditions of one's life. We have discussed how any foundational psychosocial theory would both highlight the importance of and problematize both the intimate psychic arena as well as the social structural conditions in society.

Theories of human need and potential

Writers coming from a more psychosocial perspective such as Hoggett (2000) are interested in how we can understand the core principles of welfare in relation to deeply held psychic and emotional needs. Others like Froggett (2002) and Cooper and Lousada (2005) have sought to bring in the concept of well-being into the domain of social policy in order to help highlight the value of welfare that goes beyond merely crude economic and functional relationships:

It foregrounds personal relationships, trust and participation rather than consumption, and focuses on the creation and exchange of 'social value' through relationships at the level of culture rather than economic value through contract. (Taylor, 2011: 2)

At its basis is the idea that welfare is also there to promote human personal and social development, the capabilities and capacities that allow individuals to flourish and to grow. Such views have their roots in universal theories of human need (Doyal and Gough, 1991, see Box 6.2) but they are also underpinned by philosophical perspectives in human capabilities. We shall proceed to examine some of these perspectives in the following section.

Box 6.2

Doyal and Gough (1991): a theory of human need and universal human needs

In their seminal text *A Theory of Human Need*, Doyal and Gough argue that humans have basic needs for physical health and individual autonomy, but also they have a range of intermediate needs, which are termed 'universal satisfier characteristics' that arise from these basic needs and form the basis for requiring certain goods that satisfy basic needs.

However, their view suggests that it is difficult to provide a list of human needs that are universal and applicable in all societies and cultures. Such intermediate needs include nutritional food and water, adequate protective housing, security in childhood, physical security and so on. Their view is that the list they present is a list of intrinsic and therefore universal basic needs.

In the 1980s the Indian economist Amartya Sen developed the capabilities approach to welfare and welfare economics. The principle behind the theory was that individuals should have the ability and opportunities to achieve and develop outcomes that are favourable to the person, and that these may rely on certain capabilities. This approach highlights what the person is capable of doing, and given the range of personal and material circumstances that may restrict this, which may be considerable. So, for Sen, the theory is about what individual capabilities does the individual have, to do valuable acts or to achieve valuable states of being (Sen, 1993). This emphasizes the role of individual agency and self-determination in the achievement of reaching a positive state of wellness.

Following on from some collaborative work with Sen, writers like the American philosopher Martha Nussbaum have adapted Sen's capabilities and freedoms in terms of outlining ten 'central human functioning capabilities' to highlight the kinds of areas of human capabilities that we should be trying to improve from the point of view of increasing human development in democratic societies (Nussbaum, 2000). This is the capabilities approach to human development, and the capabilities are universal in nature. The capabilities are classified in relation to different kinds of activities.

It is not necessary to list them all here but some of those capabilities are linked directly to physical health and security (similar to Maslow's 'hierarchy of needs', 1943). A few of the other capabilities bring to mind something more akin to issues surrounding well-being, such as what Nussbaum calls the 'Senses, imagination, thought'. That is, being able to imagine, to think and to reason (the concept of rationality was important to Nussbaum's work) and to do this in an informed way, and being able to have pleasurable experiences and to avoid 'non-beneficial' pain. Another capability that Nussbaum suggested was the 'emotions'; that is to say, being able to have attachments, to love and to care, being able to grieve at someone's absence, to experience longing, gratitude and justified anger. Lastly, 'play' – being able to laugh and to play and enjoy recreation – was also regarded as an important capability. All of the capabilities were intrinsically tied to well-being and personal fulfilment: the work's concern with emotion, the relational and the material makes it helpful for psychosocial thinking.

Theories of resilience

Let us look now at resilience. Resilience, and its opposite, vulnerability have become core concepts for thinking about the factors influential in 'doing well'; that is to say, who 'sinks' and who 'swims' (and why) in contemporary social science literature – and indeed in a range of other disciplines – from a variety of perspectives including the psychosocial. It is also becoming a key concept in the literature of professionalism as 'professional resilience'. For example, to look at why child protection social workers leave the job after less time and have more days of sickness than their counterparts working with adults, can be conceptualized as a matter of professional resilience (Gilligan, 2004).

In this volume we briefly discussed the concept of resilience in relation to understanding children's development in Chapter 3. However, as a central framework in relation to which well-being, the core concern of this chapter, can be understood, it is useful to look at the ideas both more generally and in more depth.

A 'standard' definition of resilience is often taken to be 'positive adaptation in the face of considerable adversity' (Wright and Masten, 2005). Whilst resilience was originally thought of as a trait (of the individual or community, for example), it now tends to be seen more as a dynamic process, where internal and external factors interact in changing ways over time, and new vulnerabilities or strengths emerge with changing circumstances. 'Protective factors' lessen the risks inherent in adverse circumstances and a person develops protection by drawing upon internal and external 'resources' (Hoggett, 2010). Previous experiences and how they were navigated, friends and family for example, might constitute internal and external resources.

Psychodynamic theories of resilience and vulnerability

The kinds of life-stage models referred to in earlier chapters also specifically Bowlby's attachment theory discussed particularly in Chapter 2 tell us a great deal about resilience, survival and resources, and particularly inner resources.

Life-stage models from, for example, Erikson or Freud tend to see damage and thriving in relation to completing life stages. 'Healthy' development involves passing through the stipulated stages and/or completing the task required of the stages. Becoming fixated or having only partially negotiated crucial life stages sets up a pattern of psychic struggles or difficulties lasting into adulthood. For psychoanalytic theorists such as Freud, Klein and Winnicott, 'difficult' mental states are encoded very early in life, so that psychic vulnerability and/or strengths and even 'clinical' problems may be pre-Oedipal (3–5 years), and a propensity to experience, for example, separation anxiety, or depressive tendencies or even psychiatric disorders have their roots in childhood.

For all of us, by the end of the childhood period universal features such as anxiety, conflict, ambivalence, emotional drives, defences and desires will have been established in person-specific patterns. The kinds of ways that each individual struggles – as we said above, for psychoanalytic thinkers all of us struggle; this is ordinary and not 'ill' or 'mad' – for example, their proneness to envy, anger or paranoia is set in place at a young age. The extent to which this is moderated, increased, mediated or changed in any way is a contentious issue in psychosocial studies. Its focus on external as well as internal influences and impacts, offers more hope for ongoing change than pure psychoanalysis. Bateman *et al.* (2010) lean more towards the psychoanalytical but even so this is not entirely arguing that nothing changes, but that our way of seeing the world is internalized early in life:

> Development does not stop here; but whether early crises have been resolved for good or for ill, towards or away from the establishment of sufficient trust, autonomy and initiative, will determine an individual's attitude and response to subsequent challenges (2010: 52–3).

Attachment theory is in one sense a rigorous consideration of how resilience and vulnerability are established inside the identity of each person. As we have already considered, the principal argument is that the need for a close attachment to one relationship in infancy with a primary carer constitutes a basic drive within humans (and some animals), not within a specific category of life stages but as a primary motivational system itself. Either the attainment of such 'attachment', or the various limitations, failures or damage to such a state, impact fundamentally on the development of the individual, through childhood and into adulthood. Attachments can be thought about as primarily divided into secure and insecure attachment and like many psychodynamic concepts 'attachment' carries experiential and theoretical overtones. To feel attached is to feel safe and secure. By contrast, an insecurely attached person may have a mixture of feelings towards their attachment figure: 'intense love and dependency, or fear of rejection, irritability and vigilance' (Holmes, 1993: 67).

Strong feelings relived in relation to adult attachments and losses may constitute vulnerabilities, as the resonances of firm, loving attachments – secure identity, a sense of being lovable, trust etc. – may contribute to resilience in individuals. Concepts such as separation and loss (from loved ones – 'attachment' figures) mourning, rejection, loneliness, can also be understood within the framework of attachment theory. However, they can also be understood more generally within an interpretation of resilience as a fundamentally relational concept. In other words, our well-being is not a separate capacity or feeling, but intertwined with relationships, friendships, love, connections: the esteem and concern of others, and of our significant groups. We raise this in relation to gender in Chapter 4. It also can be extremely useful for understanding the importance of work and the work place, of communities of well-being and esteem.

Box 6.3

The Casita (little house) model of resilience

Belgian theorists called Stefan Vanistendael and Jaqcues Lecomte, developed the Casita model working in community development in Chile and have used it for understanding and moving forward with individuals, organizations and communities since then.

Vanistendael has gone on to use the model in a wide range of disparate and extreme contexts – for example, in a children's hospice, as well as with homeless children in poor countries. One of its basic features is the predominance it gives to networks of relationships, as the building block – the base – of resilience.

Resilience:

- Is never absolute
- Is variable in time and space
- Consists of two dimensions – resistance and construction, to do the latter involves projecting oneself into the future – imaging the future
- In certain cases the capacity to transform negative events for some elements of personal growth
- Built in a life-long relationship between an individual/group and its surroundings/ environment
- Links to ethical principles – what is 'positive adaptation', what does it mean 'to adapt' to repressive regimes or difficulties?
- In trying to overcome some real problem or threat, may open up resources in a person or group, but the growth therein may also be the trigger to negative responses. In reality in difficult situations growth will sometimes happen in spite of problems, sometimes because of them and sometimes be a mixture.

The model can be used for analysis of communities and individuals, thinking with them about what is in each room, what are the other rooms, what might the attic look like and so on – a working tool to think about and increase resilience with.

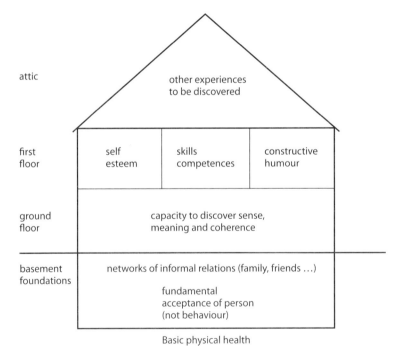

Figure 6.1   Casita: resilience building
Source: Vanistendael (1998)

Friendships and resilience

Inter-connectedness, ongoing relationships, growth and processes – the Casita model positions relationships – friends – networks, etc. at the ground floor; they are seen here as a basic underlying feature of resilience, as the hearth or the kitchen of the 'house'.

The importance of relationships, of connectedness rather than aloneness, which we discussed a little in Chapter 4, has started to filter through research in relation to all kinds of topics, as crucial for people to thrive. Local research here with children making the transition from primary school to secondary school showed the factor they overwhelming suggested that made 'being new' okay was having close friends, a best friend, a gang of friends (Frost and Hoggett, 2008). Mental health research looks at loneliness in particularly older people as causative of depression. People cut off from their cultures and homelands similarly report more isolation and despair.

In terms of resilience then, a very strong case can be made for friendship, connection and recognition as a crucial factor, and even though there seems to be very little research on friendship, there is some interesting work thinking about what we mean by friendship, what friendships mean. Freud's version seems somewhat limited here – friendship is seen as a manifestation of aim inhibited sexuality – which seems to imply a kind of pathology about it, or at least a distortion and inhibition. Early psychoanalytic readings tend to focus on friendship as a particular manifestation in childhood and adolescence, almost, it is implied, before you get to 'the real thing' and form a couple. Klein, on the other hand, suggests something more important. She speaks of 'friendship as an opportunity for revising and improving early relationships … [they can] prove that [one] is able to love and is lovable, that love and goodness exist…'. In other words, we can experience something of another's love and care in the give and take of friendships as adults (Klein, cited in Akhtar, 2009: 254–5). Salman Akhtar's work, interestingly, using psychoanalysis to think about friendship, explores the relationship between friendship and what he calls 'the immigrant experience' – so thinking about the part friendship has in mitigating loneliness and reconnecting people in new, strange or alien environments.

That friendships are powerful, are a resource, offer belonging, a chance to learn about self and other and to grow – these are the kinds of positive aspects friendships can offer, though of course the flip-side might well be self-doubt, competitiveness and fear of loss (Schulman, 2009). And this rather more psychosocial take is self-explanatory:

The self is contradictorily both private and social. The self obtains its sense of coherence and continuity from within, yet at the same time it is dependent upon the appraisal of others who can either support or disrupts the self's continuity. The private self supports the relative self-sufficiency, whereas from another perspective the self is not at all autonomous and is vulnerable in its dependence upon others for a sense of coherence and continuity (Modell, 1997).

The issue of friendships/networks is useful for understanding 'swimming and sinking' in all kinds of contexts, in transitions as well as ongoing life worlds. Much has been produced, for example, in relation to 'being occupied' – work and play (Chapter 5). Andrew and Montague's (1998) study, for example, of female friendships in a university context tries to get close to what friendship is: what are the elements that make it able to sustain well-being. They suggest that the concept is dynamic, subsumes a whole range of relationships, and may be experienced in different ways.

Some aspects might be that friends share one's values and interests, possess desirable personality traits. They may be for liking and trusting, self-disclosure (sharing personal information), joint activities and companionship and support and advice, and positive affirmation of identity. This aspect – of providing positive affirmation and a sense of self, offers some clue as to why this might be important psychosocially. Friendships mirror back to us ourselves as likeable/lovable, worth knowing so worth something: 'two people who recognize each other' (Andrew and Montague, 1998: 355).

This brings us quite squarely to the notion of 'recognition'. The work of Axel Honneth on recognition (explored more in Chapter 7) is valuable in helping us to see how recognition or self-esteem is created and how it can be sustained. What is particularly useful here is the connection of affirmation and feeling worth something, to one's place in a group, a community, a culture: in other words, in the context of people on whose esteem one seeks or depends. Honneth's notion of 'Communities of value' is really helpful for thinking about what friendships, for example at work or play, might be able to provide. Ideas of 'social capital' also offer a framework for understanding relationship, community and integration as important for well-being.

Box 6.4

Social capital

Social capital theory is built on ideas that have developed to account for the importance of social ties and networks that endure into late adulthood.

It describes both the ways in which social interaction is enabled, perhaps via the reciprocity that arises from social obligations (Bourdieu, 1986), and as a resource to draw upon (Coleman, 1988). Social capital also encapsulates the ways in which the social fabric is knitted together (Putnam, 1995, 2000).

Within economic and policy fields, it has been used to address the issue of social exclusion (Cattell, 2001), neighbourhood renewal (Cabinet Office, Social Exclusion Unit, 1998; Middleton et al., 2005), and the nature of health inequalities (Gillies, 1998). With regard to inequalities, social capital is seen as a psychosocial factor involved in the alleviation of health inequalities.

The social capital debate is an established one, and is one that largely asks questions about the relationship between individualism and community within modern societies). Putnam (1995: 65–78), for example, defines *social capital* as: 'features of social life – networks, norms and trust – that enable participants to act together more effectively to pursue shared objectives'. In a later work he introduced the concepts of 'bonding' and 'bridging': bonding' is likely to be more inward-looking and may reinforce exclusive identities and gate keeping; 'bridging' – may be more outward-looking and encompass people across different social divides.

Bridging thereby generates 'reciprocity' and togetherness across social divides, and could be seen as a key benefit of high social capital.

A sense of belonging and the experience of social networks (and the relationships of trust, mutuality and tolerance that can be involved) can bring great benefits to people, some of which may be seen in psychosocial terms.

For instance, civil attendance in an association or club also has a strong link to well-being and psychosocial health (Viswanath et al., 2006). It has also been argued that older age groups are more likely to have high levels of neighbourhood connections (Zeirsch et al., 2005).

Resilience as mentalization

The internalized security of strong early attachments, internalized strengths from successful negotiation of early life stages, internalized good objects and a flexible defensive structure all form part of what then becomes a resource in relationship with a 'threat' (pressure). The point we are making here is that resilience is present in the response to a threat; it is not therefore a quality of personality or a trait. Resources can be thought about in various ways; for example, they have also been conceptualized as 'capacities and capabilities' (as we discussed earlier with Sen's and Nussbaum's approach), which again gives the concept a more active application – that which the person is able to marshal and to bring about – almost equating agency with resilience, or at least getting near to that perspective.

Another way of thinking about this is as 'mentalization'. The concepts of mentalization and 'reflective function' were developed by Bateman and Fonagy (2004) to examine the capacity to process 'emotional experience' and render it 'thinkable'. In other words, to use reflection and consideration as part of responding to difficulties. For example, in terms of professional resilience (surviving in the workplace), some recent research has been done on how the presence of 'reflective spaces' in front-line settings has been shown to promote these capacities (Mayo *et al.*, 2007).

Mentalization is an example of what Lazarus and Folkman (1984) originally termed 'emotion focused coping', an idea they contrasted with 'problem focused coping', which refers to agency directed towards the external world rather than towards the self. Both forms of agency will have recursive effects, strengthening resources but also, at times, through 'negative chain reactions' (Rutter, 1995, 1999), compounding difficulties.

In terms of psychosocial well-being, it seems that resilience can be usefully thought of as existing in the process or relationship between individuals and particular challenges/sets of circumstances in which internal and external resources (intermingled) are accessed to produce some kind of positive or improved outcome.

Two points perhaps worth noting about 'positive outcome' would be that within our psychosocial definition this would need to be perceived as such by the individual experiencing the situation, and that notions such as 'successful' or even 'positive' can easily suggest that outcomes are either/or (either successful or unsuccessful, for example) whereas in this volume as we have shown in previous discussions, these kind of black and white absolutes are cautioned against. The outcomes and the perceptions of the outcomes are all likely to have some mixed elements of useful and less useful, satisfactory and unsatisfactory, good but up to a point. The same kind of resolution can both help and harm – at the time and because of future ramifications.

Well-being and fate

So far the above has focused on ways of understanding the dynamic relationship that we are arguing resilience is, as well as some psychoanalytic thinking about the inner resources individuals may be able to muster. For balance, then, before we conclude it may be worth briefly considering how people might come to understand their own well-being (and its opposite). The opportunities and changes that have meaning to individuals as catalysts are frequently understood as more random and fateful than we have suggested so far. Identity sociologists have been helpful for this and the work of Giddens, applied in research studies by, for example, Henderson, is helpful here.

> **Box 6.5**
>
> **'Fateful moments' and 'critical moments'**
>
> 'Fateful moments' (Giddens, 1991), attempts to look at how people tend to describe their own lives in relation to key 'turning points' or events that are seen as make or break: '... times when events come together in such a way that an individual stands, as it were, at a cross-roads in their existence; or where a person learns of information with fateful consequences' (1991: 113)
>
> Fateful moments can be destructive or (potentially) empowering, and may have consequences for ongoing/future identity.
>
> 'Critical moments' (Henderson, 2007) did not necessarily have to be recognized as 'critical' at the time. Critical moments encompass the idea of biography, timing, resources, resourcefulness, etc.
>
> Some examples of critical moments are: a chance encounter with a significant individual, 'falling' in love, a crash, political/religious epiphany, a book, a speech, an encounter with mortality.

This then suggests that the meaning individuals ascribe to their well-being may also have to do with what 'fate' or life threw at them; the moment of chance and change. As psychosocial theorists we wouldn't disagree, but might add that perhaps what they were able to do with the chance, how they shaped or resisted or embraced or prolonged or responded in any other way, might be the product of psychosocial forces.

Conclusion

This chapter has ranged widely over the topic of well-being, using what seems useful to reflect and also to construct a psychosocial approach. After some introductory thoughts, we began our discussion by looking briefly at the relationship between health and well-being. We then mentioned theories of 'capital' before going on to discuss the strengths and problems of positive psychology. Psychoanalytic notions of well-being, how it is constructed and what it means were then, by contrast, examined. Self-help was considered before we looked at the more psychosocial concepts of attachment and particularly resilience. Resilience was discussed mainly as a relational concept, and friendships and the idea of recognition were then analysed. Finally, we made a brief comment on fate and well-being. The following chapter is very much a necessary part of the discussion here, focusing as it does on the flip-side of the coin – ill-being.

7

How people struggle: social suffering and ill-being

Introduction

In the previous chapter we explored some of the ways in which well-being has been critically understood, and we began to highlight the subjective (inner) as well as social, structural (outer) dimensions in the debate about its relationship to doing well in the world. In so doing we have shown that the individual and the social are interrelated and that we can explore the individual lived experience to make sense of social circumstances and conditions. Exploring those issues separately is useful of course, but the approach to well-being we outline here aims to present a more sophisticated, integrated and meaningful discussion about the intimate concerns of individual lives and the external social, economic and political order that shapes those lives.

On a rather superficial level we might argue that the subject of ill-being is the flip-side to exploring well-being; two sides to the same coin. The greater or lesser quality of *being* is the central concern. Well-being implies a positive approach to human development, whereas ill-being suggests its opposite – the disruptive and negative life events that happen to the person and that overwhelm and/or threaten health and identity – that ensures the individual (and groups) is/are more likely to struggle or suffer in life. We highlight ill-being as a relational issue and it is experienced relationally, impacting on groups as well as individuals. Just as Clarke (2008) suggests, we cannot talk about the psycho without the social in psychosocial studies, they are inseparable; it is also the case that we cannot talk about well-being without talking about ill-being, and vice-versa. For the purposes of this book, then, they are separate 'themes', but it will be important for the reader to explore these chapters together.

In this chapter we want to continue with this theme of people and groups trying to 'do well' in the world, but explore more the downside to this and the ways in which ill-being and social suffering may be a feature of individuals' lives. Here, we consider a range of different themes about ill-being and show how the individual psyche and the social and structural circumstances overlap and are entwined. The relationship between physical illness and long-term depression on the one hand, and social deprivation, poverty, and all kinds of illnesses on the other is given substantial consideration in this chapter. That being a member of any undervalued group – working class, black, female – is likely to correlate with poor health across most dimensions is crucial to the debate. That 'social suffering' and exclusion, regardless of the life stage, is damaging is also discussed. Examples such as research into depression in women are drawn upon. How the mechanisms of stigma and other forms of exclusion, isolation, stress, anxiety and powerlessness create physical and mental distress and 'ill-being' is examined. Contemporary, consumerist 'life-style epidemics' such as anorexia are critically evaluated.

As such, in this chapter we aim to highlight the individual and social basis of social suffering and to explore that in the context of an emphasis on the emotions in social life. We explore some of the key psychosocial problems in relation to ill-being, such as hurt, loss, shame, depression and loneliness, and we highlight the psychosocial approach to health inequalities. We identify and discuss some of the contemporary consumerist 'life-style epidemics' and how we might explore these psychosocially.

What is ill-being?

Psychosocially, well-being and ill-being exist more on a continuum rather than necessarily being opposites. During the lifecourse individuals may fluctuate between the two states, experiencing greater or lesser *being* depending on a range of factors, not least social and economic circumstances but also more personal factors. We can also argue that some individuals are dealt a better hand in life and do not struggle with being in the ways that others may do. However, none of us are immune to some of those ill-being moments and events – what Giddens (1991: 112–14) calls 'fateful moments' (see Chapter 6) such as hearing the results of a medical test – but other adversities and ill-being events are more socially patterned and provide evidence about the existence and nature of a class structure and other forms of social oppression. Exploring the psychosocial issues of well-being and ill-being allows us then to present a more multifactorial and complex picture of illness, disease and suffering than would normally be available through more conventional health and epidemiological studies.

In a psychosocial sense the concept of ill-being brings to mind thoughts about the deficiencies and weaknesses of individual health and the self as well as outcomes of a difficult life, one where well-being and personal and/or social fulfilment is basically absent. There are psychic, individually determined aspects of a life that may predispose someone to ill-being in a way other individuals are not, but at the same time there are considerable social structural and more prevalent and enduring aspects to social life that impact on the individual and their relative exposure to ill-being. We must try to appreciate the increasingly individualized and atomistic nature of society (Beck, 1992; Giddens, 1991) and the effects of this in terms of dissolving or seriously altering the communal bonds that bind people together, but at the same time we are aware that some forms of structurally oriented social oppression to do with social class, gender and ethnicity, continue and endure and these have a major effect on the person's ill-being.

It is also important to make the link with both well-being and ill-being to the idea of how far these are intertwined with people's social relationships; that is to say, their social connections. Our suggestion is that increasingly more structural and economic factors influence and affect one's sense of doing well through more indirect, rather than direct, routes (Williams, 1998, 2000), and any account of those affects needs to both address the inner and outer worlds, the individual psyche and the wider social, political and cultural system, as Williams suggests: 'feelings of absurdity and alienation, bitterness and resentment, entrapment and despair are often entirely realistic and understandable responses to existing social circumstances' (1998: 65).

Theories of social suffering

Social suffering is an important theme in the psychosocial approach to understanding why some people struggle. In particular, the concept of social suffering is central to the psychosocial approach to understanding the relationship between the inner worlds of the subject and the outer world of social structure, power and oppression. It pays attention to the 'lived experience' of the suffering and damage that may be the result of living in late-capitalist societies in the early twenty-first century, and thus focuses on the feelings that experiences of social suffering produce.

It is useful to see this concept as in some ways a deviation from traditional sociological and social policy writing and discourses that have often focused exclusively on the social dimensions of suffering and the material and structural reality of the person's life, in terms of poverty, class and ethnicity (the classically used demographics in social science), although we should also note that the psychosocial approach does not choose to ignore it altogether. Rather, the psychosocial approach seeks to redefine the relationship between the objective features of social demographics (e.g. social class) and how that is located in the subjective 'lived experience' of particular individuals.

In the psychoanalyst and humanist Erich Fromm's classic book *To Have or to Be* (1976) he considers the problem of ill-being and human suffering from an interdisciplinary social theory perspective that synthesizes the work of Marx and Freud. By synthesize we mean to seek solutions to some of the major social problems in the world from a range of different, and sometimes competing, perspectives and to draw some conclusions from that. Fromm's synthesized approach has many similarities with other writers from the Frankfurt School such as Herbert Marcuse and Theodor Adorno (see Chapter 1). Historically, writers such as Marx and Freud were not seen as complementary; naturally psychoanalysis developed as a rather different philosophical position on the self from Marxism.

Box 7.1

Erich Fromm (1900–80): the sick individual and the sick society

Erich Fromm was associated with the Frankfurt School of Critical Theory but his work was very diverse. He developed critical ideas that brought together the work of psychoanalysts like Freud with sociological and humanistic philosophy, in new ways.

In particular Fromm was interested in the new forms of freedom brought about by modernity and capitalism. For Fromm, the move from more traditional, feudal societies led to some fear and anxiety due to the increase in individualism; as such, extreme ideological and political sympathies could develop (e.g. fascism). For Fromm, aspects of being an individual in modern society were problematic and the forms of belonging engendered by not being an individual (lack of freedom) in pre-modern societies meant that the person (and the group/community) was less isolated in the social structure.

He was also a practising psychoanalyst and wrote for a wider audience than most social theorists, focused as he was on issues such as personal development (e.g. *The Art of Loving*, 1957) and the ways to live a more balanced life committed to equality and fairness. Perhaps as a consequence of his popularity Fromm has been criticized as superficial, but he has also been noted as being optimistic about people's potential and therefore is a counterbalance to many traditionally psychoanalytically influenced writers.

Fromm explains that Marx, in his comprehensive analysis of class struggle and alienation, had tried to show how the working class of the day (the nineteenth-century proletariat in Europe) had suffered but due to the circumstances surrounding their suffering it was not clear to many of them that they were indeed suffering the consequences of a working situation that was both alienating and miserable. The main cause of this human suffering was not the work that they were doing per se, but the nature of the capitalist economy and the social relations on which that was based, although the workers may be under some other illusion – Marx felt that his writings were helping to free that illusion. In that respect, suffering in the form that Marx outlined would not change without a more substantial shift to the existing social structure and social order.

Freud, in comparison, suggested that the clients who visited him may also be suffering individually, and again the nature of that may be hidden from the person, and so Freud as the psychoanalyst would seek to change the nature of that illusion. As Fromm explains, for Freud much of that process of dealing with ill-being was lifting the veil over the deep-rooted causes of what was often childhood repression (see Chapter 2), but Freud's perspective missed the importance of the social both in terms of defining what is valued as important and the socially constructed nature of each individual experience. What we can understand from this preliminary sketch of Marx and Freud's respective work is that Fromm saw them as addressing the same fundamental issues about the individual self, the nature of ill-being, and the individuals' relationship to 'hidden' aspects of their individual lives (the difference between what is 'real' and what is illusion) – here, that of the psyche and the capitalist economic system and logic. This was an important contrast between what he saw as the 'sick individual' and the 'sick society' (Fromm, 1962).

Social suffering and the emotions

Let us first explain what we mean by 'lived experience'. Lived experience denotes the first-hand direct individual experience of a particular phenomenon that the individual may be 'living through' (as opposed to merely observing or thinking about). This approach to exploring individual perception and emotion is derived from an interpretative phenomenological perspective on the individual and claims that it is important to understand the subjective nature of the individual's experience in itself, as it is experienced first-hand. Furthermore, here we place importance also on the emotional life of the individual in making sense of their lived experience.

The emotions are of central importance to our understanding of ill-being and social suffering, in the forms of disease, illness, disability, pain and suffering (Williams, 1998, 2000, 2001). Thinking about the emotions also allows us to deal head-on with aspects of a person's development that do not fit comfortably within a mainstream medical model. Moreover, exploring the emotional dimension and the lived experience of social suffering and social misery is more psychosocial in its approach (Frost and Hoggett, 2008). The move towards exploring the emotions in social life has been referred to as the 'affective turn' in the humanities and the social sciences, but also has its roots in the work of Honneth and Winnicott, key figures that we have discussed in previous chapters. The affective turn gives a name to the turn or change from 'rationalist' scientific discourses to more holistic, psychoanalytically and psychosocially influenced discourses in the social sciences.

Exploring the emotions also allows us to move beyond conventional Cartesian (e.g. dichotomous) models of thinking that see mind and body, and individual and society as separate. Let us take the example of self-harm as a way of thinking about the emotions. Chandler (2012) explores how self-injury or harm can be seen as a form of embodied emotion work, which is heavily influenced by the socio-cultural contexts of the individual's world. Medical and clinical research and practice, according to Chandler, rarely takes into account such socio-cultural contexts of the emotions, preferring to see emotions as universal and unproblematic categories; emotions are treated purely as individual experiences. In a psychosocial sense, self-injury is an embodied method for managing emotions and suffering, bringing together mind and body.

The French sociologist Pierre Bourdieu (see Box 7.2) in particular has initiated a more psychosocial approach to the nature of ill-being and social suffering. Pierre Bourdieu's sociology has frequently sought to combine insights from objectivist and subjectivist approaches in the social sciences as well as different disciplines (Hage, 2011).

For Bourdieu, being (i.e. the condition of doing well and being fulfilled) is unequally distributed in society. Life is not fulfilling for everyone. Some people have more being than others. Moreover, during our lives we try to increase the fulfilment of our being and this works less or more well according to the individual and social circumstances that surrounds an individual's life. Bourdieu shows how the material circumstances surrounding individuals' access to resources, goods and services is important, but equally if not more important is the lived experience that being excluded from those material goods produces, and the emotional feelings of worthlessness and social marginality that often result (see Bourdieu, 1999; Frost and Hoggett, 2008). The social exclusion arises due to the person's place in the social world (due to social class for instance) but it is accompanied by a range of emotional consequences for the individual.

Box 7.2

Pierre Bourdieu (1930–2002): social and cultural capital

Pierre Bourdieu was a French sociologist, anthropologist and social thinker known particularly for the depth and breadth of his work on social and cultural capital and the complex power relationships in society. He was entrenched in a philosophical way of thinking (along with a writing style that was typically difficult and obfuscatory), but at the same time he was critical of the way that philosophy does not always engage in the real world. In particular, much of Bourdieu's writing tried to ambitiously bring together the traditional Marxist ideas about social structure and power with the more psychosocial ideas about the subjective experiences of the individual.

An important concept for Bourdieu, and which is relevant to our discussion here, is that of social and cultural capital, particularly the latter. The idea of cultural capital was essential to his work on class distinctions (Bourdieu, 1984). For Bourdieu, being (living a fulfilling life) was unequally distributed and accumulated, and one of the ways to accumulate this was through capital. His view was that dispositions towards forms of cultural 'taste' (as well as accumulating them), whether it is art, food, material items, education, etc., are formed at an early age, are internalized (which leads to his concept of 'habitus'), and guide people towards activities and behaviours that are appropriate for that class. As such the individual feels a deep-seated aversion to other modes of belonging and class distinction.

In the *Weight of the World* (1999) for example, Bourdieu produced an analysis (through ethnographic qualitative research) of examples of social suffering and the forms of social misery this produces, such as the experience of poor housing, unemployment, intergenerational conflict, loneliness, and so on. This book marked a shift from some of the more structural analysis Bourdieu had been writing to a more individual stories-focused narrative. For Reay (2005) this book represents one of the earliest examples of social science writing on the affective dimension of class (the psychic landscape of a social structural issue). In essence it made the focus of attention those individuals without power in society and how that must feel and what those experiences produce in the individual, in terms of powerlessness but also worthlessness. A focus on social suffering therefore allows us to consider what those without power and status endure, and not just those without economic resources.

As such, if an individual is located in a social position where they are extremely powerless, they are more likely, as a consequence of that marginality, to experience 'unpleasant' emotional modes of being and this represents a huge disadvantage for those individuals (see Freund, 1990). The social suffering of the French working class represents their lack of 'recognition' and social importance. More than that, Bourdieu shows how the powerful are able to enforce the way they see the world, some-thing which the powerless are unable to do partly as a consequence of their social exclusion and marginality. As Reay shows, the suffering falls unequally on those in the lower social and economic groups in society,

> The inequitable operations of social class damage all of us regardless of where we are positioned in the social field. But it is the most vulnerable, the working classes, who are made to bear the greatest psychological burdens of an unequal society ... class is deeply embedded in everyday interactions, in insti-tutional processes, in struggles over identity, validity, self-worth and integrity even when it is not acknowledged. Class is a powerful psychic force, the stuff of conflict, both internal and external. (Reay, 2005: 924)

In thinking about the importance of accounting for the emotions in social life and their importance to psychosocial theory, we must also iden-tify particular concepts that have been used that engage in the emotions. One particular concept to explore that is very useful to those working in the social care and health professions is that of emotional labour and emotion work (see Box 7.3). The concept of emotional labour is about recognizing and explaining the emotional 'work' that goes into types of paid work, and goes beyond the biological understanding of the emotions to one that considers what emotions and feelings actually mean in terms of the social context of work in late-capitalist society.

Box 7.3

Arlie Hochschild: emotional labour

Arlie Hochschild is an American sociologist known particularly for her work devel-oping a psychosocial and interactionist model of the emotions (see Williams, 1998, 2000). In her well-known book, *The Managed Heart*, she developed a theory of 'emo-tional labour' (Hochschild, 1983). This concept was coined to apply to the ways in which people adapt to 'feeling rules' in defining how a person's emotions should be appropriate to a particular role in society, such as an occupational group.

For example, some occupational roles require more intensive emotional labour than others. Roles where individuals are required to 'manage' their emotions in face-to-face service work or where they are needed to control others' emotions are both roles that require emotional labour. Hochschild cited flight attendants and nurses as roles that require emotional labour as both engage in a managed approach to the emotional quality of their work, albeit for different reasons. As such, Hochschild emphasizes some of the implications of emotional labour, some of which are the indirect effects on the health and well-being of the individual.

In her work on this issue, Hochschild distinguished between two general types of emotion work, evocation and suppression – evocation referring to bringing about a feeling that is absent, and suppression negating a feeling that is present (Stets and Turner, 2007). In addition to this she identified three techniques of emotion work: cognitive, bodily and expressive. As a concept it has value in sociological thinking about the problems of ill-being, and more research is being undertaken to make sense of the embodied nature of emotions as well as the cognitive and expressive aspects of the phenomena (Chandler, 2012).

Social suffering and stigma

The American sociologist Erving Goffman produced an important sociological and social psychological analysis of the social concept of stigma to explain the subjective experience of one dimension of social suffering and social hurt (1968). Goffman argued that there are unwritten views about what it means to have a 'normal' identity in contemporary society and that those who do not come up to this standard, because of physical difference, for example, are stigmatized for their identity; that is to say, the embodied nature of their difference marks them out as different from the norm and therefore their identities become discredited.

Here, stigmatized identity comes to stand for discredited identity, in that the identity of the person does not come up to standard in terms of normality. The more vital aspect of this discrediting process is that it is not just the 'embodied' aspect of their identity that becomes discredited but their whole identity – it has the effect of marking all aspects of their self. Due to their social stigma the individual internalizes the hurt and feels that their failure to match up to the 'norm' is a shameful experience. For Goffman there are a range of conditions leading to bodily difference which can ensure more or less stigmatization. Let us take an illness condition such as HIV/AIDS as an example. Goffman argued that stigma is greater, for example, if the condition is visible, it is greater if it is obstrusive (i.e. disabling, and prevents the person from fulfilling their social obligations such as employment), and it is greater if the public knowledge about the condition is low.

The example of anorexia is helpful to illuminate the psychosocial theme as it is a highly stigmatized condition (Rich, 2006). The issue of anorexia, or any other bodily disorder in society, is a particularly complex one and we must be careful not to trivialize or over-analyse the reasons behind it. Anorexia nervosa, as Giddens (1991) explains, is a particular feature of late-modernity. Here we see that anorexia nervosa and other eating disorders such as its opposite – overeating – are extreme manifestations of the need for individuals to form a particular self-identity, one where the individual wishes to claim some control over the embodied aspect of their identity, and the need to not be discredited as Goffman explains in relation to stigma.

For Giddens, anorexia is but one response to the need for control over the body that the young woman exercises in the need for control in a world of pluralistic choices about how that individual life is led. As Giddens explains, 'Anorexia represents a striving for security in a world of plural, but ambiguous, options. The tightly controlled body is an emblem of safe existence in an open social environment' (1991: 107). More significantly, there is also the issue of how anorexia is constructed as a social identity where young women resist the idea of its stigma and stereotypes, in the use of pro-anorexia websites and constructing relationships with other sufferers for example (Rich, 2006).

Psychoanalytic perspectives on social suffering

Within the psychoanalytic movement, and the UK in particular, two particular traditions emerged after the post-war period: Kleinian and Object Relations schools of thinking. Winnicott, as we have seen, is one of the foremost figures of the Object Relations School. Both schools of psychoanalytic thinking frame ill-being in terms of the individual impulse towards destructiveness. The view from both perspectives sees this as essential to human nature, and that this destructiveness originates at an early stage of child development with the infant.

Hoggett (2000) reminds us it is important to talk of the 'struggle' of development, that suffering from a psychoanalytic perspective is part of being human and that there is a danger of pathologizing 'normal' misery and not being okay in the world. For Hoggett it is a struggle with others but also with ourselves, and therefore this idea gives credence to the importance of looking both in terms of the intimate psychic aspects of people's lives and their struggles as well as the social aspect (the 'others').

The Kleinian view (1935) is this: there are two particular states of mind that are fundamental – the depressive and the paranoid-schizoid (things are either really good or really bad) – that forms the basis for human development. In many ways this suggests that people's well-being, and subsequently their ill-being, depends upon 'the quality of social relationships in which they are immersed' (Hoggett, 2000: 22).

Loss, depression and loneliness

Freud suggested that all of us at various points in our lives experience 'everyday misery', but this form of sadness that may result from a setback or a loss, sometimes as a result of change, is separate from depression. The key issues connected to psychosocial ill-being can be explored particularly well through the understanding of loss, depression and loneliness, all of which may be interconnected on a psychosocial level.

Depression, for instance, is a good example of an ill-being theme that is best explored through a psychosocial lens as more conventional and medical conceptual models do not allow for an understanding of the complexity of the issue such as engagement with the emotional quality of the person's lived experience. For many people depression is a response to adversity and this may involve complex social needs that are not being met as much as ones that are strictly psychological or physiological in nature. Many people cite a range of social circumstances and changes in personal circumstances as to the trigger for depression, particularly those connected with loss and separation – such as loss of a job, partner, or sudden loss of good health in the person or loved one. For Brown and Harris (1978) (see below) the psychosocial triggers of depression are typically loss, disappointment or failure and three of the four vulnerability factors they identify directly suggest isolation: no employment outside the home; three children under 14 years; lacking a close and intimate relationship. The fourth – a mother dying in childhood – might be both loss and isolation.

In her compelling book *Disrupted Lives* (1997), inspired by the perspective of phenomenology, Becker explains it is helpful to think about loss in terms of the physical and existential metaphors that individuals use in order to deal with the loss. In her examples the physical sense of loss concerns disruption to the individual based on physical impairment – such as stroke, disability and late-life transitions – whereas the existential sense of loss was about mid-life and in particular infertility. The key finding of Becker's work was that those dealing with existential loss were seeking ways to transform the experience, to rise above it and transcend it, whereas seeking recovery and learning to cope dealt with physical loss.

This raises some interesting issues about the nature of change and transformation and ways in which people deal with disruption to individual lives. What Becker's work does not do, however, is engage so well with the issue of how these transformation stories (narratives) may also be limited by structural social factors such as social class, gender and ethnicity.

Depression and the working class

Class is central to one particular well-known study on the topic of depression, where the higher incidence of depression amongst women and the lower social class was linked primarily to the individual's social circumstances, suggesting that poverty clearly correlates with poor mental health (Brown and Harris, 1978). The suggestion was that working-class women experience more vulnerability factors as well as difficult life events than middle-class women.

Brown and Harris conducted surveys with two groups of women in a borough of London during the period 1969–75. They highlight differences both in the prevalence and experience of depression amongst different social classes. Overall they argued that depression, as a psychosocial phenomenon, is more common amongst women and those from the lower socio-economic groups (here, defined as the working class). Social class, then, is experienced emotionally as a 'felt injury' (Reay, 2005: 916). The main thrust of Brown and Harris's study was to take C. Wright Mills' views of the role of the 'sociological imagination' to the issue of depression.

Their research did not seek to relate social class lifestyle factors to the higher incidence of depression; instead, the issue of class was used to explain the likelihood of 'vulnerability' factors that were used to explain the higher propensity of women developing depression. This was then about highlighting what they saw as the 'depressogenic' links between different agents that increased the propensity of depression. In addition to the life events experienced by the women in the previous year, these vulnerability factors included: the absence of a confiding relationship, having three or more children under 14 to look after, not having paid work outside the home, and the loss of one's mother before the age of 11. As such, clinical depression was seen as an 'understandable response to adversity ... we could imagine practically anyone developing depression given a certain set of environmental circumstances' (Brown and Harris, 1978: 46).

George W. Brown had previously carried out research studies with Michael Rutter (see Chapter 2 on childhood) and some of this work explored the issue of schizophrenia. In many ways this work on depression had mirrored this previous research although Brown and Harris were keen to see the aetiology of depression as being explained by almost exclusively social factors, unlike schizophrenia. Some of these themes were followed up and developed in their more recent book *Life Events and Illness* (1989), which focused on life events and the association with particular illness – stress, anxiety, schizophrenia, as well as more physical impairments.

Loss and shame

Let us develop this theme about loss a little, so as to show the ways in which it can further help us to see how psychosocial thinking can illuminate the relationship between the psyche (private experience) and social circumstances. For instance, some of the themes raised by Brown and Harris are dealt with in a similar way in Jimenez and Walkerdine's (2011) more recent research study (see also Chapter 5). They discuss the ways in which young working-class men deal with the impact of unemployment in a traditional ex-mining town in South Wales, and the effect this has ultimately on issues of ill-being – such as depression, shame, embarrassment and loss. As Jimenez and Walkerdine explain:

> These included a mixture of grief, pain, disappointment, disillusionment, a sense of traumatic loss, various forms of shame, depressive anxiety and even temporary forms of melancholic dispositions affecting the relationships between fathers and sons. (Jimenez and Walkerdine, 2011: 188)

This psychosocially influenced research explored the effects of the closure of the industrial steel works in South Wales and the ways in which some of the young men did not make the transition to other forms of work – specifically, service work. For many of the young men who were interviewed as part of the study they considered service-related jobs like retail 'feminine' and embarrassing; many of their views were influenced by family expectations and discourses encouraged by their fathers. The researchers used psychosocial interviewing in the study where they allowed the respondents to explore emotional issues in the interview and this helped to bring out important psychosocial themes. For instance, there was the sense that, in mourning the loss of the manufacturing steelworks and the jobs and ordered sense of gendered reality that it fostered, the young men felt shame and embarrassment at having to consider other forms of work which did not fit with the normative heterosexual working-class masculinity. This meant ultimately that the shame they felt would be related to what the work represented within the family and what was expected of them.

For Giddens this would mean that where young men take on 'feminine' work this increases the anxiety they feel about the work in relation to their forming a coherent life narrative and biography; that is to say, it fails their normative sense of who they are and who they want to be. It also makes them vulnerable to embodying a sense of shame due to the reactions of significant others.

However, the authors claimed that not all the men failed to move on; melancholia at the loss of manufacturing was not an inevitable response, but the most important implication was that in getting young men in those communities to think about new skills and retraining that such 'psychosocial' aspects of identity and belonging needed to be thought about and taken into consideration very carefully.

Giddens argues that 'shame' originates as guilt, where feelings of inadequacy and humiliation are created. Shame is about the 'integrity of the self' and relies on some early onset experiences connected to self-adequacy. As Giddens explains, 'shame bears directly on self-identity because it is essentially anxiety about the adequacy of the narrative by means of which the individual sustains a coherent biography (1991: 65). In this way some of those feelings of shame are unconsciously produced but represent something about the person that does not measure up to their expectations. It can also be that the feelings of shame are pre-empted by a loss of trust or vice versa, 'Shame and trust are very closely bound up with one another, since an experience of shame may threaten or destroy trust' (*ibid*.: 66).

The flip-side to shame is the feeling of pride, where the individual gains self-esteem from the coherence of their individual narrative. Giddens argues that the individual relies very much on the responses of others – encounter reaction – to feel a sense of either shame or pride: 'Founded in the social bond, pride is continually vulnerable to the reactions of others, and the experience of shame often focuses on that "visible" aspect of self, the body' (*ibid*.: 66).

In thinking about how we can conceptualize these young men's responses to doing service work, Honneth's writing on recognition (see also Chapter 5) can be seen as valuable in helping us to see how recognition or self-esteem is created and how it can be sustained. It may be that the young men doing what they considered feminine work may receive a more positive response in a different community to the one that is of 'value' to them – that is to say, recognition comes from the society that they feel a part of and so one cannot ignore the socially derived nature of those views.

Box 7.4

Honneth: struggles for recognition (1995)

Axel Honneth's (1995) work on recognition is important to our understanding of the psychosocial nature of development. Honneth suggested that there are three different sources of recognition that we, as humans, are looking for: the first concerns individual identity; the second and third social/group identity (Hoggett, 2000).

1   Receiving appropriate care and love helps the child develop 'self-confidence', a sense of security for one's being, similar to Winnicott's notion of 'being' as a social state. For this reason Hoggett refers to well-being as 'being well with others' (2000: 6); it implies that one cannot disentangle the social from the individual sense of well-being. Hence this level of recognition is the fundamental level from which other forms of recognition stem.

2   The second form of recognition is about gaining self-respect, but mostly in relation to the state (one's recognition of rights in the eyes of the impersonal state).

3   The third form of recognition is the need for self-esteem, recognition of the individual's qualities amongst the person's 'communities of value' to which they belong. Esteem is linked both to the person's esteem within the group to which they belong and also the value of the 'group' to the society as a whole.

Health inequalities and psychosocial stress

Traditional social science in the textbooks draws attention to the relationship between health and mental outcomes and socio-demographic factors such as poverty, social class, gender and ethnicity; the links between social oppression (what is often referred to as symbolic violence) and ill-being are emphasized. Here we suggest that a psychosocial approach redefines the relationship between the objective features of socio-demographics and the subjective 'lived experience' of particular individuals, and it is that issue we pay attention to here.

In the UK and in other Western late-capitalist societies the 'Inequalities in Health' debate has been central to a public health and epidemiological debate and discourse. This debate has developed since the well-documented *Black Report* in 1980 (Black and Townsend, 1982) – although its roots were formed much earlier during the nineteenth century – through to the New Labour government (*The Acheson Report*; Acheson, 1998) and more recently forming the backdrop to the coalition government in *The Marmot Review* (Marmot *et al.*, 2010).

Overall, much of that body of literature and research has tried to identify the relationship between the wider determinants of health (e.g. poverty, the environment – the material, structural conditions of social life) and the prevalence of mortality and morbidity rates amongst lower socio-economic groups as well as particular ethnic groups. Although there is often good evidence for the relationship (or 'correlation') between social class and health, social scientists have been more puzzled at how to explain the relationship – that is to say, 'why' is there a relationship between an individual's social class and their health, and is it a causal relationship? A number of explanations have been put forward, some more convincing than others, and each of which have led to different kinds of policy emphasis within successive governments.

Despite the range of explanations, key theories for the prevalence of health inequalities have either taken a 'material/structural' explanation, which highlights the relationship between the material conditions of social class and health; or in contrast they have taken a 'life-style/cultural' explanation, which seeks to blame the 'culture' of a social class in raising the risk factors, such as through smoking, alcohol abuse and obesity (Nettleton, 2006). Some authors have tried to find a middle ground between the material and cultural explanations; others more recently have moved beyond traditional sociological explanations of the direct effect between social class and health, to highlight the more indirect effects of class and status, such as psychosocial stress, and these debates are important in terms of how psychosocially we can think about stress, ill-being, inequality and social class.

The psychosocial approach to health inequalities

Some observers have suggested that the social structural circumstances surrounding material poverty cannot fully explain the existence of health inequalities. Across the UK there are fundamental differences in the social patterning of health, even taking into account individual psychological factors that are produced by society's reliance on differing social status. Even within relatively affluent groups of individuals, then, it is argued that there are differences in the patterning of heath and morbidity and mortality outcomes. Not only this, but once a society has reached a certain level of material wealth (passing what is called the epidemiological transition) often less direct factors account for differences in health status.

The work of Cockerham (2007), Wilkinson (1996) and Wilkinson and Picket (2009) suggests that material/structural factors combined with cultural/behavioural factors are not sufficient to explain the relationship between inequality and ill-health or ill-being. The Whitehall studies, for example, which originally took place in the 1960s but were followed up later in the 1980s and 90s, showed that within the same organization (the UK Civil Service) the senior administrators had better morbidity and mortality rates than the lower ranked administrators (Cockerham, 2007). There was therefore a strong link – or association – between the employment grade levels of the civil servants' employment and their mortality and morbidity rates from a range of causes.

Cockerham lists such psychosocial factors such as self-esteem and social status as underlining the differences and explaining why those on a lower rung of the civil service ladder experience greater psychosocial stress and ill-being – one explanation was to show that the increased stress and raised cortisol levels were enough to lower the immune response.

There are therefore subtle differences in health status between relatively better-off groups of civil servants. Marmot (2004) concluded that rates of heart disease were four times greater amongst the lower ranks of civil servants than the senior grades. Within the wealthy Western countries these differences in health status can therefore be explained by psychosocial factors, taking into account the person's material circumstances and the psychological and physiological consequences of differential social status in employment roles and society more generally.

Taking this view we can see that inequality and differences in social status (not just income and wealth) can negatively affect health and being in a number of ways. In Richard Wilkinson's work he refers to this as the ways in which inequalities in health damage social cohesion and are inherently damaging to all societies. The more unequal a society is, therefore, the more likely it will experience larger inequality gaps (Wilkinson, 1996). There are two main ways in which health can be affected; one is in relation to a lack of social cohesion and the other is a lack of self-esteem, both of which are contributory factors that are psychosocial in nature.

The upshot of these arguments is clear: having attained a basic minimum standard of living for the vast majority of the population, psychosocial rather than material factors become pre-eminent in the aetiology and social patterning of contemporary Western disease. This, in turn, places emotions centre-stage in aetiological terms, yet to date they remain a strangely neglected topic and under-theorized aspect of the inequalities debate; particularly as the 'missing link' between structure and agency, mind and body, biology and society (Williams, 2008: 60).

In the psychosocial debate about inequalities and ill-being it is argued that all unequal societies (in terms of material wealth) are less socially cohesive and more socially divisive and therefore are more likely to result in higher levels of psychosocial stress. The lack of social cohesion, then, is more likely to lead to people feeling socially isolated and experiencing higher amounts of ill-being. Those who are lower down in the social scale are less likely to feel like they can take control of the situation and therefore feel more anxiety and stress.

Box 7.5

Richard Wilkinson and Kate Pickett: 'The Spirit Level' (2009)

In terms of wealth and incomes the UK, as is the case with all major post-industrial capitalist nations, is rich enough and would not improve as a society or make people happy or give them improved health and well-being with more wealth.

The problem according to Wilkinson and Pickett is that people's wealth and income in the UK is poorly distributed, some earning vastly in excess of the mean average. Therefore the problem is not one of growth in society but merely distribution: distribution of both wealth and *being*. This is the cause of many of the problems of ill-being and unhappiness in society. Also, it is not just the poorest that are affected but all strata in society are in various ways badly affected by inequality.

Inequality, therefore, between people causes social unease and makes lives shorter as well as more stressful and unfulfilled. More equal societies, those that worry about income and wealth inequality and seek to do something about it, have better outcomes in terms of stress and status anxiety in that society – they have created their own 'spirit level' according to Wilkinson and Pickett.

However, the psychosocial explanation and perspective on health inequalities, as highlighted by writers such as Wilkinson, can be seen as a particularly Durkheimian, even Functionalist perspective on the value of social integration and social cohesion (after the French sociologist, Emile Durkheim, 1858–1917). Other examples of this kind of perspective include writing that has been referred to as structural strain theory and has drawn heavily on the work of the American sociologist Robert K. Merton, whose studies of crime and deviance underpinned the theory. The structural strain approach emphasized the role that is played by differences in social status and the impact that has on psychological health and crime and deviance. A simple account of the theory suggests that if individuals see money and material success as important and they cannot achieve this legitimately (through education and employment) they will seek to redress this in an illegitimate way – through crime, for example, which is an example of how structural strain affects individual behaviour. An early study by Faris and Dunham (1939) explored the association between people with high rates of severe mental illness (such as schizophrenia) and residence in disadvantaged neighbourhoods. Latterly, the studies of Harvey Brenner suggested that the unemployment rate correlated with a rate of persons hospitalized for mental disorders (1979) (the research had since been revisited in 2002).

Much of this work also highlights the importance of social networks and sociality more generally in helping individuals to achieve a sense of well-being. The work of Putnam, which we have referred to, as well as others such as Christakis's work on social networks (2010) have shown how such social networks have a more important role in our health and well-being than we realize and show the interdependence of material and psychological factors in producing particular health outcomes.

Conclusion

In this chapter we continued our theme of individuals trying to 'do well' in the world, but we looked more closely at the relational dimension of ill-being – the ways in which ill-being and social suffering is often a feature in the lives of both individuals and social groups. We considered a range of different psychosocial theories about ill-being such as those focused on social suffering, stigma and the emotions, as well as psychoanalytic perspectives. We expanded on themes about ill-being, such as loss and depression, and the relationship between stress and inequality, and we showed how the individual psyche and the social and structural circumstances overlap and are entwined. The relationship between physical illness and long-term depression on the one hand, and social deprivation, poverty and all kinds of illnesses on the other was given substantial consideration in this chapter. How the mechanisms of stigma and other forms of exclusion, stress, anxiety and powerlessness create physical and mental distress and 'ill-being' was examined, focusing on consumerist 'life-style epidemics' such as anorexia.

8

How people hurt and hate: violence and bullying

Introduction

For many people in contemporary society, anger, violence and abuse are the emotional and physical context in which their lives, or some part of their lives, are led. From babies being shaken to political 'dissidents' being tortured, from being ridiculed by a teacher for poor work, to being treated as less worthy because of your skin colour, some of the various kinds of damage which are inflicted on individuals and communities will be considered here.

This chapter is concerned with how best we can understand the perpetration of violence and hatred in a range of social and domestic contexts. The term 'violence and hatred' encompasses a huge range of phenomena, despite the relative lack of focus on all but domestic violence and child abuse in most standard social science texts. Here we will consider ways in which we can think psychosocially about them, using not just sociological and psychoanalytical theories but an overarching network of themes including gender, shame, inequality and anxiety. This chapter will also apply this psychosocial framework of ideas to some illustrative examples of violence and hatred – domestic violence, gang violence, racism, bullying – and suggest, as it progresses, other areas in which it is useful for understanding.

This is a complex area to think about experientially, as we try to do within the psychosocial. Chapter 1 used an example relating to violence to demonstrate what we mean by a psychosocial approach, and it may well be helpful to refer back to that to think about issues of violence. Here, though, the chapter will move on first to thinking about masculinity, followed by thinking about the concept of gender and domestic violence.

Gender and violence: masculinity

The scenario in Chapter 1, referred to above, is of male violence, and indeed if we consider violence, including domestic violence, we also need to think about masculinity. This is neither sexism nor coincidence, but reflects what we can read off from crime statistics in the Western world: that men far outweigh women in terms of crimes of violence and indeed crime generally.

Box 8.1

Gender and violence: statistics

National crime statistics tell us that 'in 2006, males were more likely than females to be found guilty of, or cautioned for, crimes in all major crime categories. Between 82 and 94 per cent of all offenders in England and Wales found guilty of, or cautioned for, violence against the person, criminal damage, drug offences and robbery and burglary were male. Although the number of offenders was relatively small, 97 per cent of those found guilty of, or cautioned for, sexual offences were also male.'

The proportions in relation to being the victim of crime – subject to violence in other words – are more varied.

The British Crime Survey in 2007/8 showed that the risk of being a victim of violent crime was 3.2 per cent, although there were differences between men and women. Young men, aged 16 to 24, were most at risk, with 13.4 per cent experiencing a violent crime of some sort in the year preceding the interview, compared with 6.4 per cent of women of the same age. For both sexes, the risk of being a victim of violent crime decreased with age. For those aged 25 to 34, 5.7 per cent of men and 3.3 per cent of women were victims of violent crime in the previous year. For those aged 75 and over, the proportions fell to 0.3 per cent and 0.2 per cent respectively.

The type of violent incident experienced by victims of violent crime also varies by sex. In 2007/8, the number of domestic violence incidents experienced by women was five times greater than for men; 85 per cent of victims of this type of violence were women compared with 15 per cent who were men. However, men were more likely than women to be a victim of violence from strangers (78 per cent of victims were men) and violence from acquaintances (58 per cent were men).

(Source: Office for National Statistics licensed under the
Open Government Licence v.1.0)

Men are considerably more likely to be just the perpetrators but also the 'victims' of most forms of violence, with the exceptions, which will be briefly considered below, of domestic and sexual violence. Leaving this aside, we can state clearly that violence is mainly the provenance of masculinity. In previous chapters we have thought about masculinity, and some of that thinking is useful here. Research such as Frosh *et al.*'s work on *Young Masculinities* (2002) point to a situation in which boys, to be seen to count in their world, feel the need to be 'hard'; that is to say, to be able to stand up for themselves and if necessary defend themselves physically. And admiration for the 'hard man' also goes much further than the playground and the territorial youth gangs of urban areas of the Western world. If a review of the images of masculinity available through film, TV, advertising, photography and so on for the last few decades were undertaken, those of men in battle, in sport, in hard physical labour (mines, pits, furnaces, factory floors, etc.), facing dangers and disasters – in other words as tough, brave, heroic, strong and embodied – would predominate. Physical prowess, toughness and also competitiveness dominate conceptions of what it is to be a man in the contemporary world. The capacity to fight to defend one's 'honour', or indeed the honour of family or group or even nation, are standard portrayals and expectations of masculinity.

This sets the social scene to explore why, when individuals and groups, families and societies turn to violence, most of the participants in these violent scenarios are men: young men taking up adult masculine identities. Of course we are not arguing that there is something about being a man that makes you violent – not biological essentialism or because of socialization – but arguing that there are links between what is ordinarily seen and even admired as being 'masculine' and physical 'hardness'. We could also think about this as being positioned by discourses of masculinity, recalling our discussion of Foucault, discourse and identity in Chapter 5.

How does that notion connect to aggression and violence? One strand of argument here might be that the high incidence of violent crime in contemporary society as opposed to, for example, two generations ago in the mid twentieth century, is because sources of masculine confidence and pride in their physical strength and bravery (and the admiration and respect that accompanies this) have become substantially reduced, particularly for working-class men. Not only did the end of compulsory National Service in 1960 take the mass of the male population of England out of the masculine world of soldiering, but the substantial decline in the manufacturing sector of the economy – the mines, the ship yards, print works, heavy machinery production and so on – 'feminize' labour, so that toughness and physical strength in the workplace are far less needed (see Chapter 5). Those who refer to a 'crisis of masculinity' (Connell, 1995; Messerschmidt, 1997) understand that most of the traditional ways that the previous generations of men had for collectively demonstrating this kind of robust gender differential have all but disappeared.

The disappearance of many ways that ordinary men come together in groups, not just at work but also as communities of workers such as fishermen or miners; as union participants; as men together at leisure and socially – 'the lads' – have left a vacuum, with two major and entwined consequences. Masculinity is less clear-cut, harder to get the hang of and to some extent less certain and confident; sources of pride and self-respect are lacking. What kind of man should you be? What does it mean to be a 'new man'? Does 'new man' infer weak, 'hen-pecked and girlie'? Men overall, and particularly those 'becoming' men (young men – the age group with the highest crime rates and also the highest suicide rates) may be far more vulnerable to feeling humiliated and disrespected (see below on 'shame and violence'), with far fewer sources for demonstrating the physical 'hardness' that has become lodged in ideas of masculine identity. Again this intersects with social class. It is possible that the routes to successful transition to manhood now so socially advocated, via the academic success of three good 'A' levels and a university career, rather than, for example, an apprenticeship in a trade respected by your Dad and the local community, is difficult to access. Jimenez and Walkerdine's research (see Chapters 5 and 7) in a deindustrialized area of Wales carefully explores feelings of shame, lack of esteem and disconnection from the traditional masculine community in precisely these circumstances (2011).

Gangs and brawls, crime and vandalism, high levels of risk-taking and jockeying for power positions, taking other men 'on', may be the arenas available in which masculinity can still be established and demonstrated – where it is possible to still feel some kind of masculine pride, though frequently with hopelessly destructive and self-destructive long-term consequences.

Drawing on established gender theorists such as Connell (1995) and Messerschmidt (1997), what it means to 'be a man' in Western societies is not only defined through the paid labour market and aggressive individualism, it is also, like all identities, constructed in relation to the rejection and subordination of certain ways of being and thinking – i.e. 'what makes me this is that I am not like that' – and with masculinity the 'not like that' is the feminine or the rejection of the qualities considered woman-like. This takes us a little way towards thinking about men's anger against and violence towards women: what is womanly is denigrated.

Gender and domestic violence

Highly visible man-on-man aggression and/or violence against property and other gangs or groups (see below) may account for some of the perceived violence we read about or see in the media on a daily basis. But some men, not all men, commit individual acts of violence, outside the context of groups, on women and sometimes children, in domestic and

'hidden' circumstances not in the public world of masculine image production. Domestic violence is by no means confined to poor areas or
working-class contexts, though clearly social stresses and deprivation
exacerbate violent situations.

However, this may need a different kind of understanding. The inflic-
tion of rage and anger onto another human being, causing pain, harm,
fear, psychic damage and occasionally ultimately death is experienced
individually through the body, emotions and meaning system of both people. In reading about it, especially sociologically, it is easy to lose that
important sense of attempting to connect with a lived experience. It is
also important that it is not just a given, even in cultures or geographical
areas where it is socially statistically less unlikely than others.
Psychosocial theory offers us a way of thinking about individuals located
within the social setting.

Psychoanalytic versions of human development, as we have seen
throughout this book, are premised on the key notion that very early life
impacts on how people are likely to be as adults. Here, then, is the notion
that differences in people's propensity to violent behaviour can be
explained by the experience of the person as a baby – that there are
destructive babyhoods which reach into the childhood and adulthood of
an individual, continuing to damage if 'untreated'.

Mothers, babies and the 'uncontained'

Rosalind Minsky's book *Psychoanalysis and Culture* (1998) offers several
psychoanalytically informed accounts of contemporary violence, some of
which also connect into social contexts and themes. Her account of Bion's
work (building on Kleinian thinking – see Chapter 2) applied to domestic
violence is helpful here, to allow us to move away from the exclusively
social. Gadd's scenario in Chapter 1 gives some clues. Stewart is overwhelmed by *uncontained* feelings and fantasies from his internal landscape; Mubarek was 'unable to contain' Stewart's pain.

Thinking about 'containment', the premise is that, going back to the
early infancy of every baby, mothers or 'good enough mothers'
(Winnicott's forgiving phrase) act as 'containers' for the utterly confusing
and powerful emotional world of infants, who have no means to differen-
tiate what feelings and fantasies are inside them and what is in the relationship with the mother or the world. The baby projects these
undifferentiated instinctual sensations, impressions etc., some of which,
if hungry or discomfited will be rage, fear and so on, and the mother
responds in ways which makes these potentially overwhelming feelings
safe and tolerable; that is to say, she 'contains' them (of course, the lan-

guage is hard to get right here because babies *experience* rather than think). Repeated experiences of this – making the unsafe feelings safe – allows the baby as it becomes a differentiated person to do this for itself, contain its own experience and eventually 'symbolize it', in phantasies and dreams and eventually convert it into words and express it safely.

Where mothers are unable to contain their baby's emotional turmoil, perhaps because of their own internal needs and what they themselves unconsciously project onto the baby, the baby has its own and the mother's sets of overwhelming and confusing emotions to endure. It cannot make sense of these psychic experiences and they remain as confusion, and turn into destructive impulses in adults. Hate and envy, mixed up with love and the dependency of unresolved needs, colour psychic life, and may reignite in relationships later on in life.

Babies need to use mothers to make psychic sense of dense feelings, but also as Winnicott discusses, older babies need to use their mothers to contain physical 'attacks' – a certain level of ordinary aggression as babies work out as part of their understanding of themselves and the mother as differentiated. Again mothers have to 'contain' not retaliate, to allow the baby to hate as well as love, to prove the possibility of resilience so the baby can inhabit a safe outside world which becomes internalized. For Winnicott and the large numbers of 'object relations' practitioners who find his ideas useful, exceptionally mothers who cannot put their baby's needs before their own, can damage them in psychic ways and this damage can be expressed sometimes violently in adulthood. That this is expressed against women – unconsciously recognized as the perceived powerful perpetrators of their own identity damage; the all-controlling source of pain and withholding – offers an account of the misogyny and violence against women of some damaged men. This goes some way to help us think about domestic violence.

However, the psychic context of these individual acts also has a resonance. All mothers are vastly more powerful than all babies, male and female, and as Minsky (1998) goes on to discuss, this 'hugeness' and dominance of women, inevitably embedded in the phantasy life of all people, elides women to quite primitive fears of annihilation. Symptoms of misogyny and fear – quick resorts to expressed criticism and suspicion of women; ready condemnation of their actions in the press and in communities, toleration of pornography etc. – are some of the hints some feminist and social commentators generally have alluded to, to suggest a level of misogyny as socially embedded in many Western societies. This may also go some way to explain the tolerance of domestic violence expressed by society including both women and men, and the notion of 'asking for it' drawn on by some perpetrators and perhaps even more shockingly, some victims.

Misogyny and domestic violence

Moving into the territory of feminist analysis might be useful here to clarify a 'political' understanding of domestic violence.

Misogyny and patriarchy

The context of male violence is misogyny and patriarchy; the unequal society in which we live is dominated, politically, economically and socially, by men, and women are subordinated in this. Men's dominant position in society is maintained by the use of, or threat of, violence, and ideologies such as 'romantic love' which traditionally led women to 'sign up for' caring, supporting, understanding and where necessary forgiving 'her' man, in the name of love.

Violence and abuse are 'normalized', ignored or under-played in patriarchal societies. What constitutes violence and domestic violence has also been defined through masculine versions of what constitutes crime.

Feminist researchers have introduced the concept of a 'continuum of abuse' inflicted within a normal range of male behaviour. Women are subject to persuasion, coercion, harassment, intimidation, threat and force, which may represent escalation or overlap, and which are all abusive – all violent.

The damage inflicted can be seen as relating to frequency of these experiences, not any notion of 'seriousness', which is argued as a less useful concept here, as all these forms are serious (Spalek, 2008).

Minsky's work draws together psychoanalytical thinking and Spalek's socio-political ideas that help us in understanding gender violence, and therefore domestic violence as an example of this, by constructing an integrated psychosocial perspective. Psychosocially, then, the fantasies from the internal world of some men – for example, of destroying the envied mother figure; an external world where men generally still have more power than women; male identification depends on rejecting/denigrating the feminine; and aggression – is connected to ordinary masculinity; all make domestic violence a possible outcome.

Before moving on it might be worth noting that the kind of thinking about violence or indeed any form of crime put forward above, not just as single incidences but as processes with stages, and thinking about prevalence rather than incidence, is not limited to feminist analysis of domestic violence but is also argued by some contemporary criminologists as useful for thinking about crime more generally (see, for example, Maguire *et al.*, 2007 for an up-to-date survey of ideas and debates in contemporary criminology).

Crime, violence and consumer culture

Box 8.3

Criminal identities and consumer societies: Hall et *al.* (2008)

This is work underpinned by primary research in very deprived communities in the North of England, by psychosocial theory from, for example,. Christopher Lasch's work on a psychoanalytic reading of contemporary consumer culture as pathologically narcissistic. It also draws on Lacanian psychoanalytic theory and the work of the Frankfurt School (see previous chapters).

It considers estates where virtually everybody is unemployed, in the context of contemporary consumer capitalist societies where only the capacity to buy material goods seems to have value.

In a society in which only individualistic market engagement is prized, the working-class communities of places like the North East have come to be debased, only seen as places to escape from, not communities worth investing in, having in themselves.

In areas like this 'crime is an instrument for achieving fantasised positions of social distinction and "respect" in consumer culture'. The criminal identity most sought after was that of international drug dealer, where high levels of risk and violence produce huge returns. Involvement in the drug trade on some level involved high numbers of young men on the estates.

Crime has come to offer the only chance of being seen as worthy and worthwhile, because it will give access to the material goods that make you 'something' in the world.

Hall's work, in Box 8.3, in many senses follows a long tradition of criminology in which the materiality of society along with its exclusion of those who cannot fully partake of its goods is used to think about crime and deviance. Merton's theory of social strain (see Chapter 7) written in the 1950s, also suggests that in societies like the US where wealth is an attribute promoted as desirable to/by all but without the access to the routes that allow its accumulation distributed to all, then other means – criminal means – will be taken to acquire it. This of course may not necessarily connect into violence – what is being discussed here is the acquisition of property, but writers like Hall would suggest that violence and crime, particularly in relation to drugs, and one also might want to add pornography, trafficking people and so on, are inseparable now from violence. Violence establishes and maintains the power hierarchies through which huge fortunes are built. The context of consumer capitalism, itself produces identities which are superficial, manipulative, have a very weak sense of self and a need for a great deal of external validation, a deep sense of emptiness lying at the heart of the self, forged in that pervasive emptiness which characterizes contemporary consumer culture. Not just 'goods' to fill the void at whatever cost: glossy and superficial relationships that preclude empathy, but are valued primarily for what they can reflect back – what shoring up of a hedonistic ego they can provide, or what deep seated void they might seem to satisfy (Lasch, 1979; Frosh, 1991).

Violence, hatred and shame

Lasch's psychosocial critique of identities in consumer capitalism is highly critical of the contemporary world, and can also seem disengaged from the experience of inhabiting this demonized space. This chapter is now going to consider the experience of occupying a place in that world – or at least one damaging element of the experience: shame. Shame and its opposite, pride, as psychosocial emotions will be considered as central elements to help us understand issues of aggression and violence, including the forms and contexts of violence already presented above. Shame plays a central role in relation to the gendered nature of violence. This has been touched on in previous chapters. By shame what is meant here is something like feeling diminished or reduced by our own perception of the perception of others, as explained by, for example, Goffman, as 'I am what I think you think I am' (1990 [1959]). If what people think they are seeing – what they seem to be 'getting back' – is belittling or demeaning, it is damaging to the systems people use to consciously and unconsciously shore themselves up, for example ego and esteem. Shame is a very personal feeling in a perceived public arena, internalized and taken home afterwards, metaphorically and literally (as a concept it has also been drawn on to consider domestic violence). We are lowered in status in the eyes of the world.

What, then, are the elements of feeling ashamed/shamed? First, there is how we already feel about ourselves inside – our existing sense of our selves and our vulnerability – whether, for example, we were made to feel excessively shamed from early in life. There may be a shamed child always near the surface, released very quickly and easily: in other words, in more psychoanalytical language, we may already inhabit a world of persecutory/critical object relations as the 'lens' through which we must view the social. Secondly, what kind of social circumstances we live in are important. We may be part of unequal societies – part of already denigrated groups (e.g. are we old in ageist societies, are we poor where material goods seem to define people's value). Thirdly, the kinds of experiences thrown up by our lives – the individual and collective sources of shame we are exposed to. Perhaps we are located in an education system that designates failure to some students; employment that chews some people up and spits them out.

Shame is a complex psychosocial emotion, but is beginning to be understood as a key factor in aggression and violence, as well as the human suffering that may be implicated. In Richard Wilkinson and Kate Pickett's controversial book on social inequality (2009), their chapter on violence is tellingly titled 'Violence: gaining respect' (see Chapter 7 for more discussion of Wilkinson and Pickett's work).

Wilkinson and Picket argue, drawing on a range of contemporary sociological and psychological sources and on research that shows that crime rates, along with a plethora of other social problems, are at their worst in the most unequal ('developed'/relatively wealthy overall) societies.

In relation to violence they make a strong case that it is in countries where people already feel disrespected, looked down on, humiliated, excluded and/or undervalued – shamed in other words – that violence most easily erupts. Like a range of, loosely, psychosocial theorists currently at work, the central argument suggests that acts of aggression and violence are,

> ... attempts to ward off or eliminate the feeling of shame or humiliation – a feeling that is painful and can even be intolerable and overwhelming – and replace it with its opposite, the feeling of pride (Gilligan in Wilkinson and Picket, 2009: 133).

This kind of understanding of violence, as an attempt to transcend feelings of humiliation and rage, could of course be used to understand a range of kinds of aggression and violence, but Wilkinson and Picket use it to explain the particularly high rates of crime and violence between young men, statistically evident in all Western societies and the particularly high rates of assaults and even murders in the most unequal societies and even in the most deprived areas of the cities within these unequal societies.

James Gilligan's US-based work is extremely good at evoking the power and strength of the emotional experience involved in violence, the overwhelming personal desperation and pain in the context of worlds in which there is little access to sources of self-worth (2001). Minsky adds to our psychosocial understanding the notion of a 'cycle': the 'shame, blame, grudge and retribution' cycle, which links this powerful internal feeling with actions of aggression in relation to the damaged lives of, for example, children who have been subject to abuse and their adulthoods in which such a cycle may (but not always) come to be played out, but also in relation to the politics of conflict such as latterly that of Northern Ireland or the Middle East (Minsky, 1998).

Violence in the 'gang'

Thinking about violence and gangs links to the section on masculinity, above, to some extent, as gang behaviour is a gendered phenomenon. Living in situations of poverty and unemployment, it is evident that others own the goods that are markers of social status, others have the opportunities for better lives, have multiple sources for gaining pride, status and self-esteem. If 'those who have' suffer a humiliation in one area – the husband runs off with a younger woman; the promotion went to a younger man – there are usually other sources of consolation to buffer against the blows.

However, for many on the worst end of the inequality scale, what status and sources of pride are available may be far more limited and also fragile. Being 'top dog' or a valued member of a group of men, the gang may be the only place offering the respect of others, and the forum in which to be 'someone' is crucial. Threats to it, lack of it, and loss of it: these are the triggers that seem useful to explore. Respect and its opposite, diss(respect)ing become life and death issues, where individual 'honour' becomes interwoven with group honour, and individual grievance becomes group grievance.

Gangs, whether formal or informal, provide opportunities to shore up masculinity and, functioning in the same ways as the traditional male unit of affiliation and identity – the regiment, the public school 'house', the college fraternity, the football club supporters network – create security and acceptance, and also mark out outsiders, 'others', the 'not me'. Any shame at inadequate masculinity, such as not having the good job, the authority, the individual achievements and the respect that gives, is redirected or 'displaced'.

Box 8.4

Freud and the gang

A Freudian understanding of young men being in gangs draws on his thinking about identification and the Oedipal phase (see Chapter 3).

Freud's work applied here, tends to focus on the roles of the gang member and the gang leader – symbolically cast as the father – in relation to each other. This is a mutual identification that substitutes for absent (real or symbolically absent) fathers.

The gang leader becomes the desired object in place of the father (we could substitute the notion of admired and identified with, loved even).

This strong emotional bond unites the members, and excludes non-members. Sibling rivalry for the love of the 'father' may also present in group rivalries 'male relationships are often rivalrous [because] … male identity is forged in the continuing Oedipal phantasy that life is about being a victor or victim, winner or loser, "another's gain is my loss", so all outsiders may henceforth be regarded as potential annihilators of identity' (Minsky, 1998: 160).

Gangs mostly flourish in deprived and denigrated areas, and can act as a defence against feelings of powerlessness, worthlessness and hopelessness, and substitute the sense of a potent identity. Thinking about the gang or the group is helpful also for looking at 'mass' hatreds. From this point the chapter will look at racism, hate crimes and other forms of social exclusion and 'othering'.

Racism and hating 'other' groups

Racism is both a statistically evident, almost tangible, feature of twenty-first-century life in Western societies, and it also denotes a subtle set of innuendos, impressions and hints. It is about how 'society' treats people and how individuals treat people, and it is about projections and phantasies, and kicks and blows, about shame and disappointed hopes; history and the present. This section will suggest some psychosocial understandings of this form of violence, as an example of the mass hatred of groups perceived as 'others'.

As we noted above, Freud helps explain some useful things about gangs, with the understanding of leaders as symbolic fathers, and also then with thinking about interactions within the membership as analogous with the more everyday concept of 'intense sibling rivalry'. However, it is Melanie Klein's work on the psychic defence mechanism of 'splitting' that usually forms one of the key starting points of discussions of racism in contemporary society. Racism and other forms of hatred have become a key area of study in psychosocial work, and draws on writing by, for example, Judith Butler (2004), Simon Clarke (2003) as well as David Gadd and Bill Dixon (2010) in thinking about these forms of violence.

As explained in Chapter 2, the early stages of a baby's development for Klein involve intense emotional anguish, fear and primitive emotions, which gradually become 'ordered' though never completely. Part of this ordering or patterning involves moving from a position where bad feelings and good feelings are not understood as interlinked, but as separated. This includes the set of comforting, feeding, warming sensations of being held close to the mother and fed, distinct from the sensations of abandonment, cold, hunger, produced by the absence of contact with the mother. These sets of feelings must be reconciled, as the baby understands that this source of pain and joy is the same 'object': that good and bad are part of one whole. In Klein's work this is called moving from the paranoid-schizoid position to the depressive position. The argument is, then, that for many adults and indeed as standard in groups, the reconciliation of good and bad 'objects' is not always or wholly attained.

Groups can be used to explore or to simply get rid of emotions that cannot be tolerated. The bad feelings are projected outward, onto other individuals and groups, so that a sense of good, wholly good, can be maintained, and the other is objectified. This is a process called 'splitting': dividing up and separating off what psychically is seen as good and what bad, and evacuate the bad, getting rid of the anxiety that the good will be contaminated, which can be seen as a paranoid phantasy (left over from the paranoid-schizoid phase outlined in the last paragraph). An example would be the fairly ordinary notion of 'scapegoating', meaning the group members concur with 'our group is great, but this particular member is rubbish/lowers the standard/doesn't really fit in', and so on. The 'victim' is forced psychically to take in the anxiety, fear and guilt of the projecting group. Projective identification is the mechanism, and hatred, and all forms of inferiority are ascribed to 'the other' – that which is not me and mine – which could be a gender, a 'colour', a culture or a religion.

And as with all psychosocial thinking, these psychic processes are integrated with a political and social situation in which groups have the power to project onto, define and control the identities and beings of others. Groups may also, as recent research by Hoggett *et al.* (2013) suggests, have deprivations and grievances which make them feel aggrieved, angry, shamed – bad about themselves, in other words – which then becomes that 'bad' which is split off and projected onto the other. The classic cry of 'they come over here, take all our jobs, get everything from the council, never do a day's work' and so on is the kind of destructive and pervasive resentment (he refers to it as 'resentment' – meaning something more enduring and structural than a passing and relatively easy to shake off resentment) stoked by a sense of rejection, abandonment and loss (their sense that 'authorities' never give them help, recognition, good housing, good jobs etc.) projected onto what they would call 'outsiders'. Racism can be explained, then, with reference to the dynamic socio-political context (historical, local and national, the psychic processes of hatred and 'othering') and the internal and external flows of identification and identity formation that are generated within these.

Box 8.5

Frantz Fanon (1925–61): post-colonial studies

Frantz Fanon was writing from the perspective of both the white colonizer and the black colonized. Fanon drew on psychoanalysis, philosophy (particularly existentialism) and sociology to discuss the legacy of colonial oppression, the root as he saw it, of racism.

Fanon was trying to understand the emotional states produced within the terrible suffering of the physical, political, personal and embodied practices of slavery and colonization. He was interested in the capacity of the colonizers to define the identities of those they oppressed in ways that disallow the oppressed recognition, integration, pride and self-worth.

Economic oppression is accompanied by the internalization of projected images of inferiority. White men project into black men their own repressed desires and fantasies of sexual licence, violence, physical strength.

Racist culture, not just the family, should be seen as breeding adult neurosis (Elliott, 2002).

That racism endures in social systems, such as education, criminal justice, health and so on, is evident in a significant body of research, with high-profile incidents attracting criticism and inquiries regularly (e.g. The Stephen Lawrence Inquiry – Macpherson, 1999) but it is difficult to register what change is produced by knowledge in these institutions.

For example, the British Crime Survey throughout the previous decade reported that far more Asian people are the victims of racist crimes than white people, and African Caribbean people fall between these two groups. Far more young black men populate English prisons than proportionally would be expected to be the case. In the statutory mental health system, the proportion of African Caribbean men is nine times what would be expected, and this has been researched and acknowledged for more than a generation, but change is unforthcoming. More black children, particularly boys, leave school without the qualifications they need to progress their lives. More black children are in the care system. Social structures are not producing greater equality. More black people die in poverty, in prisons, in psychiatric hospitals, the victims of direct and indirect psychic and often physical damage – the victims of violence indeed (Gadd and Dixon, 2010).

Moving the chapter on from its consideration of gender, domestic violence, gang violence, shame and racism, another overarching psychosocial concept, which has been prevalent in the literature for the last two decades will be considered: the notion of 'fear of crime'.

Fears of violence, aggression and crime

The differences between the perception of aggression and violence, and the actual incidence of aggression and violence, have attracted a considerable degree of concern from the police, policy-makers and criminologists over several decades. As incidences of violent crime decreased in the last decade of the twentieth century, fear of crime seemed to be on the increase. And within that the groups less likely to be the victims of crime, for example, women and the elderly, seem to live a life most limited by their fears of harassment and assault. This is no simple matter of just a distorted belief about statistical incidence, like fear of flying (as opposed to driving on the motor way – a far more dangerous but much less feared form of transport) that might ruin an occasional holiday, but for some an ongoing dread, so that the streets or neighbourhood, certainly after dark, become inaccessible, and isolation and loneliness as well as the gruelling mental state of anxiety might be the consequence.

Perceptions of violence, aggression and civil and community disturbances (things like public drunkenness, groups of young men hanging about, graffiti, abuse and so on) impact on how substantial numbers of people feel and how they act, in quite profound ways. Fear of possible harm can be understood from a variety of perspectives. First, if one accepts the 'risk society' thesis (Beck, 1992) that in the context of globalization, information overload, media sensationalism, breakdown of faith in abstract and tangible systems of established order, trust etc. where 'unknowability' – living with few sources of certainty – is simply ordinary, then it is easy for everyday possibilities to become frightening. Garland, a criminologist, sums this up usefully:

> For some, the crime problem has become a source of anxiety and frustration: an urgent daily reminder of the need to impose control, to take care, to secure oneself and one's family against the dangers of the modern world. (Garland, cited in Jackson and Grey, 2010: 4)

In other words the world is perceived as dangerous and unpredictable and fear of crime is part of this.

These kinds of fears can also be seen to reflect the vulnerability of certain groups to certain kinds of pressures and oppressions in a general sense, and what such potential assaults or intrusions might 'mean'. If you are a young man, is being punched in the face by another young man in a brawl experienced in the same way as an elderly woman being punched in the face by a frustrated carer who loses patience? Fears might connect to a different range of meanings, and to a different level of vulnerability. The issue pointed out above in Box 8.2 on 'domestic violence' about inhabiting worlds which include insults, harassment, intimidation and so on, arguably what those with relatively little power may experience in relation to those with far more power, is the lived daily experience in which 'fear of crime' is an obvious and ordinary component. Also, importantly, central to women's fears, this kind of thinking would argue, lies a dread of sexual assault, grounded in both primitive phantasies and the realities of the incidence, the horror and their particular vulnerability.

A third more straightforwardly psychological position to emerge is the idea that 'fear of crime' can not only be seen as negative and limiting, but, like any kind of source of wariness, can be a useful spur to sensible precaution and self-protection, to taking action rather than being a victim. Although this view may well match the ordinary reality many people employ of putting extra locks on houses and cars and staying out of parks at night, it could be argued that it entirely denies or ignores the emotional aspects of the lived experience of anxiety and fear.

Psychosocial literature has also emerged in relation to 'fear of crime', with Hollway and Jefferson's work contributing to the debate in the 1990s and 2000s. This thinking draws on the contemporary socio-political construction of the issues, including their differential impact on certain groups who may then be more 'vulnerable', and the personal biographies, including 'psychic' processes and states, of the individuals for whom this is a particular struggle. Thinking about fear of crime psychosocially, the idea that 'risk' is primarily a scientifically quantifiable and understandable and avoidable phenomenon is taken as a flawed understanding, and indeed as a defence against anxiety. We like to think risks can be controlled, that uncertainty can be eliminated, and that risks are largely a product of deliberate malevolent actions or negligence on the part of culpable people, but this is largely because the alternative – random chance, unknowable factors, fate and our own inevitable vulnerability in the face of the world – is impossible to contemplate. Postmodern risk societies tend to generate uncertainties, which we anxiously defend against with impossible faith in order, control and the elimination of risk. 'The battle against crime' and the 'zero tolerance' rhetoric, and also the pathologizing of the 'fear of crime' is one context.

Also in this psychosocial model are the kinds of ideas about 'splitting' and 'othering' that we considered above. Why do some kinds of crime and some groups become 'demonized' more than others? Why do groups of young men (especially if black) hanging about get seen as threatening so easily? The stereotypes of 'the hoodie' and of 'stranger danger' is what is constructed as a threat to society, rather than, for example, dumping toxic waste. How crime gets represented and which groups become associated with it are part of the wider socio-political context.

Importantly, though, the psychosocial theorists are saying that we have to also (the 'also' is important) pay attention to the individuals who are feeling the dread – their lived experiences including their internal worlds – to understand what is going on here.

Anxiety, as we have noted at various points in this text, is a psychic phenomena not pathological in the sense that, certainly for Freudians, anxiety is perceived as ordinary. Anxiety and the defence mechanisms drawn on to contain/control anxiety are the product of all psychic development.

However, the ongoing impact of anxiety can also be seen as variable, in the sense that 'containing' infant and childhoods, in which trust and security become internalized within good parent–child relations (Winnicott, 1964 is useful here) are by no means the experience of all, and a person's levels of trust, anxiety, perception of risk etc. relate to their specific internal state – their unconscious fears and phantasies as well as the external situation. Hollway and Jefferson express this particularly well:

> Fear of crime is an unconscious displacement of other fears which are far more intractable and do not display the modern characteristics of knowability and decisionability … which add up to the belief in one's capacity to control the external world. (Hollway and Jefferson, 1997: 263)

The fears unconsciously displaced by the focus on crime may have primitive roots, and can be exacerbated by circumstances and contexts – fears like ageing and loss of capacity, meaninglessness and inconsequence. Connected to broad social contexts, individual circumstances and individual internal worlds, fear of violence and aggression, of intrusions and harassments, are multi-dimensional and best explained psychosocially.

Bullying

The final part of this chapter will briefly consider bullying as an example of much of what has gone before. Subject to much social sensationalization and over-simplification – 'splitting' evident in ideas of 'blameless victims and evil perpetrators' – the 'bully' can be seen as the projective identification of unwanted and hateful group emotions onto the despised 'other' in facilitating social circumstances.

This section will focus on bullying within the school system, in relation to children. The notion of workplace bullying, however, may also be illuminated by the discussion – the mechanisms at work are similar.

At this point in time public and indeed private debates on education and on children regularly veer towards discussions of 'bullying'. The concept seems to encapsulate a broad variety of meanings and projections for contemporary society. Cyber-bullying is the new face of this so-called phenomena, the 'mean-girl' of popular media and cultural studies research the new 'demon' personification.

Popular press use 'bullying' as a catch-all single explanation – a paranoid projection, psychoanalytically explained – to account simply for highly complex tragedies such as suicide in young people, which can lay the blame at the feet of some pathological extra-familial individual and neatly avoids the often social or familial explanations that young people themselves offer for their struggles and miseries. As we outlined in Chapter 2, much research in child and adolescent psychiatry attests to young people experiencing multi-faceted causes of grief and depression, often including losses of friendship, family and relationship breakdowns generally, but rarely mentioning bullying.

The statistic claimed by organizations concerned with bullying per se tend to suggest that bullying is ubiquitous: an everyday event for nearly 7 out of 10 children, and that parents perceive there to be far more bullying, and physical violence than children do.

Box 8.6

Bullying – a moral panic?

According to Bullying UK's 2006 National Bullying Survey (the largest, most comprehensive survey of its kind at the time):

- 69 per cent of children in the UK report being bullied
- 87 per cent of parents report that their child had been bullied in the past 12 months
- 20 per cent report bullying others
- 85 per cent had witnessed bullying.

Bullying is not the same as disputes and squabbles between equals or friends – though these can and do cross the line sometimes. Bullying is an unprovoked, sustained campaign of aggression towards someone in order to hurt them for the sake of it.

It is estimated that at least 20 children and adolescents a year commit suicide because of being bullied – this is a conservative estimate based on documented cases known to us. It is likely that the actual number is higher, perhaps much higher (these figures also do not take into account the numbers of young people who attempt suicide but survive).

According to the National Bullying Survey, more than half of those who reported being bullied had been physically hurt (parents report over 71 per cent).

(Accessed online 22 February 2011).

If one simply takes these statistics at face value the world of children must be almost intolerable. However, the work above on 'fear of crime' is informative here too. We live in a society in which the perception of risk far outstrips the actual risks in everyday life. Fear of crime may be one of a range of 'ontological insecurities' that have been included in a generalized criticism of fearful or 'overprotective' parents who may inadvertently curtail their children's growth towards independence (Giddens, 1991; Hollway and Jefferson, 2001; Furedi, 2001).

Psychosocial discourses of 'bullying' resonate with the kinds of media-fuelled fears of wicked 'others' – strangers to parents and the family- victimizing the good and the familiar – the helpless and innocent child. Kleinian 'splitting', outlined above, gives us access to understanding this projection of paranoid fantasies, of anxiety and fear, outside the intimate group of the family or the community, onto the unknown 'other', introjected into the othered and named as bad, evil, violent. Neatly 'black and white', neatly 'not our fault' – random individual acts by screwed-up children/people.

This contrasts somewhat with NSPCC statistics which suggest 'Children who were abused or neglected by their parents were consistently more likely than others to experience bullying, discrimination, or being made to feel different by their peers. For example, 70% of those who were sexually abused by parents were also bullied by other children. 60% of those who were physically abused by parents, and 58% of those who experienced absence of physical care, also reported being bullied' (Cawson, 2002). We could understand this bullying pattern, perhaps, in relation to the above, as the fearful perceptions of those for whom fear has become part of their psychic landscape, and/or also as a relational interaction: the damaged capacity to make trusting relationships as part of a pattern which might lead to excluding children from friendship groups. This is different from innocent victims and wicked perpetrators, and implicates the families, schools and broader social factors which puts and leaves the damaged, poorly parented child in potentially further damaging situations.

Being alone, rather than with a group, or indeed having a close friend, seems to be the psychic territory in which fears and perceptions of bullying (probably far outweighing the actual incidence of bullying) are generated. The author's research in 2004 with children just arrived at secondary school listened to anxieties which pinned so much dread and concern on 'bullies', so much hope and reassurance on having a friend or friends – beyond any rational or experiential perceptions. Thinking about this through psychosocial 'lenses' from above, fears of bullying might well be seen as the displacement of other fears – of abandonment, aloneness etc. – the full expression of the primitive terrors of the baby in the Kleinian paranoid–schizoid position.

Lucey and Reay's psychosocial studies of schools underline this. Whilst agreeing that children see their friends as protective against, for example, bullying, they also present the issue of friendships as a psychic defence against such fears (2001). 'Safety' as the psychic alleviation of anxiety is to be found in the company of others.

But why then is group membership so fundamental to bullying issues? Adlerian group relations work (psychoanalytical theory applied within the context of groups) provides a further way of understanding bullying psychosocially, and is useful here to flesh out why the 'in' or 'out' position in relation to the group, has a strong connection with bullying. Adler starts from a position that membership of groups is a fundamental element of humanity and that the exclusion from a group, for whatever reasons, forces the individual into a narcissistic position whereby either the individual avoids the group, is outside the group and a victim identification taken up, or will attempt to force re-entry into the group as the bully (Greenwood, 2005).

As has been seen at various points in the text already, the psychosocial importance of the friendship group – being esteemed, connected, contained – is evident.

A final word then on school-based bullying fears – the 'rescuers'. From a psychosocial perspective, teachers function in quite specific spaces in children's fantasy worlds. Whereas notions of victims and bullies carefully separate and demarcate ideas of good and bad well away from each other – idealization and 'demonization' perhaps again – the children's perceptions of teachers, like those they may have of parents, include complex elements of persecutor and rescuer: symbolized perhaps as 'demon headmasters' and classroom 'good fairies'. Shaw describes schools as 'a social setting where the parenting motif is profound and incorporated into institutional arrangements' (hence well suited to the application of psychoanalytic theory) (Shaw, 1995: 16). The demand that teachers should be in control of, and the terror that they will be unable to be in control of, fears and anxieties (such as those personified in the notion of 'dangerous bullying big kids') has been made evident in school-based research. Children, and indeed parents, may invest teachers with powerful fantasies of containment of anxiety and prevention from being overwhelmed. No wonder fears of 'bullying' are usually connected to schools – no wonder teachers are often blamed.

Conclusion

The chapter has attempted to offer a psychosocial discussion of some key areas of violence of concern to contemporary society, though this is not an attempt at a comprehensive coverage. In the chapter we initially offered an illustrative example of how violence and hatred might be considered psychosocially, to encapsulate some of the ideas we went on to examine.

The chapter then looked at gender and violence, and argued that the expectations of contemporary masculinity set the scene against which aggression becomes possible. It also looked at how the 'uncontained' baby and the residual fears and anxieties may also play a strong part in violence in individuals. Misogyny and domestic violence was also considered as gendered psychosocial states. Racism was the next concern here, in itself but also as a protracted example of positioning some groups as outsiders and as then projecting hatred and 'bad' feelings onto them. After this we examined the psychosocial work on crime and the fear of crime, thinking through what the social and internal elements of this modern phenomena might be. Finally the chapter considered what psychosocial thinking might add to our understanding of the contemporary 'moral panic' of bullying. In this area particularly – violence and crime – it is evident that the body of work is expanding rapidly and a rich field is emerging in the UK and the USA.

9

How people age and die: disengagement, disruption and loss

Introduction

Significant transformations taking place within our society have led towards a diversity of experience for people entering older age. Older people are not all the same, they are not a homogeneous group, but the social experiences of those individuals entering a particular age cohort through much of the twentieth century tended to be similar. These individual and social experiences have changed in more recent decades and socio-cultural shifts in society continue to transform the nature of older age, and also death and dying.

In some ways older people today are more visible, more politically and economically significant, more out there in the world than any other generation, though paradoxically often it is only their capacity to look and act young that accords them respect and admiration. Valuing ageing for its greater wisdom and experience may have taken a back seat to valuing ageing for its capacity to imitate youth, in relation to, for example, sexual attractiveness or physical fitness. The lived experience of ageing is hemmed in by the unavoidable knowledge that as far as possible you need to hide it. We live in a society, it could be argued, where people do not want to be reminded of ageing and death, and where there are deep-seated attitudes that represent the fear of ageing and of death. We explore some of these themes in this chapter.

Ageing is a continuous process, there is no sudden change of direction or rupture at age 50 or 60 or 70 or 80. The gradations of ageing make little sense, as Woodward (1991) suggests, culturally there exists more of a 'binary' opposite of age and youth; individuals belong to one or the other camp. Yet it is important to understand something of the diversity of experience for older people and the reality of their lives. Misconceptions have to do with the perception of ageing in our society, and the status of growing old; ageing associated with the culturally embedded fear (and perhaps denial) of dependency, death and decay. As Woodward clearly states, when people speak personally about their experience of ageing and of their own fears of ageing and death, the common response of others is to reject what they have to say: 'nervous anxiety is masked by a denial of another's subjectivity in a way that appears to be reassuring but is in reality silencing and repressive' (1991: 3).

Beliefs about ageing prevalent in a society will also of course be the beliefs to which older people themselves have been exposed. In an ageist world (see below) old people may have to experience themselves as the victims of prejudice; may inhabit devalued identities. For some this will be a new experience of a 'subaltern' identity; for others additional devaluing. The version of themselves being reflected back – the stereotypes about ageing – may be an uncomfortable fit, or even in conflict with self-perceptions about their identity and the complexity of their lives.

For some people the struggle to assert their own version of who they are, and therefore how they can feel about themselves, may become far more of a challenge: a psychosocial identity issue we will look at later in the chapter. However, the psychic struggles involved here will, as we have seen in relation to the previous chapters, be mediated by both the *social* and the pre-existing *psychic* landscapes. Ageing, experienced in poverty and struggle (ill-being), with existing early histories of mistrust and rejection, and with few resources or supports, will be experienced very differently from ageing when a person is 'comfortably off', confident and well supported.

Primarily, then, this chapter considers the context of how societies create old age as an undervalued part of life, and the impact this has on individuals' emotions and inner states, for example their confidence and sense of self-worth and esteem will be looked at. How people strive to counterbalance the various losses of status, power, income, looks and physical capacity are considered. The potential losses of contact through leaving work, a grown-up family, bereavement of friends, and the psychosocial impact of these are looked at, as are the fluctuations in relationships within communities and the possibility of loneliness and aloneness. It goes on to examine death and dying in the context of grief and loss, psychosocial themes that are pertinent here.

The meaning of ageing

In Woodward's seminal text on the social construction of ageing, taken from a psychoanalytic perspective, the author cites an earlier French book, *Histoire de Louise: des viellards en hospice* (*The Story of Louise: Old People in a Nursing Home*) and its intriguing focus on the biography of a woman who frequented a bistro across from the nursing home and made it her 'home':

> In spite of her broken voice Louise was singing songs from the beginning of the century at the top of her lungs. The three others followed. Between songs they downed their liquor straight, laughed and exchanged the most outrageous collection of obscenities. Louise was at the time seventy-seven years old, strong, compact enough that you could see her body under the old coat she always wore; her dishevelled platinum blond hair flew in all directions; her dark lipstick outlined a mouth well beyond its natural borders, just up to a moustache. Her face was covered with spots that at first I thought were traces of pigmentation but were in fact for the most part filth. Her nails were black, half painted with an old dark polish. Louise was astonishingly dirty and possessed a lack of all restraint that was incited by provocation; by herself she managed to animate the entire room of the bar. (Dacher cited in Woodward, 1991: 158).

Is this old age? In this scenario Louise has passion, energy, flamboyance and a lack of conformity to being a 'nice old lady'. She is noisy, spirited and public, filthy, lewd and drunken. She also represented something that the authors found admirable, as they believed that the nursing home was suffocating its inhabitants through control and containment. But do we find characters like Louise sad, repellent or admirable? Perhaps they evoke mixed feelings. Perhaps they demonstrate something of our ambivalence about age and ageing and maybe also reveal something about their gendered nature. What they also suggest is that sloughing off the identities that have been formed and re-formed over 60 or 70 years is not likely to be straightforward or painless. Dates on a calendar do not, we suggest, bring about identity change.

A good starting point for this chapter is to think about the meaning of ageing and older age more specifically, as a prelude for thinking about questions of death and dying in the context of the lifecourse. Our understanding of and feelings about old age and about ageing are undoubtedly shaped by the society that we live and grow up in, as well as by the socio-cultural beliefs, norms and values that underpin our understanding of the lifecourse (the social context). These beliefs, norms and values differ, sometimes fundamentally, according to the society that we are a part of, as well as by the more specific family, community and intergenerational norms that impact on individuals. In similar fashion to our discussion about childhood and adulthood, these social and cultural variations in the perception of ageing bring to light the *social construction* of age and dependency; ageing does not therefore just denote particular biological and physiological processes. As we discussed in relation to babies and childhood in Chapter 2, the lived experience of occupying a body that is subject to considerable ongoing change, may be a source of considerable preoccupation and concern that inhabiting the superficially more static, more under control, bodies of early and mid-adulthood does not provoke.

One of the key social changes of the twentieth century has been the rise in life expectancy and particularly healthy life expectancy, as well as a significant change to social welfare systems (see Phillipson, 1998) (with an increasing emphasis on private provision), in addition to the ageing and coming into late adulthood of what we might refer to as the 'consumer' generation (those born in the period shortly after 1945). Significant changes to health and healthcare for the 55–65 age group have been emphasized and there have been many improvements in that respect. Life expectancy in the UK is currently 77 for men and 82 for women, but of course what this statistic masks is differences across social classes and ethnic groups, as well as geographical areas, and that the older you become the longer you can expect to live (see www.ons.gov.uk for current statistics). This also masks issues of identity for older adults; age limits and age boundaries only tell part of the story. What we can also note is that substantial increases in life expectancy in ageing in Western societies and the UK have not yet not equated with changes to what it means to grow older and to age; that is to say, it does not tell us about the lived experience of growing older and ageing.

Thinking about ageing and dying psychosocially

So far the existing psychosocial work on ageing, marrying issues of social context with the inner psychic phenomena and the experiential, is limited. As with some sections of previous chapters we tentatively build psychosocial approaches from integrating existing social theories and insight from psychoanalysis and other related theory. Besides, many texts on social gerontology as well as those of a more sociological emphasis exploring ageing and society, have focused primarily on the area of ageing populations and the implications of those for modern societies, most of which have been characterized as negative (Coleman, 1993). This work has presented a negative view of ageing, focusing on decline and the welfare challenges of an ageing society. As we saw in Chapter 5, theories about how people are occupied in later life (and with ageing) had focused either on looking at how older people disengage from society as an inevitable response to how older people's roles change, or it was seen as a period where older people successfully change their roles in the pursuit of new activities (disengagement and role theory). In this disengagement process the individual prepares for the final disengagement – death – and as such there is a certain amount of emotional and psychic preparation:

> … late adulthood coincides with an important moment of transition towards a life phase substantially marked by conclusion of the plan guiding the main choices made in youth. In this logic, old age does not represent so much a phase of potential new planning as a time for weighing up the balance; where the dimension of the present is mainly defined by first looking back at the past instead of forward to the future. This logic goes hand in hand with the affirmation of the *disengagement* model. (Facchini and Rampazi, 2009: 355)

Many of these perspectives have seen ageing as both an individual and a social problem. Other more critical sociological perspectives have challenged some of these hypotheses by highlighting the social construction of ageing and dependency (see Hockey and James, 1993), suggesting that the meanings of ageing are historically and culturally contingent. A significant change in recent years is that the debate about ageing is suddenly about how to grow old 'successfully' (Bowling and Dieppe, 2005) and that older age is itself an important consumer and commoditized social role internalized with the attendant problems of all consumer identities. This debate is set against the backdrop of a generally medical and medicalized view of ageing and the notion of 'successful', and therefore by implication 'unsuccessful', ageing. This view suggests that we need to optimize life expectancy and healthy life expectancy, whilst minimizing disability as we grow older. In contrast, psychosocial approaches would acknowledge no such thing as 'successful' in this context. Within a broadly psychosocial approach we would acknowledge that there are losses and gains, struggles and achievements like the rest of life. The view that one ought to be successful at ageing is in itself 'double suffering' – feeling bad about feeling bad.

In some ways our perspective is similar to Gilleard and Higgs (1998, 2000). They argue that formulating standardized definitions of ageing based on old demarcations (a characteristic feature of Western industrial societies) is no longer useful and that the old certainties about ageing have given way to a multidimensional period; in essence, many older adults today face a multitude of choices and futures, whilst others are aware of those choices and futures, without being able to access them, making any lack of possible agency all the more disconcerting.

Psychoanalytic theory

Psychoanalytically old age in itself has attracted less theoretical attention than, for example, childhood, as it is the events of childhood that are seen as explanatory of human development. Childhood is a starting point and a continual reference point for psychoanalytical discussions about identity. Psychoanalysis, particular Freudian, is traditionally a theory of childhood that presents and reinforces a negative view of ageing, focusing as it does on the themes of anxiety, fear, denial and repression (Woodward, 1991: 4). Traditional psychoanalysis has therefore taken little interest in the kinds of identity developments of later age and particularly old age, tending to argue that the essential psychic structures – for example, defensive systems and object-relations – are put in place in early childhood, and that later life events, even perhaps those which are traumatic, have a relatively superficial impact compared to attachment phenomena, for example, in dictating who one can be, the extent to which one is resilient, the likelihood of ego damage, mental illness and so on. Freud argued that prevalent attitudes about the anxiety and fear of death were not about death per se, but about fear of the loss of others; that is, fear of separation and absence brought about by attachment.

As we saw in Chapter 2, the psychic worlds of Kleinian babies are teaming with phantasy images and drives. And yet Klein sees ageing more as a period of (renewed) latency: more passive than active. Psychoanalytic concepts such as splitting are useful in understanding the culturally significant binary opposites of youth and ageing as either good or bad. Tolerance towards and understanding of the ambivalence of both youth and old age would show appreciation of the complexity of ageing, but Western societies do not promote that view in that there is little ambiguity in how we represent ageing (Woodward, 1991).

Freud's analysis of ageing was deeply pessimistic, linking to psychic notions of castration and increasing physical and psychological inertia. For example, in terms of intellectual and creative 'potency', vitality, energy and so on, Freud argued that the best has gone and so much psychoanalytic thinking is about how the creative and productive phase slows down as we age. Famously, Freud believed that there was little point in attempting psychoanalytic change with patients in middle age, or older, as the over 50s were 'uneducable'. Erikson, though, specifically designated a life stage in his model in which far more optimistic outcomes are achievable though not always achieved, which we will examine and critique below. Themes such as mourning and loss are evoked in psychoanalytical work on ageing; loss will be highlighted later in the chapter.

Contemporary psychosocial work that looks at how 'subaltern' identities (i.e. those without power and status) are psychically damaged by their oppression and under-valuation in society also offers a potentially productive seam of thought to mine for thinking about age and ageism.

Erikson's life stages: ego integrity

The psychoanalytic perspective on ageing and loss is developed and given a different emphasis in the work of Erikson. Here, loss of identity is connected to retirement and the different gendered expectations of future family roles. Erikson, whose life-stage work we considered in Chapter 2, unusually for his generation of psychoanalytically trained theorists, extended his stage model so that ageing into later life was incorporated. Erikson thus pointed to the ongoing evolution of identity during adulthood and more generally the lifecourse:

> A sense of 'I' becomes a most sensitive matter again in old age, as an individual's uniqueness gradually and often suddenly seems to have lost any leeway for further variations such as those which seemed to open themselves with each previous stage. Now, non-Being must be faced 'as is'. (Erikson, 1984: 102)

Not dissimilarly to the Facchini and Rampazi (2009) quote above, a certain 'weighing up' pervades this view. As we saw previously, Erikson developed a view about development that was counter to the prevailing ideas about stages of development. The area of developmental psychology, for example, is explicitly devoted to the study of child development. However, Erikson knew that psychological development in later life could not be seen in epigenetic ways; that is to say, later life development was more attuned to the social environment and not the psychic landscape.

Box 9.1

Erikson: ego integrity vs despair

Erikson's notion of ego integrity vs despair is the final stage in his schema and is perhaps the least understood of his stage constructs (James and Zarrett, 2006).

Here it is argued that adults look back at what they have done with their lives (a process of evaluation), and integrate this with their vision of community (personal history or biography is reunited with experience of larger community). There is the tendency to review one's life at this stage.

> Ego integrity is very much about getting the *inner life* in order (the psyche) and to come to acceptance. Erikson's view is that individuals, as they negotiate life, try to balance out the inner psychic tensions as well as the external social tensions.
>
> Erikson's view is that in oscillating between the two extremes of integrity and despair, most people achieve something of a balance. For those who succeed at integrating these tensions and coming to some resolution they gain a sense of order and meaning over their lives; those who don't develop wisdom will feel despair, yet some despair is inevitable – through suffering misfortunes, or loss of friends and family.

In his psychosocial thinking Erikson bridges the gap from pure psychoanalytic thinking to applied psychosocial theory and notions of identity, which we will now give further consideration to. His views about ego integrity in particular have been criticized for reflecting a middle-class bias and may reflect the concerns of the well-educated (James and Zarrett, 2007). Others have suggested that his stage theory overall, but particularly around ego integrity, is too prescriptive (Woodward, 1991).

Identity theory

Alongside the visible biological and physiological changes which ageing brings are particular and variable experiences that accompany those changes, experiences that shape what we might understand as how the psychosocial impacts on ageing. For identity theorists drawn from sociology and social psychology, ageing is understood as a key process for producing social identity, and the general consensus in the sociological literature is that our society has produced restrictive ideas about ageing which are internalized and impact on how older people see themselves. In the process of infantilizing older people we have denied individuals the 'full personhood' that they would normally take for granted (Hockey and James, 1993: 33). This could also be argued about traditional psychoanalysis.

Many of our existing definitions of what actual years constitute older age or what has become known as the 'third age' have come from the male state pension age of 65, though the age at which people retire tends to vary according to gender, profession and social circumstances. But of course chronological age is not always a good marker for understanding and making sense of the meanings of old age, especially the psychosocial themes that are central to this book. Also, the changing relationship between work and identity, as well as the shifting nature of employment in society has meant that the meaning of retirement has shifted over time – what we might term the *lifestylization* of post-retirement has meant a move towards a more active notion of independence and identity making in older age (see Chapter 5 for a fuller discussion of this issue). As such, individuals nearing retirement today may have very different ideas about what is expected of that period from previous generations.

As with our other life stages, any discipline that explores the nature of being a person, for example, literature and philosophy, can be helpful in thinking psychosocially about ageing. The French writer and feminist Simone de Beauvoir (*The Coming of Age*, 1975) wrote thoughtfully about how in almost all societies ageing brings along a change in status to the individual, and in the majority of cases this is something negative; ageing is thus accompanied by a disregarding and de-personalizing process that strips older people of their rights, their livelihood and their social status, in similar and related ways to that noted by Erving Goffman in his social-psychological analysis of total institutions such as asylums (1970 [1961]).

Like Goffman, de Beauvoir was interested in processes that prevent individuals' ongoing construction of their own identities, and instead have depersonalization forced on them. This notion of a forced depletion of individuality and status is similar to Hockey and James' (1993, 2003) concept that ageing is accompanied by stereotypes about older people that serve to deny the individual full personhood – and can be seen in themselves as ageist. What we can add to this is that the meanings of age vary across societies and across points in history: ageing is socially and culturally constructed. For example, social anthropology is helpful in explaining how in age set societies (such as in most tribal parts of East Africa) the experiences and activities of those of a similar age and identity tend to be similar as they pass through age set statuses over the lifecourse (Keesing, 1981). For Hockey and James (2003: 58–9) in contemporary Western societies the traditional age boundaries and lifecourse stages are becoming blurred and the lifecourse is a more 'fluid' endeavour.

Postmodern approaches to ageing and dying: continuity and disruption

Fluidity is a central theme in understanding the postmodern approach to ageing. Maintaining a sense of continuity of identity and biography, as people enter older age, is an issue that the postmodern (or late-modern) approach finds more problematic. Some writers who explore health and well-being connected to later life as well as those who find their life biographies 'disrupted' by significant life events and serious illnesses explain that any sense of coherent life 'biography' can be altered and so any future sense of self has to make sense of those 'unanticipated' changes to the life plan (see Becker, 1997). As Polivka explains:

> According to this perspective, the aging experience is not inherently meaningful or constitutive of certain kinds of wisdom. It is rather an experience not only of physical decline *a la* the medical model, it is also more fundamentally characterized by increasingly limited capacities to act, to change, to consume, to experience joy, to play, to shift and experiment with identity, to create and modify or radically amend the narrative of one's own life at will. (2000: 228)

Ageing brings one to a re-evaluation of the psychosocial self. Ageing is part of a reflexive project of the self. This discussion resonates with Hoggett's psychosocial thinking about identity in that he suggests as much as there is continuity within identity there is also a 'fluidity and contingency' (Hoggett, 2000: 89); that is to say, continuity of self cannot always be relied upon as one ages and so there is movement. He continues, 'One's identity may be a collage of experiences from the past – some remembered, some forgotten, some idealised, some spoiled – but it is also constantly moulded by the present' (Hoggett, 2000: 89).

For people in old age there is a balance that they engage in, between reminiscence and re-imaginings of the past, but these are seen in the light of contemporary 'of the now' social experience. Movement and fluidity is central to this psychosocial theme. The contemporary Western lifecourse, once rooted in debates about fixed 'crises' (e.g. Erikson) has therefore become more fluid, and the notion of individual choice emphasized more at all stages of the lifecourse.

Encouraging psychosocial, emotional connection is central to development in our late-modern consumer society. Hoggett also suggests that 'For development to occur there must be some emotional contact with the other' (2000: 42), which he suggests is so that the individual who wishes to offload with emotional anger, fear, hatred or disappointment can do so with another who acts as the 'container' for such emotions. This is the case at any stage of development and clearly also relates to older age. This then is also highly significant in relation to the issue of loss and isolation discussed above: it posits another reason why people need to be with others in reciprocal relationships.

Box 9.2

A post-modern/late-modern theory of ageing: Featherstone and Hepworth

Featherstone and Hepworth (1998) argue that the late twentieth century marked the end of ageing. Biotechnology and other techno-culture developments make it possible for older people to take full advantage of the multiple, shifting identities characteristic of postmodern culture. They see a greater freedom and room for agency in a lengthened middle age (extending beyond the 'artificial' retirement period, ending in a 'deep' old age (over 80 or older). (Featherstone and Hepworth, 1998; Gilleard and Higgs, 2000)

Anthony Giddens, the sociologist of late-modernity, argues that there are particular questions that concern existential issues about anxiety and ontological security (see Chapter 2) and which come to light in late modernity (Giddens, 1991). Late-modern societies, as opposed to traditional societies, are ones that are oriented towards the future, where individuals plan and map out their life biography. Hence there is a particular avoidance of discussing death in a society in which, as Giddens states, death (as well as sickness) is 'sequestrated'; that is to say, death has been separated off from everyday life. This is a particular feature of late-modern societies as opposed to 'traditional' ones.

One of the existential issues that Giddens speaks about is subjective death, which in the psychoanalytic perspective he suggests we have no intrinsic understanding of. In the psychoanalytic perspective the unconscious cannot conceive of its own death, as it has no sense of time. Giddens contrasts this with his view about the existential contradiction of being, that humans are aware of the inanimate world and yet set against it as self-conscious beings aware of our finite nature: '…consciousness of finitude, which human beings develop with increasing cognitive mastery of temporal categories, is associated with anxieties of an utterly fundamental sort' (1991: 50).

In addition, increased knowledge of that finitude in terms of heightened awareness of one's own or significant other's death may be experienced as a 'fateful moment' (see Chapter 6). For example, receiving a diagnosis of terminal illness may be regarded as a fateful moment and brings to the fore finitude and the existential questions, as the individual knows the outcome is their own death.

The ageing body, gender and stigma

The above discussion offers some insights into what kinds of psychoanalytical and sociological theories can inform a psychosocial discussion of ageing. What is missing from this discussion is embodiment, which is surely central in offering a psychosocial approach to ageing. To understand embodiment is to understand the experience of the lived body, as opposed to the 'natural' and medicalized body. Reductionist approaches to the body, ones that medicalize the body in different ways, serve to reinforce stereotypes about ageing and disembody lived experiences of ageing that can be understood psychosocially. Stigma that arises from embodied ageing reflects back uncertainty and ambivalence about ageing: 'The painfulness of sudden stigmatisation can come not from the individual's confusion about his identity, but from knowing too well what he has become' (Goffman cited in Featherstone and Hepworth, 1986: 86).

As part of a postmodernist critique, Featherstone and Hepworth, through their discussion about the 'mask' of age, argued that the image of the mask was a way of undermining traditional age-related categories. From this they went on to highlight a range of important issues about ageing that were specific to this period: tensions associated with the self and personal identity; the current resistance to ageism and ageist stereotypes; and lastly the baby boomers' attempt to develop 'a new public language to challenge and destabilise traditional cultural images of middle age' (Featherstone and Hepworth, 1989: 151). In many ways one could argue that Featherstone and Hepworth foresaw that a new language would be created as those who enter the third agers take on the challenges of post middle age.

At an individual level resistance to traditional versions of ageing – 'staying young' – are predominantly linked to preserving, enhancing and grooming the body, and it is in relation to the body that many men and women are judged as 'doing well for their age' and looking 'younger' than they are. For men the capacity to continue to be seen as strong and sporty, and for women slim and 'attractive', may be the defining arenas in which they are subject or not to ageism and under-valuing, how they can avoid feeling undermined or shamed. Not only is the ('healthy') body and its prolonged capacity to access action and activity a definitive feature of whether and how people experience ageing/ageism, but the visual aspects of the body, in reality not separable from its capacities, are intrinsic to how it is valued.

Psychosocially the emotional dimensions of anxiety at one's capacity to 'pass' as not old, or shame at failing to pass, can be viewed as inflicting psychic damage (we discuss shame more in Chapters 7 and 9). Psychosocially, too, the cultural capital and material resources to access bodily enhancement are by no means equally distributed. The rich have greater access to the means of continuing to inhabit the body beautiful (and healthy), and the social admiration and internalized self-esteem this generates. The issue may also be gendered, with women's capacity to remain attractive seen as more crucial to her identity and ageing appearance inevitably rendering women less valued, less noticed and less important; men may become increasingly subject to the same judgements.

Not all gender themes in ageing are to do with the physical. Let us think about adults in 'traditional' roles for a moment. For women, being the hub of family life may change as children grow up and leave and further children become biologically impossible. The parents of the young-old may be frail or indeed often die at this stage, severing further attachments and loving bonds. Life in older age may have less everyday loving and caring, less emotional labour and less nurturing. A sense of being at the centre of a network of close emotional bonds may be replaced with feeling disconnected, isolated and unneeded.

Thinking about late 50s onwards and a more or less traditional notion of masculinity, then physical strength, competitiveness and sexual success may all become less available, and this is also likely to impact on men's confidence and self-esteem. The fantasies of what one might have become have to be put away. Parents dying and children leaving home may further disrupt identity in the twenty-first century where 'new men's' relationship to family is more involved.

The above suggests that gender is a significant feature in the (possible) transition of old age, but thinking psychosocially, other structural features such as class and ethnicity *and* the individual psyche of the subject concerned are also likely to impact. Physical strength and endurance, for example, plays far more of a part in job success in some social classes than others. The capacity to do long hours of manual labour are needed to produce extra income in some work, so for working-class men not only a sense of self-worth but actual earnings might decline in old age. However, in some prestigious, middle-class occupations, for example, law, it is not at all unusual for status and earnings to increase in a man's late 50s and the greater choices available in retirement to the financially secure – for example, to disengage with the 9–5 but fulfil creative ambitions such as to write, take up a musical instrument or paint instead – may be possible only where ongoing income is 'comfortable' and one can turn one's hand to creative possibilities.

Culturally options and possibilities may vary; for example, the role of women in relation to children and grandchildren differs according to ethnicity, and the extent to which families (including family businesses) remain intact. However, for many men and women, loss may be a significant product of ageing and it is this issue to which we now turn our attention.

Ageing, dying and loss

In old age the issue of loss has significant resonance in terms of the internal, intimate concerns of individual lives and the external social order that shapes those lives. Loss is undoubtedly a key defining feature of later life and older age – loss of a parent, loss of friends and family, loss of career and direction, loss of looks and youthful signs, retirement, physical ageing and its losses of bodily capacity, psychological disruption – sources of recognition and self-worth alter the psychic and socio-cultural landscape of later life. Facchini and Rampazi (2009) suggest that this is a 'triple loss': of health; loss of economic well-being and loss of social role due to retirement; and loss of emotional attachment and affections (partner death, children leaving home). These can be physical losses – death or loss of a house – or more psychosocial ones – those that are more intangible such as divorce, retirement or unemployment.

Not only are there more losses – that is to say, more need for mourning in the Freudian sense of grieving and its normal, necessary and painstaking psychic processes of eventual detachment from that which has been lost so that we can replace it – but also, if Woodward's argument is correct, 'the process of mourning becomes both increasingly more difficult and yet paradoxically more familiar as we grow older, as losses inevitably accumulate around us, and as we find ourselves coming closer to death ourselves.' (1991: 113). The gradual loss of relationships and connections, perhaps some due to retirement, or friends ageing and dying, or no longer having children at home or close by is a key feature of ageing and loss, and perhaps a fear for many of us as we age. Woodward suggests that we may not wish to 'let go' of friends and family whom have died, we may no longer want to get over them, but instead keep the memories of them and the affective ties with them – 'when we are very old we may not wish to replace what we have lost' (*ibid.*: 126).

Perhaps this presents too bleak a picture and that older people have a higher rate of satisfaction than younger people, much of which could be explained due to greater acceptance of life situations. Retirement for those with comfortable pensions and a good standard of health does not so much constitute a loss but an opportunity to travel, change direction (write that novel, learn a language or an instrument), have time for projects and relationships that previously had to be sandwiched in to small amounts of free time, perhaps even take up part-time or voluntary work in a different sector to one's former employment. For many, retirement from full-time employment is sought early and embraced; with financial security its meaning is not loss but gain.

Our society places great importance on, and often attaches the meaning of 'social success' to sociality and being connected with others: to be without others signifies a social death. Emotionally, as we have seen in other chapters in relation to key life changes – for example, moving schools, changing jobs, being forced to flee one's country – having close emotional bonds with a friend, friends, family or someone to love are highly valued and aloneness dreaded. The primitive Kleinian fears of being 'alone in the dark' and the social fears of being seen to be a 'Johnny no-mates', inter-twine. In this context loneliness is both stigmatizing and psychically damaging. Intimate relationships are therefore central to how we understand ageing. Our understanding of loneliness can be set within the family context and the changes to families over the last half century. One key change has been the diversity of modern families so that the conventional age 'boundaries' between age classifications have altered – grandparents, for example, can range in age from 35 to 100. Our notions of what it is to be a grandparent and how that might define later life experience is thus more complex.

Grief and loss

Grief takes many forms, and any discussion of grief will be unable to encapsulate the complexity and diversity in how it manifests. However, many of the discussions about grief incorporate some recognition of loss. As we saw earlier, Giddens explained how death had become sequestered under late modernity, but more than that – what was once a public event under traditional societies has become a private and privatized experience, where death has moved away from the public and community realm. As such, grief and mourning itself has become privatized in Western societies, unused as we are to thinking about suffering and grief in a community and social context.

Grief is the term commonly used to describe a person's emotional response to the death of a loved one, which is experienced as a loss. The area of study and research on grief, suffering, and death and dying is a significant and large one, but many of the studies coalesce around central themes and issues. One of those themes is about how people come to some form of acceptance at the loss and that without this acceptance it is difficult for the grieving person to find any peace in their own life.

An earliest theory of grief and loss includes Freud's *Mourning and Melancholia* (1917), which is still very influential and seen as a classic psychoanalytic text on bereavement. For Freud the individual experiencing the loss needs to withdraw energy from the deceased (cathexis) – to decathect': that is to say, withdraw one's feelings of attachment and emotional energy from the loss object and 'cathect' (i.e. attach and refocus emotional energies) elsewhere. As Freud explains, 'Mourning has a quite precise psychical task to perform: its function is to detach the survivor's hopes and memories from the dead' (Freud, 1917: 268). And yet Freud felt that this process was never complete; there is a deep psychological need for a connection to a loved one.

Freud was essentially the first to link loss to depression where the attachment is not given up and feelings of emotional links are not yet withdrawn, and he referred to this as melancholia. Because of this, much of the work on grief and disorder stems from Freud's view that there were normal and pathological responses to grief and loss. Adopting a Freudian perspective, the work of Melanie Klein also considered grief and mourning. Klein (1940) linked mourning and the manic-depressive states (see Chapter 2) in that in the process of mourning the individual re-works the movement in infancy from paranoid-schizoid to depressive state. Experiencing grief is about the letting go of bad internal objects, and the experience of grief as problematic stems from the failure in childhood from establishing 'internal' good objects and feeling secure in the world. Psychoanalytical and psychodynamic theory of loss has focused on the psyche, the internal aspects of grief that emphasize the psychological but individual meanings of the loss are not seen as relevant. Such theories have been hugely influential in theories of grief and mourning.

In referring to his theory of attachment John Bowlby wrote about loss (*Attachment and Loss*, 1982). Bowlby outlined the mother-infant bond and the rupture of this bond is outlined in his views about the 'separation response syndrome' and it is here that he discusses grief. During the process of attachment any unwanted separation from the attachment figure would cause distress and grief. This 'separation response' usually occurs sometime after the first six months of life and is a three-stage process from protest, despair (characterized by grief and mourning) and then detachment (1982). For Bowlby, then, grief in adults was about separation anxiety.

Furthermore, Bowlby referred to what he called the four stages of the grief process: numbness, denial and a sense of unreality; yearning and protest; despair and disorganization; reorganization and investment in the future. The difficulty with this theory and other similar theories of grief is that individuals may experience chronic grief and never achieve the kind of acceptance suggested. Some have referred to this as a disorder and that it is pathological, like a mental health condition, but this is problematic as an interpretation. There are also wider cultural influences that further impact on how grief is experienced that are ignored here in an attempt to describe the universal and could be seen as ethnocentric (see below).

The work of Kubler-Ross (Box 9.3) led the way in many of these studies and influenced countless others. Kubler-Ross has had a key influence on much of the work on grief and bereavement and the problems associated with people's awareness of death. She pioneered studies into death and dying with her work with dying patients, and in particular developed the five stages of grief, forming a critique of traditional psychiatry using techniques from psychoanalysis and culminated in the most well-known publication *On Death and Dying* (1970).

> **Box 9.3**
>
> **Elizabeth Kubler-Ross (1926–2004): five stages of grief (1970)**
> The five stages of grief were proposed as being applied to the experience of the dying, but later was seen also as a system of adjustment to grief. These included:
>
> 1 Denial
> 2 Anger
> 3 Bargaining
> 4 Depression
> 5 Acceptance
>
> She argued that individuals experienced most of these stages and in no particular order, though acceptance usually coming at the end of a process.

Kubler-Ross was critical of what she saw as medicalized dying (see Szasz, 1961 and Illich, 1976 for critique of medicalization) and would have been in agreement with Giddens' formulation of the problem in terms of how death and dying has been sequestered from everyday life. Kubler-Ross was at one point a member of the American Holistic Medical Association and we could argue that the popularity and use of complementary and alternative medicine for individuals are so as to give hope and meaning to individuals facing death and dying such as in the case of terminal illness or cancer (McClean *et al.*, 2012).

As well as reflecting a deep inner process with the psyche, grief is also a social experience, one that can be mediated and managed by the social networks and social support that individuals come to rely on. More than that, many of the perspectives that focus exclusively on the psyche, the inner experience of grief, ignore the importance and enduring significance of death and grief in the context of social relationships. Depending on the nature of these social relationships, as well as issues to do with class and ethnicity, this will impact variably on the individual lived experience of grief. We must also place in a social context in the West, which holds the view that death is an embarrassment in a society that privileges and valorizes the place of youth and vitality.

The sociologist Tony Walter has taken what has been called the postmodern perspective on death and grief (Walter, 2001; Klass and Walter 2001) and, along with the work of Klass, Silverman and Nickman on 'continuing bonds' represented a welcome change from the classic Western grief theory (Klass *et al.*, 1996; Árnason, 2012). For Walter

(2001) our psychosocial experience of death is permeated by contradictory and paradoxical influences: on the one hand we have a cultural aversion to and deep-seated fear of death, yet at the same time we have a view that sees loss of a loved one as unbearable. These are the social and cultural contexts that frame how death, dying and in particular bereavement, is experienced. The work of the sociologist Walter has contributed to this debate in terms of what he has called the biographical model and the individualization of loss (i.e. there is no overarching grief process). In this the grieving person, rather than seeking to move on and accept through the 'emotion work' of bereavement counselling, seeks to give permanence to their memories of the dead person by constructing a biography of those memories in its narrative retelling. This involves talking to as many people as possible who had connection to that person. This is different from the closure models outlined above in that the aim of grief is a biographical construction of the dead than can endure, not weaken, for everything has changed and the past cannot be altered.

In a powerful and evocative account of the death of his father, the writer and journalist Matthew Parris recalls how the memory of his father did not wither and he did not gain acceptance. This account perhaps presents the most personal representation of the 'continuing bonds' view of grief, and it shows the relevance of Walter's perspective in our late-modern times:

> Death is not a 'wound' to be 'healed' or a 'scar' to 'fade'. Once someone has been in the world, they have always been in the world; and once they have gone their absence will be in the world forever, part of the world; in Dad's case part of mine. This is a good thing. How foolish, then, is all this talk of 'getting over' death. How empty, how wrong-headed the exhortations we make to those who love us that they should try not to miss us when we're gone. Why not? You do miss someone you love, don't you, when they're gone? How self-negating is the wish that others should not feel sad when they remember us. Of course they should feel sad! They can't talk to us any more. It is right that we make an imprint on the minds and lives of others, right that we should be needed while still alive; and therefore right that the imprint remains and the loss hurts, and continues hurting. (Parris, 2009).

For Parris the deceased has a continued (and wanted) presence in their life (Árnason, 2012). Walter's view also shows the importance of understanding cultural perspectives on grief, death and dying, which are absent from stage theories and disengagement views of grief from Bowlby, Kubler-Ross, and the like who demonstrate the Western ideology of individualism and individual autonomy in their socially constructed worldview (Árnason, 2012).

Attitudes and beliefs towards and experiences of death and grief vary enormously across cultures and it may be that rather than emphasizing independence of the person (and therefore disengagement from others) that people may see themselves as interdependent with others. A psychosocial response involves thinking about the internal dimension of the person as well as their social position. An example of this is the notion that loss or losses, of a whole range and nature, need to be mourned and then let go of, because unhappiness from grief prevents a person from being able to change and move forward, put simply. From his perspective as a practising psychotherapist as well as a political activist and social theorist, Hoggett comments that 'one of the paradoxes we face as human beings is that we often find it immensely difficult to give up our own unhappiness' (see Box 9.4).

Box 9.4

Paul Hoggett: loss, grief and change
Three core elements make up Hoggett's argument:

1 That people find letting go of the past, and mourning loss, harder than grieving, letting go and moving forward.
2 That grief can easily become grievance, and that groups and individuals can find satisfactions in this kind of anger and resentment: a kind of righteous indignation, a sense of being wronged victims, keeping old wounds open.
3 For change to occur loss has to be worked through which involves:
   ■ Mourning for the part of the self, e.g. the unhappy child that needs to be given up and left behind.
   ■ A 'settling of accounts' with the past, a taking on board (remembering, internalizing) what was good and letting go of what was bad
   ■ This might require forgiveness, of both self and others. (Hoggett, 2010)

Conclusion

As the final chapter we have set out to consider how we can make psychosocial sense of the later stages of people's lives. Specifically, we have discussed the meaning of later life, ageing, and death and dying, particularly taking into account a range of theories and approaches that can shed light on the lifecourse issues as a psychosocial theme. As such, theories from psychoanalysis, identity theory, Erikson's life-stage approach, and the postmodern approach have been brought in to help us develop an integrated and interdisciplinary psychosocial view. The major theme of loss – of status, power, looks, losses of contact through leaving work, grown-up family, bereavement of friends, and so on, were examined; death and dying has also been highlighted in the context of grief and loss.

Concluding thoughts

Knowing quite how to end a book such as this is something of a dilemma, in the sense that there are no specific conclusions, and if it is simply a summary that we opt for, each chapter already has those built in. Saying what you are going to do, doing it and saying what you did only goes so far. However, simply stopping at the end of Chapter 9 also seems a little brusque and a little unfinished. We have decided then to simply make a handful of what we hope are useful final points here in relation to how we think this book has developed psychosocial thinking, and what we hope you the reader might be able to make with that.

What we wanted to achieve with this book is to offer a way of thinking about the major stages, transitions, relations and struggles in life; in essence, the most important elements that make up a life, and from a psychosocial approach. In other words using the most helpful perspectives from sociology, psychology, psychoanalysis and occasionally philosophy together, to think in multi-dimensional ways rather than stay within the confines of one discipline alone.

The reason and hopefully the use of this, is that after many years of working with students and often practitioners in welfare occupations, and with colleagues whose research is frequently coming from a social justice perspective, we have never felt that any one discipline in isolation gives us, or them, *enough* to take into practice. They do not work with people whose problems are only psychological or only structural, we would argue, but mostly people whose lives struggle across the boundaries of social issues and internalized perceptions, and so it seems only right and useful to offer theories and ideas which can be applied 'whole' as it were, not separately to bits of the problem. It isn't that the individual disciplines aren't helpful. For example, in understanding why a woman does not necessarily leave an abusive partner it is crucial to think about economic issues and power issues, but not instead of, but as well as to think about gendered identity concerns, emotional and relational factors, and the capacity of the person's internal world to sustain them resiliently in the face of change, separation and loss. This kind of multi-faceted exploration seems worthwhile.

Psychosocial theory is for us, and we hope the reader agrees, practical, sensible and useful. It seems to start with 'real people' and then work backwards through the theory to come to a kind of realization – 'ah yes, this helps us understand what it might be like for them in their situation/us in our situation'. We have been able to use it in our work with students who then use it in their work, but also to understand elements of life going on around us that are puzzling or profound. We have already found some of the work we have put forward here immensely helpful, and we hope we have been able to both represent that work, and build some more that the reader can feel enlightened by.

Indeed, our own students representing a range of health and social welfare fields of study, frequently puzzle over the big issues of life – for example, can people change; how can people change; why do some people seem to work against their own interests; why is it that of many children who have abused and deprived childhoods only some go on to be abusers? And we hope what we have offered here are a variety of ways of thinking about these issues that try to avoid simple reductionism or obscurity, but that can offer ways of thinking with breadth, with a tentative and exploratory ethos, and with a strong relationship to the experience of both the enquirer and the enquired about.

In the introduction and in Chapter 1 we emphasized that psychosocial theory, though having sound roots in the twentieth century, was also in the process of being revisited, revised and rebuilt, and that this book contributes to this process. To the reader it may be worth saying if this book has stimulated your interest, 'keep an eye out' for what else is emerging in this area as every year the texts and subjects thought about psychosocially multiply. Not just England, but Norway and the USA, are prolific in the area, with a wide range of other European countries, for example, Portugal, Greece and Italy also applying psychosocial thinking to 'local' and international issues.

The last UK psychosocial studies network conference, in London in December 2012 – some measure of who is doing what new work in the subject area – presented psychosocial analyses and discussion on, for example, anti-Mafia activism in Italy, climate change denial in Norway and the UK, human rights denial, digital technology use, gender, inhabiting the role of prison officer, inhabiting the role of artist, and so on. A swathe of psychosocial papers appeared at the British Sociological Association Annual Conference in April 2013, from, for example, 'Atrocities children: towards a psychocultural understanding of post traumatic generations', from A. Stein, and 'Foreclosures from Freud to Fannie Mae', from L. Andrews, both from the USA, and 'Women's experience of living in an unequal society: the place of shame, social comparison and neoliberal discourse', from M. Peacock, UK and 'Love at the office: thinking psychosocially about resilience and recognition', from L. Frost.

However, developing psychosocial knowledge is not just a scholarly pursuit, but also that of 'scholarly practitioners'. Work is emerging from practice – a notable example would be Scanlon and Adlam's prolific work on homelessness and self-harm (e.g. 2011, 2009) – and, as we noted previously, from any of the range of applied disciplines that connect into the psychosocial. As new problems emerge so does a new analysis: psychosocial work on gender and unconscious affect is already appearing in relation to the UK 'riots' of the summer of 2012 (Jones, 2013). The Breivik massacres in Norway in 2012 are, similarly, attracting a psychosocial analysis (Krüger, 2013; Richards, 2013).

We cannot claim our text here to be that of 'scholarly practitioners', but hope a term like 'practice aware scholars' might cover what our ethos is. We hope our text can help you, the reader, be able to think 'into' and about practice situations, real world problems, and the nature of being human in contemporary society. We have found the psychosocial approach a most useful way of contemplating many aspects of the lifecourse – our own and other peoples – and we trust you can find it equally helpful.

Bibliography

Acheson, D. (1998) *Independent Inquiry into Inequalities in Health: The Acheson Report* (London: HMSO).

Adorno, T., Frenkel-Brunswick, E., Levison, D. J. and Sanford, R. N. (1950) *The Authoritarian Personality* (New York: Harper Row).

Ainsworth, M. D. S., Blehar, M. C., Waters, E., and Wall, S. (1978) *Patterns of Attachment: A Psychological Study of the Strange Situation* (Hillsdale, NJ: Erlbaum).

Akhtar, S. (2009) Friendship, socialization and the immigrant experience. *Psychoanalysis, Culture and Society*, 14(3): 253–72.

Andrew, A and Montague, M. (1998) Women's friendship at work. *Women's Studies International Forum*, 21(4): 355–61.

Árnason, A. (2012) Individuals and relationships: on the possibilities and impossibilities of presence. In D. J. Davies and C. Park (eds.), *Emotion, Identity and Death: Mortality across Disciplines* (Farnham: Ashgate).

Bateman, A., Brown, D., and Peddar, J. (2010) *An Introduction to Psychotherapy: An Outline of Psychodynamic Principles and Practice* (London: Routledge).

Bateman, A. and Fonagy, P. (2004) *Psychotherapy for Borderline Personality Disorder: Mentalization-based Treatment* (New York; Oxford University Press).

Beall, A. and Sternberg, R. (1995) The social construction of love. *Journal of Social and Personal Relationships*, 12(3): 417–38.

Beck, U. (1992) *Risk Society: Towards a New Modernity* (London: Sage).

Becker, G. (1997) *Disrupted Lives* (Berkeley, CA: University of California Press).

Biblarz, T. J. and Savci, E. (2010) Lesbian, gay, bisexual and transgender families. *Journal of Marriage and the Family*, 72: 480–97.

Black, D. and Townsend, P. (1982) *Inequalities in Health: The Black Report* (London: Penguin).

Blackman, S. (1995) *Youth: Positions and Oppositions: Style, Sexuality and Schooling* (Aldershot: Avebury).

Bollas, C. (1987) *The Shadow of the Object: Psychoanalysis of the Unthought Known* (London: Free Association Books).

Bourdieu, P. (1984) *Distinction: A Social Critique of the Judgement of Taste* (London: Harvard University Press).

Bourdieu, P. (1986) The forms of capital. In J. Richardson (ed.), *Handbook of Theory and Research for the Sociology of Education* (New York: Greenwood Press).

Bourdieu, P. (1999) *The Weight of the World: Social Suffering in Contemporary Society* (Cambridge: Polity Press).

Boushel, M., Fawcett, M. and Selwyn, J. (eds.) (2000) *Focus on Early Childhood: Principles and Realities* (Oxford: Blackwell).

Bowlby, J. (1951) *Maternal Care and Mental Health: A Report on Behalf of the World Health Organisation* (Geneva: WHO).

Bowlby, J. (1958) The nature of the child's ties to his mother. *International Journal of Psychoanalysis*, 39: 350.

Bowlby, J. (1982 [1969]) *Attachment and Loss*: Vol. 1. *Attachment* (New York: Basic Books).

Bowling, A. and Dieppe, P. (2005) What is successful ageing and who should define it? *British Medical Journal*, 331: 1548–51.

Brenner, H. M. (1979) Influence of the social environment on psychology: the historical perspective. In J. E. Barrett (ed.), *Stress and Mental Disorder* (New York: Raven University Press).

Brown, G. W. and Harris, T. (1978) *The Social Origins of Depression: A Study of Psychiatric Disorder in Women* (London: Tavistock Publications).

Brown, G. W. and Harris, T. (eds.) (1989) *Life Events and Illness* (New York: Guilford Press).

Brown, S. and Stenner, P. (2009) *Psychology without Foundations: History, Philosophy and Psychosocial Theory* (London: Sage).

Butler, J. (2004) *Precarious Life: The Powers of Mourning and Violence* (London: Verso).

Cabinet Office, Social Exclusion Unit (1998) *Bringing Britain Together: A National Strategy for Neighbourhood Renewal*, Cm 4045 (London: HMSO).

Cairns, K. (2002) *Attachment, Trauma and Resilience: Therapeutic Caring for Children* (London: British Association of Fostering and Adoption).

Carlisle, S., Henderson, G. and Hanlon, P. W. (2009) Wellbeing: a collateral casualty of modernity. *Social Science and Medicine*, 69(10): 1556–60.

Cassidy, J. and Shaver, P. R. (eds.) (1999) *Handbook of Attachment: Theory, Research, and Clinical Applications* (New York: Guilford Press).

Cattell, V. (2001) Poor people, poor places, and poor health: the mediating role of social networks and social capital. *Social Science and Medicine*, 52(10): 1501–16.

Cawson, P. (2002) *Child Maltreatment in the Family: The Experience of a National Sample of Young People* (London: NSPCC).

Chandler, A. (2012) Self-injury as embodied emotion work: managing rationality, emotions and bodies. *Sociology*, 46(3): 442–57.

Chodorow, N. (1978) *The Reproduction of Mothering: Psychoanalysis and the Sociology of Gender* (Berkeley, CA: University of California Press).

Ciscel, D. and Heath, J. (2001) To market, to market: imperial capitalism's destruction of social capital and the family. *Review of Radical Political Economics*, 33(4): 401–14.

Cixous, H. (1976) The laugh of the Medusa. In E. Marks and I. de-Courtivon (eds.), *New French Feminisms* (Brighton: Harvester).

Clare, A. (2000) *On Men: Masculinity in Crisis* (London: Chatto and Windus).

Clarke, S. (2003) *Social Theory, Psychoanalysis and Racism* (Basingstoke: Palgrave Macmillan).

Clarke, S. (2005) *From Enlightenment to Risk, Social Theory and Contemporary Society* (Basingstoke: Palgrave Macmillan).

Clarke, S. (2008) 'Psycho-social research: relating self, identity and otherness', in S. Clarke, H. Hahn and P. Hoggett (eds.), *Object Relations and Social Relations: The Implications of the Relational Turn in Psychoanalysis* (London: Karnac).

Clarke, S. and Hoggett, P. (2011) *Researching beneath the Surface: Psycho-social Research Methods in Practice* (London: Karnac).

Cockerham, W. C. (2007) *Social Causes of Health and Disease* (Cambridge: Polity Press).

Cohen, S. (1973) *Folk Devils and Moral Panics* (St Albans: Paladin).

Cohen, S (2001) *States of Denial: Knowing about Atrocities and Suffering* (Cambridge: Polity Press).

Coleman, J. S. (1988) Social capital in the creation of human capital. *American Journal of Sociology*, 94 (supplement): S95–120.

Coleman, P. (1993) Adjustment in later life. In J. Bond, P. Coleman, and S. Peace (eds.), *Ageing in Society: An Introduction to Social Gerontology*, 2nd edn (London: Sage).

Connell, R. W. (1995) *Masculinities* (Cambridge: Polity Press).

Cooper, A. and Lousada, J. (2005) *Borderline Welfare: Feeling and Fear of Feeling in Modern Welfare* (London: Karnac).

Csikszentmihalyi, M. (1990) *Flow: The Psychology of Optimal Experience* (New York: Harper Collins).

Cummings, E. and Henry, W. E. (eds.) (1961) *Growing Old: The Process of Disengagement* (New York: Basic Books).

Delamont, S. (1991) The HIT LIST and other horror stories: sex roles and school transfer. *Sociological Review*, 39(2): 238–59.

De Beauvoir, S. (1996) *The Coming of Age* (London: W.W. Norton & Co).

Dicks, H. V. (1967) *Marital Tensions: Towards a Psychological Theory of Interaction* (London: Routledge).

Doyal, L. and Gough, I. (1991) *A Theory of Human Need* (Basingstoke: Palgrave Macmillan).

Ehrenreich, B. (2010) *Smile or Die: How Positive Thinking Fooled America and the World* (London: Granta Books).

Elliott, A. (2002) *Psychoanalytic theory*, 2nd edn (Basingstoke: Palgrave).

Elliot, A. and Lemert, C. (2009) *The New Individualism: The Emotional Costs of Globalisation* (Abingdon: Routledge).

Erikson, E. H. (1963) *Childhood and Society*. 2nd edn (New York: Norton).

Erikson, E. H. (1995) *Childhood and Society* (London: Vintage).

Erikson, E. H. (1968) *Identity: Youth and Crisis* (London: Faber).

Erikson, E. H. (1984) Reflections on the last stage – and the first. *Psychoanalytic Study of the Child*, 39: 155–65.

Facchini, C. and Rampazi, M. (2009) No longer young, not yet old: biographical uncertainty in late-adult temporality. *Time and Society*, 18: 351.

Faris, R. E. L. and Dunham, H. W. (1939) *Mental Disorders in Urban Areas: An Ecological Study of Schizophrenia and other Psychoses* (Chicago, IL: Chicago University Press).

Featherstone, M. and Hepworth, M. (1998) Ageing, the lifecourse and the sociology of embodiment. In G. Scambler and P. Higgs (eds.), *Modernity, Medicine and Health* (London: Routledge).

Ferguson, H. (2005) Working with violence, the emotions and the psycho-social dynamics of child protection: reflections on the Victoria Climbié case. *Social Work Education*, 24(7): 781–95.

Field, F. (2010) *The Field Review: Independent Review on Poverty and Life Chances* (York: Joseph Rowntree Fund).

Foucault, M. (1972) *The Archaeology of Knowledge* (London: Tavistock).

Foucault, M. (1980) *Power/Knowledge* (Brighton: Harvester).

Frazer, J. G. (1922) *The Golden Bough* (New York: Macmillan).

Freud, S. (1917) *Mourning and Melancholia*, Standard Edition, vol. 14, 237–58 (London: Hogarth Press).

Freud, S. (1927) *The Future of an Illusion* (London: Hogarth Press).

Freund, P. (1990) The expressive body: a common ground for the sociology of the emotions and health and illness. *Sociology of Health and Illness*, 12(4): 452–77.

Froggett, L. (2002) *Love, Hate and Welfare: Psychosocial Approaches to Policy and Practice* (Bristol: Policy Press).

Fromm, E. (1957) *The Art of Loving* (London: Thorsons).

Fromm, E. (1962) *Beyond the Chains of Illusion* (London: Abacus).

Fromm, E. (1976) *To Have or to Be* (London: Abacus).

Frosh, S. (1991) *Identity Crisis: Modernity, Psychoanalysis and the Self* (Basingstoke: Macmillan).

Frosh, S. (2012) *A Brief Introduction to Psychoanalytic Theory* (Basingstoke: Palgrave Macmillan).

Frosh, S., Phoenix, A. and Pattman, R. (2002) *Young Masculinities: Understanding Boys in Contemporary Society* (London: Macmillan).

Frosh, S., Pheonix, A. and Pattman, R. (2003) Taking a stand: using psychoanalysis to explore positioning of subjects in discourse. *British Journal of Social Psychology*, 42(1): 39–53.

Frost, L. (2001) *Young Women and the Body: A Feminist Sociology* (Basingstoke: Palgrave).

Frost, L. (2003) Doing bodies differently: gender, youth appearance and damage. *Journal of Youth Studies*, 6(1): 53–70.

Frost, L. (2008) Why teach social work students psychosocial studies? *Social Work Education*, 27(3): 243–61.

Frost, L. and Hoggett, P. (2004) Transitions from primary to secondary school. Unpublished paper.

Frost, L. and Hoggett, P. (2008) Human agency and social suffering. *Critical Social Policy*, 28(4): 438–60.

Furedi, F. (2001) *Paranoid Parenting: Why Ignoring the Experts May Be Best for your Child* (London: Allen Lane).

Furedi, F. (2003) *Therapy Culture: Cultivating Vulnerability in an Uncertain Age* (London: Routledge).

Gadd, D. and Dixon, B. (2010) *Losing the Race: Thinking Psychosocially about Racially Motivated Crime* (London: Karnac).

Gadd, D. (2011) Murderer, mad man, misfit? Making sense of the murder of Zahid Mubarek. *Journal of Psycho-social Studies*, 5(1): 139–62.

Giddens, A. (1991) *Modernity and Self Identity: Self and Society in the Late Modern Age* (Cambridge: Polity Press).

Giddens, A. (1992) *The Transformation of Intimacy: Sexuality, Love and Eroticism in Modern Societies* (Cambridge: Polity Press).

Giddens, A. (2009) *Sociology*, 6th edn (Cambridge: Polity Press).

Gilleard, C. and Higgs, P. (1998) Old people as users and consumers of healthcare: a third age rhetoric for a fourth age reality? *Ageing and Society Volume*, 18(2): 233–48.

Gilleard, C. and Higgs, P. (2000) *Cultures of Ageing: Self, Citizen and the Body* (Harlow: Pearson Education).

Gillies, P. A. (1998) Social capital and its contributions to public health. *FORUM Trends in Experimental and Clinical Medicine*, 8(5): 47–51.

Gilligan, J. (2001) *Preventing Violence* (New York: Thames and Hudson).

Gilligan R. (2004) Promoting resilience in child and family social work: issues for social work practice, education and policy. *Social Work Education: The International Journal*, 23(1): 93–104.

Gilligan, R. (2009) *Promoting Resilience: A Resource Guide on Working with Children in the Care System* (London: British Association of Fostering and Adoption).

Gilroy, P. (2004) *After Empire: Melancholia or Convivial Culture* (London: Routledge).

Goffman, E. (1990 [1959]) *The Presentation of Self in Everyday Life* (London: Penguin).

Goffman, E. (1968) *Stigma: Notes on the Management of Spoiled Identity* (London: Penguin).

Goffman, E. (1970 [1961]) *Asylums: Essays on the Social Situation of Mental Patients and other Inmates* (London: Penguin).

Golombok, S. and Badger, S. (2010) Children raised in fatherless families from infancy: a follow-up of children of lesbian and single heterosexual mothers in early adulthood. *Human Reproduction*, 25(1): 150–7.

Goodwin, M. (2006) *The Hidden Life of Girls: Games of Stance, Status and Exclusion* (Malden, MA: Blackwell).

Goodyer, I., Wright, C. and Altham, P. (1990) The friendships and recent life events of anxious and depressed school-age children. *British Journal of Psychiatry*, 156: 689–98.

Greenwood, L. (2005) *Violent Adolescents: Understanding the Destructive Impulse* (London: Karnac).

Griffin, C. (1985) *Typical Girls? Young Women from School to the Labour Market* (London: Routledge and Kegan Paul).

Hage, G. (2011) Social gravity: Pierre Bourdieu's phenomenological social physics. In G. Hage and E. Kowal (eds.), *Force, Movement, Intensity: The Newtonian Imagination in the Humanities and Social Sciences* (Melbourne: Melbourne University Press), 80–93.

Hakim, C. (2011) *Honey Money: The Power of Erotic Capital* (London: Allen Lane).

Hall, S. (2001) Foucault, power and knowledge. In M. Wetherall (ed.), *Discourse Theory and Practice* (London: Oxford University Press and Sage).

Hall, S., Winlow, S. and Ancrum, C. (2008) *Criminal Identities and Consumer Culture: Crime, Exclusion and the New Culture of Narcissism* (Cullompton: Willan Publishing).

Haworth, J. and Hart, G. (eds.) (2007) *Well-being: Individual, Community and Social Perspectives* (Basingstoke: Palgrave Macmillan).

Henderson, S. (2007) *Inventing Adulthoods: A Biographical Approach to Youth Transitions* (London: Sage).

Hey, V. (1997) *The Company She Keeps: An Ethnography of Girl's Friendships* (Buckingham: Open University Press).

Higgs, P. F., Hyde, M., Gilleard, C. J., Victor, C. R., Wiggins, R. D. and Jones, I. R. (2009) From passive to active consumers? Later life consumption in the UK from 1968–2005. *Sociological Review*, 57(1): 102–24.

Hill, M. (1989) The role of social networks in the care of young children. *Children and Society*, 3(3): 195–211.

Hochschild, A. R. (1983) *The Managed Heart: The Commercialization of Human Feeling* (Berkeley, CA: University of California Press).

Hockey, J. and James, A. (1993) *Growing Up and Growing Old: Ageing and Dependency in the Life Course* (London: Sage).

Hockey, J. and James, A. (2003) *Social Identities across the Life Course* (Basingstoke: Palgrave Macmillan).

Hoggett, P. (2000) *Emotional Life and the Politics of Welfare* (Basingstoke: Macmillan).

Hoggett, P. (2001) Agency, rationality and social policy. *Journal of Social Policy*, 30(1): 37–56.

Hoggett, P. (2010) Grief and grievance (Bristol: University of the West of England, unpublished).

Hoggett, P., Wilkinson, H. and Beedell, P. (2013) Fairness and the politics of resentment. *Journal of Social Policy*, in press.

Holland, J., Ramazanoglu, C., Sharper, S. and Thomas, R. (1998) *The Male in the Head: Young People, Heterosexuality and Power* (London: Tufnell Press).

Hollway, W. (1998) Gender difference and the production of subjectivity. In J. Henriques, W. Hollway, C. Urwin, C. Venn and W. Walkerdine (eds.),

Changing the Subject: Psychology, Social Regulation and Subjectivity, 2nd edn (London: Routledge).

Hollway, W. (2011) Psycho-social writing from data. *Journal of Psycho-social Studies*, 4(2): 92–101.

Hollway, W. and Jefferson, T. (1997) The risk society in the age of anxiety: situating fear of crime. *British Journal of Sociology*, 48(2): 255–66.

Hollway, W. and Jefferson, T. (2000) *Doing Qualitative Research Differently: Free Association, Narrative and the Interview Method* (London: Sage).

Hollway, W. and Jefferson, T. (2012) *Doing Qualitative Research Differently: A Psychosocial Approach*, 2nd edn (London: Sage).

Holmes, J. (1993) *John Bowlby and Attachment Theory* (London: Routledge).

Honneth, A. W. (1995) *The Struggle for Recognition: The Moral Grammar of Social Struggles* (Cambridge: Polity Press).

Idle, T., Wood, E. and Desmarais, S. (1993) Gender role socialisation in toy play situations: mothers and fathers with their sons and daughters. *Sex Roles*, 28(11/12): 679.

Illich, I. (1976) *Limits to Medicine. Medical Nemesis: The Expropriation of Health* (Harmondsworth: Penguin Books).

Irigaray, L. (1977) This sex which is not one. In C. Zanardi (ed.), *Essential Papers on the Psychology of Women* (New York: New York University Press).

Jackson, J. and Grey, E. (2010) Functional fear and public insecurities about crime. *British Journal of Criminology*, 50: 1–22.

James, A. and Prout, A. (1997) *Constructing and Reconstructing Childhood: Contemporary Issues in the Sociological Study of Childhood* (London: Routledge).

James, A., Jenks, C. and Prout, A. (1998) *Theorizing Childhood* (Cambridge: Polity Press).

James, A. and James, A. L. (2004) *Constructing Childhood: Theory, Policy and Social Practice* (Basingstoke: Palgrave Macmillan).

James, J. and Zarrett, N. (2006) Ego integrity in the lives of older women. *Journal of Adult Development*, 13(2): 61–75.

James, O. (2007) *Affluenza* (London: Vermillion).

James, O. (2010) *Britain on the Couch* (London: Vermillion).

Jimenez, L. and Walkerdine, V. (2011) A psychosocial approach to shame, embarrassment and melancholia amongst unemployed young men and their fathers. *Gender and Education*, 23(2): 185–99.

Jones, D. (2013) Putting the psyche into 'cultural criminology': psychosocial understandings of masculinity, shame violence and looting. *Journal of Psychosocial Studies*, online, forthcoming.

Jones, I. R., Hyde, M., Victor, C. R., Wiggins, R. D., Gilleard, C. and Higgs, P. (2008) *Ageing in a Consumer Society: From Active to Passive Consumption in Britain* (Bristol: Policy Press).

Keesing, R. M. (1981) *Cultural Anthropology* (London: Harcourt Brace).

Klass, D. and Walter, T. (2001) Processes of grieving: how bonds are continued. In M. Stroebe, R. Hansson, W. Stroebe and H. Schut (eds.), Handbook of

Bereavement Research: Consequences, Coping, and Care (Washington, DC: American Psychological Association), 431–48.

Klass, D., Silverman, P. R. and Nickman, S. L. (eds.) (1996) *Continuing Bonds: New Understandings of Grief* (Washington, DC: Taylor & Francis).

Klein, M. (1935) A contribution to the psychogenesis of manic-depressive states. *International Journal of Psychoanalysis*, 16: 145–74. Reprinted in *The Collected Writings of Melanie Klein* (London: Hogarth, 1975), vol. I, 262–89.

Klein, M. (1940) Mourning and its relation to manic-depressive states. *International Journal of Psychoanalysis*, 21: 125–53. Reprinted in *The Collected Writings of Melanie Klein* (London: Hogarth, 1975), vol. I, 344–69.

Klein, M. (1975) *The Collected Writings of Melanie Klein. Vol. 3: Envy and Gratitude* (London: Hogarth Press).

Kline, S. (2005) Countering children's sedentary lifestyles: an evaluative study of a media-risk education approach. *Childhood*; 12: 239–58.

Krüger, S. (2013) My own private 22/07: a depth hermeneutic analysis of the Norwegian online service Min 22. Juli (22 July). Conference paper, BSA April.

Kubler-Ross, E. (1970) *On Death and Dying* (London: Tavistock).

Langan, M. and Lee, P. (eds.) (1989) *Radical Social Work Today* (London: Unwin Hyman).

Langman, L. (1992) Neon cages: shopping for subjectivity. In R. Shields (ed.), *Lifestyle Shopping: The Subject of Consumption* (London: Routledge).

Lasch, C. (1979) *The Culture of Narcissism* (New York: Norton).

Lawlor, S. (2008) *Identity: Sociological Perspectives* (Cambridge: Polity Press).

Lazarus, R. and Folkman, S. (1984) *Stress, Appraisal and Coping* (New York: Springer).

Lewis, P. (2009) Every step you take: UK underground centre that is spy capital of the world. *The Guardian*, 2 March.

Lucey, H. and Reay, D. (2002) A market in waste: psychic and structural dimensions of school-choice policy in the U.K. and children's narratives on 'demonized' schools. *Discourses: Studies in the Cultural Policy of Education*, 23(3): 23–40.

Lyons-Ruth, K. and Jacobvitz, C. (1999) Attachment disorganization: unresolved loss, relational violence, and lapses in behavioral and attentional strategies. In J. Cassidy and P. R. Shaver (eds.), *Handbook of Attachment: Theory, Research and Clinical Applications* (New York: Guilford Press), 89–111.

Macpherson, W. (1999) *The Stephen Lawrence Inquiry* (London: The Stationery Office).

Maguire, M. (2004) *Men, Women, Passion and Power: Gender Issues in Psychotherapy* (Hove: Brunner-Routledge).

Maguire, M., Morgan, R. and Reiner, R. (eds.) (2007) *The Oxford Handbook of Criminology* (Oxford: Oxford University Press).Marmot, M. (2004) *Status Syndrome: How your Social Standing Directly Affects your Health and your Life Expectancy* (London: Bloomsbury).

Marmot, M., Allen, J., Goldblatt, P. *et al.* (2010) *Fair Society, Healthy Lives (The Marmot Review): Strategic Review of Health Inequalities in England post-2010* (London: UCL Institute of Health Equity).

Marmot, M. G., Davey Smith, G. and Stansfield, S. (1991) Health inequalities among British civil servants: the Whitehall II study. *Lancet* 337(8754): 1387–93.

Maslow, A.H. (1943) A theory of human motivation. *Psychological Review*, 50: 370–96.

Mayall, B. (2002) *Towards a Sociology for Childhood: Thinking from Children's Lives* (Buckingham: Open University Press).

Mayo, M., Hoggett, P. and Miller, C. (2007) Navigating the contradictions of public service modernisation: the case of community engagement professionals. *Policy and Politics*, 35(4): 667–81.

McClean, S., Bunt, L. and Daykin, N. (2012) The healing and spiritual properties of music therapy at a cancer care centre. Journal of Alternative and Complementary Medicine, 18(4): 402–7.

McClean, S. and Moore, R. (2013) Money, commodification and complementary health care: theorising personalised medicine within de-personalised systems of exchange. *Social Theory and Health*, 11(2): 194–214.

McIntosh, I. and Punch, S. (2009) 'Barter', 'deals', 'bribes' and 'threats': exploring sibling interactions. *Childhood*, 16(1): 49–65.

Messerschmidt, J. (1997) *Crime as Structured Action* (London: Sage).

Middleton, A., Murie, A. and Groves, R. (2005) Social capital and neighbourhoods that work. *Urban Studies*, 42(10): 1711–38.

Minsky, R. (1998) *Psychoanalysis and Culture: Contemporary States of Mind* (Cambridge: Polity Press).

Modell, A. (1997) The private self and relational theory. In E. R. Shapiro (ed.), *The Inner World in the Outer World* (New Haven, CT: Yale University Press).

Nettleton, S. (2006) *The Sociology of Health and Illness*, 2nd edn (Cambridge: Polity Press).

Noyes, A. (2003) School transfer and social relocation. *International Studies in the Sociology of Education*, 13(3): 261–80.

Nussbaum, M. C. (2000) *Women and Human Development: The Capabilities Approach* (Cambridge: Cambridge University Press).

Office of National Statistics (2009) *Social Trends*, 39, http://www.ons.gov.uk/ons/rel/social-trends-rd/social-trends/social-trends-39/index.html

Office of National Statistics (2010) *General Lifestyle Survey 2008* http://www.ons.gov.uk/ons/rel/ghs/general-lifestyle-survey/2008-report/index.html

Parris, M. (2009) I didn't want to 'get over' my father's death. *The Spectator*, 12 August.

Patterson, C. J. (2000) Family relationships of lesbians and gay men. *Journal of Marriage and the Family*, 62: 1052–69.

Pease, B. and Fook, J. (1999) *Transforming Social Work Practice* (London: Routledge).

Phillipson, C. (1998) *Reconstructing Old Age: New Agendas in Social Theory and Practice* (London: Sage).

Polivka, L. (2000) Postmodern aging and the loss of meaning. *Journal of Aging and Identity*, 5(4): 225–35.

Prendergast, S. and Forrest, S. (1997) Hieroglyphs and the heterosexual: learning about gender in school. In L. Segal (ed.), *New Sexual Agendas* (Basingstoke: Palgrave).

Price, H., Choi, J. and Vinokur, A. D. (2002) Links in the chain of adversity following job loss: how financial strain and loss of personal control lead to depression, impaired functioning, and poor health. *Journal of Occupational Health Psychology*, 7(4): 302–12.

Putnam, R. (1995) Bowling alone: America's declining social capital. *Journal of Democracy*, 6(1): 65–78.

Putnam, R. (2000) *Bowling Alone: The Collapse and Revival of American Community* (New York: Simon and Schuster).

Reay, D. (2005) Beyond consciousness: the psychic landscape of social class. *Sociology*, 39(5): 911–28.

Rich, E. (2006) Anorexia dis(connection): managing anorexia as an illness and an identity. *Sociology of Health and Illness*, 28(3): 284–305.

Richards, B. (2013) Lessons from the Brevik case: a psychosocial analysis. Conference paper, BSA April.

Ridge, T. (2002) *Childhood Poverty and Social Exclusion* (Bristol: Policy Press).

Riley, S., Burns, M., Frith, H., Wiggins, S. and Markula, P. (eds.) (2008) *Critical Bodies: Representations, Identities and Practices of Weight and Body Management* (Basingstoke: Palgrave Macmillan).

Robinson, L. (2007) *Cross-cultural Child Development for Social Workers* (Basingstoke: Palgrave Macmillan).

Roker, D. (1998) *Worth More than This: Young People Growing Up in Family Poverty* (London: The Children's Society).

Rorty, R. (1989) *Contingency, Irony and Solidarity* (Cambridge: Cambridge University Press).

Rutter, M. and Rutter, M. (1993) *Developing Minds: Challenge and Continuity across the Life Span* (London: Penguin).

Rutter, M. (1995) *Psychosocial Disorders in Young People: Time Trends and their Causes* (Chichester: John Wiley and Sons).

Rutter, M.L. (1999) Psychosocial adversity and child psychopathology. *The British Journal of Psychiatry*, 174: 480–93.

Ryan, R. M., and Deci, E. L. (2001) On happiness and human potentials: a review of research on hedonic and eudaimonic wellbeing. *Annual Review of Psychology*, 52: 141–66.

Scanlon, C. and Adlam, J. (2009) Why do you treat me this way? Reciprocal violence and the myth of deliberate self harm. In A. Motz (ed.), *Managing Self-Harm: Psychological Perspectives* (Hove: Routledge).

Scanlon, C. and Adlam, J. (2011) Cosmopolitan minds and metropolitan societies: social exclusion and social refusal revisited. *Psychodynamic Practice: Individuals, Groups and Organisations*, 17(3): 241–54.

Schulman, R. (2009) Commentary on friendship. In S. Akhtar (ed.), *Good*

Feelings: Psychoanalytical Reflections on Positive Attitudes and Emotions (London: Karnac).

Seligman, M. (1990) *Learned Optimism: How to Change your Mind and your Life* (New York: Free Press).

Selwyn, J. (2000) Infancy. In M. Boushel, M. Fawcett and J. Selwyn (eds.), *Focus on Early Childhood: Principles and Realities* (Oxford: Blackwell).

Sen, A. (1993) 'Capability and well-being. In M. Nussbaum and A. Sen (eds.), *The Quality of Life* (New York: Oxford Clarendon Press), 30–53.

Shaw, J. (1995) *Education, Gender and Anxiety* (London: Taylor Francis).

Sointu, E. (2005) The rise of an ideal: tracing changing discourses of wellbeing. *The Sociological Review*, 53(2): 255–74.

Sointu, E. (2006) The search for wellbeing in alternative and complementary health practices. *Sociology of Health and Illness*, 28(3): 330–49.

Spalek, B. (2008*) Communities, Identities and Crime* (Bristol: Policy Press).

Stets, J. E. and Turner, J. H. (eds.) (2007) *Handbook of the Sociology of the Emotions* (New York: Springer).

Stevens, R. (2008) *Erik Erikson* (Basingstoke: Palgrave).

Szasz, T. (1961) *The Myth of Mental Illness: Foundations of a Theory of Personal Conduct* (London: Secker).

Taylor, D. (2011) Wellbeing and welfare: a psychosocial analysis of being well and doing well enough. *Journal of Social Policy*, 40(4): 777–94.

Thompson, J. B. (1995) *The Media and Modernity: A Social Theory of the Media* (Stanford, CA: Stanford University Press).

Trevithick, P. (2003) Effective relationship-based practice: a theoretical explanation. *Journal of Social Work Practice*, 17(2): 163–76.

Turner, B. (1984) *Body and Society: Explorations in Social Theory* (Oxford: Blackwell).

Turner, R. (1962) Role-taking: process versus conformity. In A. Rose (ed.), *Human Behaviour and Social Processes* (London: Routledge).

Vanistendael, S. (1998) *Growth in the Muddle of Life: Resilience Building on People's Strength* (International Catholic Child Bureau).

Vericker, T., Macomber, J. and Golden, O. (2010) *Infants of Depressed Mothers Living in Poverty: Opportunities to Identify and Serve* (Washington, DC: The Urban Institute).

Viswanath, K., Breen, N., Meissener, H., Mosser, R., Hesse, B., Steel, W. and Rakowski, W. (2006) Cancer knowledge and disparities in the information age. *Journal of Health Communication: International Perspectives*, 11(1): 1–17.

Walker, S. (2003) Social work and child mental health: psychosocial principles in community practice. *British Journal of Social Work*, 33: 673–87.

Walker, S. (2004) Community work and psychosocial practice – chalk and cheese or birds of a feather? *Journal of Social Work Practice*, 18(2): 161–75.

Walkerdine, V. and Jimenez, L. (2012) *Gender, Work and Community after De-Industrialisation: A Psychosocial Approach to Affect* (Basingstoke: Palgrave).

Walkerdine, V., Lucey, H. and Melody, J. (2001) *Growing Up Girl: Psycho-social Explorations of Gender and Class* (Basingstoke: Palgrave).

Walter, T. (2001) Mourning. In J. Michie (ed.), Reader's Guide to the Social Sciences (London: Fitzroy Dearborn).

Weeks, J., Heaphy, B. and Donovan, C. (2004) The lesbian and gay family. In J. Scott *et al.* (eds.), *The Blackwell Companion to the Sociology of Families* (Oxford: Blackwell).

Weintrobe S. (ed.) (2013) *Engaging with Climate Change Psychoanalytic and Interdisciplinary Perspective* (London: Routledge).

Weitz, R. (ed.) (1998) *The Politics of Women's Bodies: Sexuality, Appearance and Behaviour* (Oxford: Oxford University Press).

Whiteman, S. D., McHale, S. M. and Crouter, A. C. (2007) Competing processes of sibling development: observational learning and sibling de-identification. *Social Development*, 16: 642–61.

Wilkinson, R. (1996) *Unhealthy Societies: The Affliction of Inequality* (London: Routledge).

Wilkinson, R. and Picket, K. (2009) *The Spirit Level: Why Equality Is Better for Everyone* (Harmondsworth: Penguin).

Williams, S. J. (1998) Emotions, equity and health. In A. Peterson and C. Waddell (eds.), *Health Matters: A Sociology of Illness, Prevention and Care* (Buckingham: Open University Press).

Williams, S. J. (2000) Emotions, social structure and health: re-thinking the class inequalities debate. In S. J. Williams, J. Gabe and M. Calnan (eds.), *Health, Medicine and Society: Key Theories, Future Agendas* (London: Routledge), 296–314.

Williams, S. J. (2001) *Emotion and Social Theory* (London: Sage).

Willison, K. D. and Andrews, G. J. (2004) Complementary medicine and older people: past research and future directions. *Complementary Therapies in Nursing and Midwifery*, 10(2): 80–91.

Winnicott, D. W. (1953) Transitional objects and transitional phenomena: a study of the first not-me possession. *International Journal of Psychoanalysis*, 34: 89–97.

Winnicott, D. W. (1964) *The Child, the Family and the Outside World* (London: Pelican Books).

Woodhead, M. (1999) Reconstructing developmental psychology – some first steps. *Children and Society*, 13: 3–19.

Woodward, K. (1991) *Aging and its Discontents: Freud and other Fictions* (Bloomington, IN: Indiana University Press).

World Health Assembly (1948) *Preamble to the Constitution of the World Health Organization as Adopted by the International Health Conference New York* (Geneva: World Health Organization).

Worth, H., Reid, A. and McMillan, K. (2002) Somewhere over the rainbow: love, trust and monogamy in gay relationships. *Journal of Sociology*, 38(3): 237–53.

Wright, M. O. and Masten, A. (2005) Resilience processes in development. In S. Goldstein and R. Brooks (eds.), *Handbook of Resilience in Children* (New York: Kluwer Academic/Plenum), 17–37.

Zeirsch, A. M., Baum, F. E., MacDougall, C. and Putland, C. (2005) Neighbourhood life and social capital: the implications for health. *Social Science and Medicine*, 60: 71–86.

Zeller, M., Reiter-Purtill, J. and Ramey, C. (2008) Negative peer perceptions of obese children in the classroom environment. *Obesity*, 16(4): 755–62.

Index